SOURCE
The Prentice Hall
ENGINEERING SOURCE

Graphics Concepts
with Pro/ENGINEER®

Richard M. Lueptow
Northwestern University

Jim Steger
Michael T. Snyder

Prentice Hall
Upper Saddle River, NJ 07458

Library of Congress Cataloging-in-Publication Data

Lueptow, Richard M.

    Graphics concepts with Pro/ENGINEER / Richard M. Lueptow, Jim Steger, Michael Snyder.
      p. cm. — (ESource—the Prentice Hall engineering source)
    Includes bibliographical reference and index.
    ISBN 0–13–014154–2
    1. Engineering graphics. 2. Pro/ENGINEER. I. Steger, Jim. II. Snyder, Michael. III. Title. IV. Series.

T353.L868 2000
620'.0042'028566—dc21

00.029802

Vice-president of editorial development, ECS: **MARCIA HORTON**
Acquisitions editor: **ERIC SVENDSEN**
Associate editor: **JOE RUSSO**
Vice-president of production and manufacturing: **DAVID W. RICCARDI**
Executive managing editor: **VINCE O' BRIEN**
Managing editor: **DAVID A. GEORGE**
Editorial/production supervisor: **LAKSHMI BALASUBRAMANIAN**
Cover director: **JAYNE CONTE**
Manufacturing buyer: **PAT BROWN**
Editorial assistant: **KRISTEN BLANCO**
Marketing manager: **DANNY HOYT**

© 2001 by Prentice-Hall, Inc.
Upper Saddle River, New Jersey 07458

The author and publisher of this book have used their best efforts in
preparing this book. These efforts include the development, research,
and testing of the theories to determine their effectiveness.
Printed in the United States of America.

10 9 8 7 6 5 4 3 2 1

ISBN 0-13-014154-2

Prentice-Hall International (UK) Limited, *London*
Prentice-Hall of Australia Pty. Limited, *Sydney*
Prentice-Hall Canada, Inc., Toronto
Prentice-Hall Hispanoamericana, S.A., *Mexico*
Prentice-Hall of India Private Limited, *New Delhi*
Prentice-Hall of Japan, Inc., *Tokyo*
Pearson Education (Singapore) Pte. Ltd., *Singapore*
Editoria Prentice-Hall do Brasil, Ltda., *Rio de Janeiro*

About ESource

ESource—The Prentice Hall Engineering Source
—www.prenhall.com/esource

ESource—The Prentice Hall Engineering Source gives professors the power to harness the full potential of their text and their first-year engineering course. More than just a collection of books, ESource is a unique publishing system revolving around the ESource website—www.prenhall.com/esource. ESource enables you to put your stamp on your book just as you do your course. It lets you:

Control   You choose exactly what chapter or sections are in your book and in what order they appear. Of course, you can choose the entire book if you'd like and stay with the authors' original order.

Optimize   Get the most from your book and your course. ESource lets you produce the optimal text for your students needs.

Customize   You can add your own material anywhere in your text's presentation, and your final product will arrive at your bookstore as a professionally formatted text.

ESource ACCESS

Starting in the fall of 2000, professors who choose to bundle two or more texts from the ESource series for their class, or use an ESource custom book will be providing their students with complete access to the library of ESource content. All bundles and custom books will come with a student password that gives web ESource ACCESS to all information on the site. This passcode is free and is valid for one year after initial log-on. We've designed ESource ACCESS to provides students a flexible, searchable, on-line resource.

ESource Content

All the content in ESource was written by educators specifically for freshman/first-year students. Authors tried to strike a balanced level of presentation, an approach that was neither formulaic nor trivial, and one that did not focus too heavily on advanced topics that most introductory students do not encounter until later classes. Because many professors do not have extensive time to cover these topics in the classroom, authors prepared each text with the idea that many students would use it for self-instruction and independent study. Students should be able to use this content to learn the software tool or subject on their own.

While authors had the freedom to write texts in a style appropriate to their particular subject, all followed certain guidelines created to promote a consistency that makes students comfortable. Namely, every chapter opens with a clear set of **Objectives**, includes **Practice Boxes** throughout the chapter, and ends with a number of **Problems**, and a list of **Key Terms**. **Applications Boxes** are spread throughout the book with the intent of giving students a real-world perspective of engineering. **Success Boxes** provide the student with advice about college study skills, and help students avoid the common pitfalls of first-year students. In addition, this series contains an entire book titled ***Engineering Success*** by Peter Schiavone of the University of Alberta intended to expose students quickly to what it takes to be an engineering student.

Creating Your Book

Using ESource is simple. You preview the content either on-line or through examination copies of the books you can request on-line, from your PH sales rep, or by calling 1-800-526-0485. Create an on-line outline of the content you want, in the order you want, using ESource's simple interface. Either type or cut and paste your own material and insert it into the text flow. You can preview the overall organization of the text you've created at anytime (please note, since this preview is immediate, it comes unformatted.), then press another button and receive an order number for your own custom book. If you are not ready to order, do nothing—ESource will save your work. You can come back at any time and change, re-arrange, or add more material to your creation. You are in control. Once you're finished and you have an ISBN, give it to your bookstore and your book will arrive on their shelves six weeks after they order. Your custom desk copies with their instructor supplements will arrive at your address at the same time.

To learn more about this new system for creating the perfect textbook, go to www.prenhall.com/esource. You can either go through the on-line walkthrough of how to create a book, or experiment yourself.

Supplements

Adopters of ESource receive an instructor's CD that contains professor and student code from the books in the series, as well as other instruction aides provided by authors. The website also holds approximately **350 Powerpoint transparencies** created by Jack Leifer of Univ. of Kentucky—Paducah available to download. Professors can either follow these transparencies as pre-prepared lectures or use them as the basis for their own custom presentations.

Titles in the ESource Series

Introduction to UNIX
0-13-095135-8
David I. Schwartz

Introduction to AutoCAD 2000
0-13-016732-0
Mark Dix and Paul Riley

Introduction to Maple
0-13-095133-1
David I. Schwartz

Introduction to Word
0-13-254764-3
David C. Kuncicky

Introduction to Excel, 2/e
0-13-016881-5
David C. Kuncicky

Introduction to Mathcad
0-13-937493-0
Ronald W. Larsen

Introduction to AutoCAD, R. 14
0-13-011001-9
Mark Dix and Paul Riley

Introduction to the Internet, 3/e
0-13-031355-6
Scott D. James

Design Concepts for Engineers
0-13-081369-9
Mark N. Horenstein

Engineering Design — A Day in the Life of Four Engineers
0-13-085089-6
Mark N. Horenstein

Engineering Ethics
0-13-784224-4
Charles B. Fleddermann

Engineering Success
0-13-080859-8
Peter Schiavone

Mathematics Review
0-13-011501-0
Peter Schiavone

Introduction to C
0-13-011854-0
Delores Etter

Introduction to C++
0-13-011855-9
Delores Etter

Introduction to MATLAB
0-13-013149-0
Delores Etter with David C. Kuncicky

Titles in the ESource Series

About the Authors

No project could ever come to pass without a group of authors who have the vision and the courage to turn a stack of blank paper into a book. The authors in this series worked diligently to produce their books, provide the building blocks of the series.

Delores M. Etter is a Professor of Electrical and Computer Engineering at the University of Colorado. Dr. Etter was a faculty member at the University of New Mexico and also a Visiting Professor at Stanford University. Dr. Etter was responsible for the Freshman Engineering Program at the University of New Mexico and is active in the Integrated Teaching Laboratory at the University of Colorado. She was elected a Fellow of the Institute of Electrical and Electronics Engineers for her contributions to education and for her technical leadership in digital signal processing. In addition to writing best-selling textbooks for engineering computing, Dr. Etter has also published research in the area of adaptive signal processing.

Sanford Leestma is a Professor of Mathematics and Computer Science at Calvin College, and received his Ph.D. from New Mexico State University. He has been the long-time co-author of successful textbooks on Fortran, Pascal, and data structures in Pascal. His current research interest are in the areas of algorithms and numerical computation.

Larry Nyhoff is a Professor of Mathematics and Computer Science at Calvin College. After doing bachelor's work at Calvin, and Master's work at Michigan, he received a Ph.D. from Michigan State and also did graduate work in computer science at Western Michigan. Dr. Nyhoff has taught at Calvin for the past 34 years—mathematics at first and computer science for the past several years. He has co-authored several computer science textbooks since 1981 including titles on Fortran and C++, as well as a brand new title on Data Structures in C++.

Acknowledgments: We express our sincere appreciation to all who helped in the preparation of this module, especially our acquisitions editor Alan Apt, managing editor Laura Steele, developmental editor Sandra Chavez, and production editor Judy Winthrop. We also thank Larry Genalo for several examples and exercises and Erin Fulp for the Internet address application in Chapter 10. We appreciate the insightful review provided by Bart Childs. We thank our families—Shar, Jeff, Dawn, Rebecca, Megan, Sara, Greg, Julie, Joshua, Derek, Tom, Joan; Marge, Michelle, Sandy, Lory, Michael—for being patient and understanding. We thank God for allowing us to write this text.

Mark Dix began working with AutoCAD in 1985 as a programmer for CAD Support Associates, Inc. He helped design a system for creating estimates and bills of material directly from AutoCAD drawing databases for use in the automated conveyor industry. This system became the basis for systems still widely in use today. In 1986 he began collaborating with Paul Riley to create AutoCAD training materials, combining Riley's background in industrial design and training with Dix's background in writing, curriculum development, and programming. Dix and Riley have created tutorial and teaching methods for every AutoCAD release since Version 2.5. Mr. Dix has a Master of Education from the University of Massachusetts. He is currently the Director of Dearborn Academy High School in Arlington, Massachusetts.

Paul Riley is an author, instructor, and designer specializing in graphics and design for multimedia. He is a founding partner of CAD Support Associates, a contract service and professional training organization for computer-aided design. His 15 years of business experience and 20 years of teaching experience are supported by degrees in education and computer science. Paul has taught AutoCAD at the University of Massachusetts at Lowell and is presently teaching AutoCAD at Mt. Ida College in Newton, Massachusetts. He has developed a program, Computer-aided Design for Professionals that is highly regarded by corporate clients and has been an ongoing success since 1982.

Scott D. James is a staff lecturer at Kettering University (formerly GMI Engineering & Management Institute) in Flint, Michigan. He is currently pursuing a Ph.D. in Systems Engineering with an emphasis on software engineering and computer-integrated manufacturing. Scott decided on writing textbooks after he found a void in the books that were available. "I really wanted a book that showed how to do things in good detail but in a clear and concise way. Many of the books on the market are full of fluff and force you to dig out the really important facts." Scott decided on teaching as a profession after several years in the computer industry. "I thought that it was really important to know what it was like outside of academia. I wanted to provide students with classes that were up to date and provide the information that is really used and needed." *Acknowledgments*: Scott would like to acknowledge his family for the time to work on the text and his students and peers at Kettering who offered helpful critiques of the materials that eventually became the book.

Charles B. Fleddermann is a professor in the Department of Electrical and Computer Engineering at the University of New Mexico in Albuquerque, New Mexico. All of his degrees are in electrical engineering: his Bachelor's degree from the University of Notre Dame, and the Master's and Ph.D. from the University of Illinois at Urbana-Champaign. Prof. Fleddermann developed an engineering ethics course for his department in response to the ABET requirement to incorporate ethics topics into the undergraduate engineering curriculum. *Engineering Ethics* was written as a vehicle for presenting ethical theory, analysis, and problem solving to engineering undergraduates in a concise and readily accessible way.
Acknowledgments: I would like to thank Profs. Charles Harris and Michael Rabins of Texas A & M University whose NSF sponsored workshops on engineering ethics got me started thinking in this field. Special thanks to my wife Liz, who proofread the manuscript for this book, provided many useful suggestions, and who helped me learn how to teach "soft" topics to engineers.

David I. Schwartz is an Assistant Professor in the Computer Science Department at Cornell University and earned his B.S., M.S., and Ph.D. degrees in Civil Engineering from State University of New York at Buffalo. Throughout his graduate studies, Schwartz combined principles of computer science to applications of civil engineering. He became interested in helping students learn how to apply software tools for solving a variety of engineering problems. He teaches his students to learn incrementally and practice frequently to gain the maturity to tackle other subjects. In his spare time, Schwartz plays drums in a variety of bands.
Acknowledgments: I dedicate my books to my family, friends, and students who all helped in so many ways. Many thanks go to the schools of Civil Engineering and Engineering & Applied Science at State University of New York at Buffalo where I originally developed and tested my UNIX and Maple books. I greatly appreciate the opportunity to explore my goals and all the help from everyone at the Computer Science Department at Cornell. Eric Svendsen and everyone at Prentice Hall also deserve my gratitude for helping to make these books a reality. Many thanks, also, to those who submitted interviews and images.

Ron Larsen is an Associate Professor of Chemical Engineering at Montana State University, and received his Ph.D. from the Pennsylvania State University. He was initially attracted to engineering by the challenges the profession offers, but also appreciates that engineering is a serving profession. Some of the greatest challenges he has faced while teaching have involved non-traditional teaching methods, including evening courses for practicing engineers and teaching through an interpreter at the Mongolian National University. These experiences have provided tremendous opportunities to learn new ways to communicate technical material. He tries to incorporate the skills he has learned in non-traditional arenas to improve his lectures, written materials, and learning programs. Dr. Larsen views modern software as one of the new tools that will radically alter the way engineers work, and his book *Introduction to Mathcad* was written to help young engineers prepare to meet the challenges of an ever-changing workplace.
Acknowledgments: To my students at Montana State University who have endured the rough drafts and typos, and who still allow me to experiment with their classes—my sincere thanks.

Peter Schiavone is a professor and student advisor in the Department of Mechanical Engineering at the University of Alberta, Canada. He received his Ph.D. from the University of Strathclyde, U.K. in 1988. He has authored several books in the area of student academic success as well as numerous papers in international scientific research journals. Dr. Schiavone has worked in private industry in several different areas of engineering including aerospace and systems engineering. He founded the first Mathematics Resource Center at the University of Alberta, a unit designed specifically to teach new students the necessary *survival skills* in mathematics and the physical sciences required for success in first-year engineering. This led to the Students' Union Gold Key Award for outstanding contributions to the university. Dr. Schiavone lectures regularly to freshman engineering students and to new engineering professors on engineering success, in particular about maximizing students' academic performance. He wrote the book *Engineering Success* in order to share the *secrets of success in engineering study*: the most effective, tried and tested methods used by the most successful engineering students.

Acknowledgements: Thanks to Eric Svendsen for his encouragement and support; to Richard Felder for being such an inspiration; to my wife Linda for sharing my dreams and believing in me; and to Francesca and Antonio for putting up with Dad when working on the text.

Mark N. Horenstein is a Professor in the Department of Electrical and Computer Engineering at Boston University. He has degrees in Electrical Engineering from M.I.T. and U.C. Berkeley and has been involved in teaching engineering design for the greater part of his academic career. He  devised and developed the senior design project class taken by all electrical and computer engineering students at Boston University. In this class, the students work for a virtual engineering company developing products and systems for real-world engineering and social-service clients. Many of the design projects developed in his class have been aimed at assistive technologies for individuals with disabilities.

Acknowledgments: I would like to thank Prof. James Bethune, the architect of the Peak Performance event at Boston University, for his permission to highlight the competition in my text. Several of the ideas relating to brainstorming and teamwork were derived from a workshop on engineering design offered by Prof. Charles Lovas of Southern Methodist University. The principles of estimation were derived in part from a freshman engineering problem posed by Prof. Thomas Kincaid of Boston University.

Kirk D. Hagen is a professor at Weber State University in Ogden, Utah. He has taught introductory-level engineering courses and upper-division thermal science courses at WSU since 1993. He received his B.S. degree in physics from Weber State College and his M.S. degree  in mechanical engineering from Utah State University, after which he worked as a thermal designer/analyst in the aerospace and electronics industries. After several years of engineering practice, he resumed his formal education, earning his Ph.D. in mechanical engineering at the University of Utah. Hagen is the author of an undergraduate heat transfer text. Having drawn upon his industrial and teaching experience, he strongly believes that engineering students must develop effective analytical problem solving abilities. His book, *Introduction to Engineering Analysis*, was written to help beginning engineering students learn a systematic approach to engineering analysis.

Richard M. Lueptow is the Charles Deering McCormick Professor of Teaching Excellence and Associate Professor of Mechanical Engineering at Northwestern University. He is a native of Wisconsin and received his doctorate from the Massachusetts Institute of Technology in 1986. He teaches design, fluid mechanics, and  spectral analysis techniques. "In my design class I saw a need for a self-paced tutorial for my students to learn CAD software quickly and easily. I worked with several students a few years ago to develop just this type of tutorial, which has since evolved into a book. My goal is to introduce students to engineering graphics and CAD, while showing them how much fun it can be." Rich has an active research program on rotating filtration, Taylor Couette flow, granular flow, fire suppression, and acoustics. He has five patents and over 40 refereed journal and proceedings papers along with many other articles, abstracts, and presentations.

Acknowledgments: Thanks to my talented and hard-working co-authors as well as the many colleagues and students who took the tutorial for a "test drive." Special thanks to Mike Minbiole for his major contributions to Graphics Concepts with SolidWorks. Thanks also to Northwestern University for the time to work on a book. Most of all, thanks to my loving wife, Maiya, and my children, Hannah and Kyle, for supporting me in this endeavor. (Photo courtesy of Evanston Photographic Studios, Inc.)

Jack Leifer is an Assistant Professor in the Department of Mechanical Engineering at the University of Kentucky Extended Campus Program in Paducah, and was previously with the Department of Mathematical Sciences and Engineering at the University of South Carolina—  Aiken. He received his Ph.D. in Mechanical Engineering from the University of Texas at Austin in December 1995.

His current research interests include the modeling of sensors for manufacturing, and the use of Artificial Neural Networks to predict corrosion.

Acknowledgements: I'd like to thank my colleagues at USC—Aiken, especially Professors Mike May and Laurene Fausett, for their encouragement and feedback; Eric Svendsen and Joe Russo of Prentice Hall, for their useful suggestions and flexibility with deadlines; and my parents, Felice and Morton Leifer, for being there and providing support (as always) as I completed this book.

David C. Kuncicky is a native Floridian. He earned his Baccalaureate in psychology, Master's in computer science, and Ph.D. in computer science from Florida State University. He has served as a faculty member in the Department of Electrical Engineering at the FAMU–FSU College of Engineering and the Department of Computer Science at Florida State University. He has taught computer science and computer engineering courses for over 15 years. He has published research in the areas of intelligent hybrid systems and neural networks. He is currently the Director of Engineering at Bioreason, Inc. in Sante Fe, New Mexico.

Acknowledgments: Thanks to Steffie and Helen for putting up with my late nights and long weekends at the computer. Thanks also to the helpful and insightful technical reviews by Jerry Ralya, Kathy Kitto, Avi Singhal, Thomas Hill, Ron Eaglin, Larry Richards, and Susan Freeman. I appreciate the patience of Eric Svendsen and Joe Russo of Prentice Hall for gently guiding me through this project. Finally, thanks to Susan Bassett for having faith in my abilities, and for providing continued tutelage and support.

Jim Steger is currently Chief Technical Officer and cofounder of an Internet applications company. He graduated with a Bachelor of Science degree in Mechanical Engineering from Northwestern University. His prior work included mechanical engineering assignments at Motorola and Acco Brands. At Motorola, Jim worked on part design for two-way radios and was one of the lead mechanical engineers on a cellular phone product line. At Acco Brands, Jim was the sole engineer on numerous office product designs. His Worx stapler has won design awards in the United States and in Europe. Jim has been a Pro/Engineer user for over six years.

Acknowledgments: Many thanks to my co-authors, especially Rich Lueptow for his leadership on this project. I would also like to thank my family for their continuous support.

David I. Schneider holds an A.B. degree from Oberlin College and a Ph.D. degree in Mathematics from MIT. He has taught for 34 years, primarily at the University of Maryland. Dr. Schneider has authored 28 books, with one-half of them computer programming books. He has developed three customized software packages that are supplied as supplements to over 55 mathematics textbooks. His involvement with computers dates back to 1962, when he programmed a special purpose computer at MIT's Lincoln Laboratory to correct errors in a communications system.

Michael T. Snyder is President of Internet startup Appointments123.com. He is a native of Chicago, and he received his Bachelor of Science degree in Mechanical Engineering from the University of Notre Dame. Mike also graduated with honors from Northwestern University's Kellogg Graduate School of Management in 1999 with his Masters of Management degree. Before Appointments123.com, Mike was a mechanical engineer in new product development for Motorola Cellular and Acco Office Products. He has received four patents for his mechanical design work. "Pro/Engineer was an invaluable design tool for me, and I am glad to help students learn the basics of Pro/Engineer."

Acknowledgments: Thanks to Rich Lueptow and Jim Steger for inviting me to be a part of this great project. Of course, thanks to my wife Gretchen for her support in my various projects.

Stephen J. Chapman received a BS in Electrical Engineering from Louisiana State University (1975), an MSE in Electrical Engineering from the University of Central Florida (1979), and pursued further graduate studies at Rice University. Mr. Chapman is currently Manager of Technical Systems for British Aerospace Australia, in Melbourne, Australia. In this position, he provides technical direction and design authority for the work of younger engineers within the company. He is also continuing to teach at local universities on a part-time basis.

Mr. Chapman is a Senior Member of the Institute of Electrical and Electronics Engineers (and several of its component societies). He is also a member of the Association for Computing Machinery and the Institution of Engineers (Australia).

Reviewers

ESource benefited from a wealth of reviewers who on the series from its initial idea stage to its completion. Reviewers read manuscripts and contributed insightful comments that helped the authors write great books. We would like to thank everyone who helped us with this project.

Concept Document

Naeem Abdurrahman *University of Texas, Austin*
Grant Baker *University of Alaska, Anchorage*
Betty Barr *University of Houston*
William Beckwith *Clemson University*
Ramzi Bualuan *University of Notre Dame*
Dale Calkins *University of Washington*
Arthur Clausing *University of Illinois at Urbana –Champaign*
John Glover *University of Houston*
A.S. Hodel *Auburn University*
Denise Jackson *University of Tennessee, Knoxville*
Kathleen Kitto *Western Washington University*
Terry Kohutek *Texas A&M University*
Larry Richards *University of Virginia*
Avi Singhal *Arizona State University*
Joseph Wujek *University of California, Berkeley*
Mandochehr Zoghi *University of Dayton*

Books

Stephen Allan *Utah State University*
Naeem Abdurrahman *University of Texas, Austin*
Anil Bajaj *Purdue University*
Grant Baker *University of Alaska—Anchorage*
Betty Burr *University of Houston*
William Beckwith *Clemson University*
Haym Benaroya *Rutgers University*
Tom Bledsaw *ITT Technical Institute*
Tom Bryson *University of Missouri, Rolla*
Ramzi Bualuan *University of Notre Dame*
Dan Budny *Purdue University*
Dale Calkins *University of Washington*
Arthur Clausing *University of Illinois*
James Devine *University of South Florida*

Patrick Fitzhorn *Colorado State University*
Dale Elifrits *University of Missouri, Rolla*
Frank Gerlitz *Washtenaw College*
John Glover *University of Houston*
John Graham *University of North Carolina—Charlotte*
Malcom Heimer *Florida International University*
A.S. Hodel *Auburn University*
Vern Johnson *University of Arizona*
Kathleen Kitto *Western Washington University*
Robert Montgomery *Purdue University*
Mark Nagurka *Marquette University*
Romarathnam Narasimhan *University of Miami*
Larry Richards *University of Virginia*
Marc H. Richman *Brown University*
Avi Singhal *Arizona State University*
Tim Sykes *Houston Community College*
Thomas Hill *SUNY at Buffalo*
Michael S. Wells *Tennessee Tech University*
Joseph Wujek *University of California, Berkeley*
Edward Young *University of South Carolina*
Mandochehr Zoghi *University of Dayton*
John Biddle *California State Polytechnic University*
Fred Boadu *Duke University*
Harish Cherukuri *University of North Carolina –Charlotte*
Barry Crittendon *Virginia Polytechnic and State University*
Ron Eaglin *University of Central Florida*
Susan Freeman *Northeastern University*
Frank Gerlitz *Washtenaw Community College*
Otto Gygax *Oregon State University*
Donald Herling *Oregon State University*
James N. Jensen *SUNY at Buffalo*
Autar Kaw *University of South Florida*
Kenneth Klika *University of Akron*
Terry L. Kohutek *Texas A&M University*
Melvin J. Maron *University of Louisville*
Soronadi Nnaji *Florida A&M University*
Michael Peshkin *Northwestern University*
Randy Shih *Oregon Institute of Technology*
Neil R. Thompson *University of Waterloo*
Garry Young *Oklahoma State University*

Contents

1

Engineering Graphics

OVERVIEW

Engineering designs start as images in the mind's eye of an engineer. Engineering graphics has evolved to communicate and record these ideas on paper both two- and three-dimensionally. In the past few decades, the computer has made it possible to automate the creation of engineering graphics. Today engineering design and engineering graphics are inextricably connected. Engineering design is communicated visually using engineering graphics.

SECTIONS

OBJECTIVES

After reading this chapter, you should be able to:

- Describe visual thinking
- Differentiate perspective, isometric, and orthographic projections
- Understand the basis of CAD
- Understand the relationship between design and CAD

1.1 THE IMPORTANCE OF ENGINEERING GRAPHICS

"Visualizing" a picture or image in your mind is a familiar experience. The image can be visualized at many different levels of abstraction. Think about light and you might see the image of a light bulb in your "mind's eye." Alternatively, you might think about light versus dark. Or you might visualize a flashlight or table lamp. Such visual thinking is necessary in engineering and science. Albert Einstein said that he rarely thought in words. Instead, he laboriously translated his visual images into verbal and mathematical terms.

Visual thinking is a foundation of engineering. Walter P. Chrysler, founder of the automobile company, recounted his experience as an apprentice machinist where he built a model locomotive that existed "within my mind so real, so complete, that it seemed to have three dimensions there."

Yet, the complexity of today's technology rarely permits a single person to build a device from his own visual image. The images must be conveyed to other engineers and designers. In addition, those images must be constructed in such a way that they are in a readily recognizable, consistent, and readable format. This assuress that the visual ideas are clearly and unambiguously conveyed to others. *Engineering graphics* is a highly stylized way of presenting images of parts or assemblies.

A major portion of engineering information is recorded and transmitted using engineering graphics. In fact, 92 percent of the design process is graphically based. Written and verbal communications along with mathematics account for the remaining eight percent. To demonstrate the effectiveness of engineering graphics compared to a written description try to visualize an ice scraper based on this word description:

> An ice scraper is generally in the shape of a 140 × 80 × 10 mm rectangular prism. One end is beveled from zero thickness to the maximum thickness in a length of 40 mm to form a sharp edge. The opposite end is semicircular. A 20 mm diameter hole is positioned so the center of the hole is 40 mm from the semicircular end and 40 mm from either side of the scraper.

It is evident immediately that the shape of the ice scraper is much more easily visualized from the graphical representation shown in Figure 1.1 than from the word description. Humans grasp information much more quickly when that information is presented in a graphical or visual form rather than as a word description.

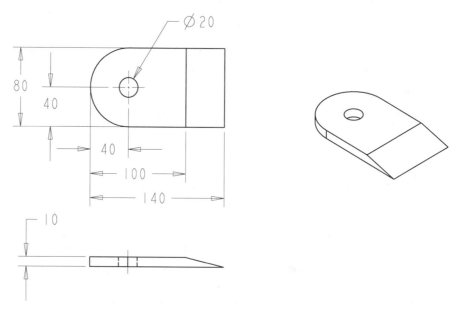

Figure 1.1.

Engineering drawings, whether done using a pencil and paper or a computer, start with a blank page or screen. The engineer's mind's eye image must be transferred to the paper or computer screen. The creative nature of this activity is similar to that of an artist. Perhaps the greatest example of this is Leonardo da Vinci, who had exceptional engineering creativity devising items such as parachutes and ball bearings, shown in Figure 1.2, hundreds of years before they were re-invented. He also had exceptional artistic talent, creating some of the most famous pictures ever painted such as *Mona Lisa* and *The Last Supper*.

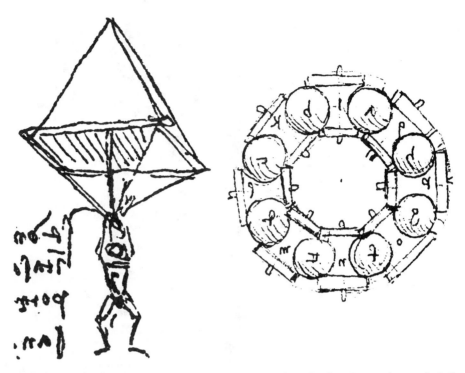

Figure 1.2.   The creative genius of da Vinci is evident in these sketches of a parachute and a ball bearing, both devised hundreds of years before they were re-invented. (Parachute used with permission of the Biblioteca–Pinacoteca Ambrosiana, Milan, Italy. Property of the Ambrosian Library. All rights reserved. Reproduction is forbidden. [*The Inventions of Leonardo da Vinci*, Charles Gibbs-Smith, Phaidon Press, Oxford, 1978, p. 24.] Ball bearing used with permission of EMB-Service for Publishers, Lucerne, Switzerland. [*The Unknown Leonardo*, edited by Ladislao Reti, McGraw-Hill, 1974, p. 286])

1.2   ENGINEERING GRAPHICS

The first authentic record of engineering graphics dates back to 2130 BC, based on a statue now in the Museum of the Louvre, Paris. The statue depicts an engineer and governor of a small city-state in an area later known as Babylon. At the base of the statue are measuring scales and scribing instruments along with a plan of a fortress engraved on a stone tablet.

Except for the use of pen and paper rather than stone tablets, it was not until printed books appeared around 1450 that techniques of graphics advanced. Around the same time, *pictorial perspective* drawing was invented by artist Paolo Uccello. This type of drawing presents an object much like it would look to the human eye or in a photograph, as shown in Figure 1.3. The essential characteristic of a perspective drawing is that parallel lines converge at a point in the distance like parallel railroad tracks seem to converge in the distance. Copper-plate engravings permitted the production of finely detailed technical drawings using pictorial perspective in large numbers. The pictorial perspective drawings were crucial to the advancement of technology through the Renaissance and until the beginning of the Industrial Revolution. But these drawings could not convey adequately details of the construction of an object. One solution to this problem was the use of the *exploded view* developed in the 15th century and perfected by Leonardo da Vinci. The exploded view of an assembly of individual parts shows the parts spread out along a common axis, as shown for the hoist in Figure 1.4. The exploded view reveals details of the individual parts along with showing the order in which they are assembled.

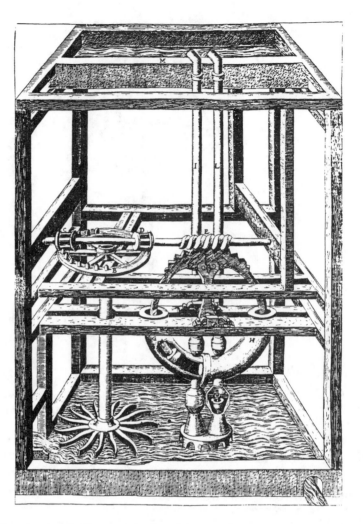

Figure 1.3. An example of pictorial perspective by Agostino Ramelli in 1588. (Used with permission of the Syndics of Cambridge University Library. [*The Various and Ingenious Machines of Agostino Ramelli (1588)*, translated by Martha Teach Gnudi, Johns Hopkins University Press, 1976. p. 83.])

The Industrial Revolution brought with it the need to tie more closely the concept of a design with the final manufactured product using technical drawing. The perspective drawing of a simple object in Figure 1.5a shows pictorially what the object looks like. However, it is difficult to represent accurately dimensions and other details in a perspective drawing. *Orthographic projections*, developed in 1528 by German artist Albrecht Dürer, accomplish this quite well. An orthographic projection typically shows three views of an object. Each view shows a different side of the object (say the front, top, and side). An example of an orthographic projection is shown in Figure 1.5b. Orthographic projections are typically easy to draw, and the lengths and angles in orthographic projections have little distortion. As a result, orthographic drawings can convey more information than a perspective drawing. But their interpretation takes more effort than a pictorial perspective, as is evident from Figure 1.5. French philosopher and mathematician René Descartes laid the foundation for the mathematical principles of projections by connecting geometry to algebra in the 17th century. Much later Gaspard Monge, a French mathematician, "invented" the mathematical principles

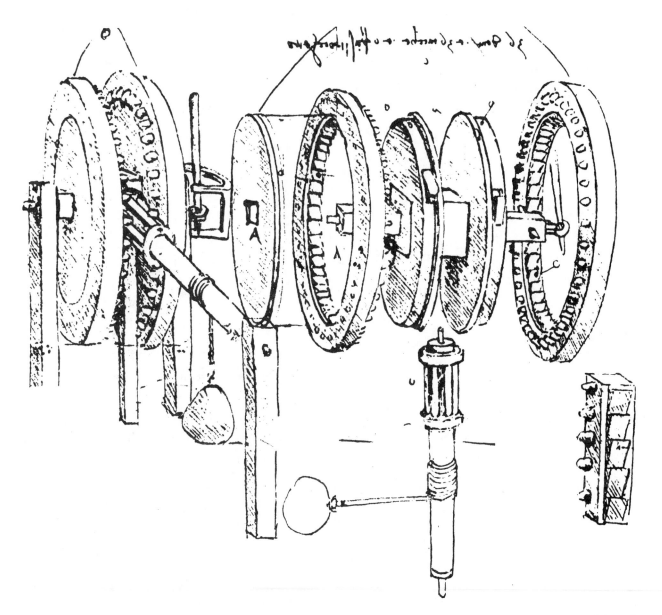

Figure 1.4. Assembled and exploded view of a hoist by Leonardo da Vinci, circa 1500. (Used with permission of the Biblioteca-Pinacoteca Ambrosiana, Milan, Italy. Property of the Ambrosian Library. All rights reserved. Reproduction is forbidden. [*The Inventions of Leonardo da Vinci*, Charles Gibbs-Smith, Phaidon Press, Oxford, 1978, p. 64.])

of projection known as *descriptive geometry*. These principles form the basis of engineering graphics today. But because these principles were thought to be of such strategic importance, they remained military secrets until 1795. By the 19th century, orthographic projections were used almost universally in mechanical drawing, and they are still the basis for engineering drawings today.

The *isometric view* is used more often today than the pictorial perspective view. Historically, it was used for centuries by engravers. Then in the early 19th century, William Farish, an English mathematician, formalized the isometric view and introduced it to engineers. The isometric view simplifies the pictorial perspective. In an isometric view, parallel lines remain parallel rather than converging to a point in the distance, as shown in Fig. 1.5c. Keeping parallel lines parallel distorts the appearance of the object slightly. But the distortion in an isometric view is negligible for objects of limited depth. For situations in which the depth of the object is large, such as an architectural view down a long hallway, the pictorial perspective is preferable. The advantage of the isometric view, though, is that it is much easier to draw than a pictorial perspective view.

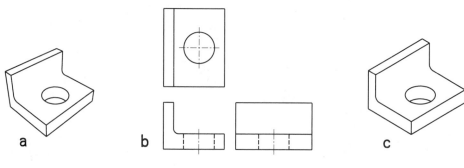

Figure 1.5.

1.3 CAD

The introduction of the computer revolutionized engineering graphics. Pioneers in computer-aided engineering graphics envisioned the computer as a tool to replace paper and pencil drafting with a system that is more automated, efficient, and accurate. The first demonstration of a computer-based drafting tool was a system called SKETCHPAD developed at the Massachusetts Institute of Technology in 1963 by Ivan Sutherland. The system used a monochrome monitor with a light pen for input from the user. The following year IBM commercialized computer-aided drafting.

During the 1970s, computer-aided drafting blossomed as the technology changed from scientific endeavor to an economically indispensable industrial tool for design. Commands for geometry generators to create commonly occurring shapes were added. Functions were added to control the viewing of the drawing geometry. Modifiers such as rotate, delete, and mirror were implemented. Commands could be accessed by typing on the keyboard or by using a mouse. Perhaps most importantly, three-dimensional modeling techniques became a key part of engineering graphics software.

By the 1980s, computer-aided drafting became fully developed in the marketplace as a standard tool in industry. In addition, the current technology of solids modeling came about. Solids models represent objects in the virtual environment of the computer just as they exist in reality, having a volume as well as surfaces and edges. The introduction of Pro/ENGINEER® in 1988 and SolidWorks® in the 1990s revolutionized computer-aided design and drafting. Today solids modeling remains the state-of-the-art technology.

What we have been referring to as computer-aided drafting is usually termed *CAD*, an acronym for Computer Aided Design, Computer Aided Drafting, or Computer Aided Design and Drafting. Originally the term Computer Aided Design included any technique that uses computers in the design process including drafting, stress analysis, and motion analysis. But over the last 35 years CAD has come to refer more specifically to Computer Aided Design and Drafting. Computer Aided Engineering (CAE) is used to refer to the broader range of computer-related design tools.

1.4 DESIGN AND CAD

Inextricably connected with engineering graphics is the *design process* in which an engineering or design team faces a particular engineering problem and devises a solution to that problem. Often the design team includes persons responsible for engineering, product design, production system design, manufacturing, marketing, and sales. The idea is to simultaneously develop the product and the manufacturing process for the product. This is known as *concurrent engineering* or *integrated product and process design*. Key to the success of concurrent engineering is communication of information. Engineering graphics is one of the primary methods used by concurrent engineering teams to record and transfer information during the design process.

The process of bringing a product to market is shown in Figure 1.6. The process begins with the identification of a market, or user need. After this, the design process is the key to bridging the gap between a user need and the manufacture and sales of a product. The design process can be broken down into three parts as indicated in Figure 1.6.

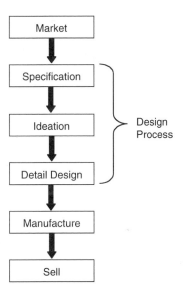

Figure 1.6.

The first part is the *specification* of the problem. The *design specification* is a list of requirements that the final product must meet, including size, performance, weight, and so on. The second part of the design process is called *ideation* or conceptual design. In this phase, the design team devises as many ideas for solutions to the design problem as possible and then narrows them down to the best one based on the specification. In many cases, a designer or engineer will quickly sketch ideas to explore or communicate the design concept to the rest of the design team. These freehand sketches form the basis for the details of the design that are laid down in the third phase of the design process. It is in this last phase of the *design process*, known as *detail design*, that CAD is crucial. The conceptual ideas for the product that were seen in a designer's mind's eye or are on paper as rough sketches must then be translated into the visual language of engineering graphics. In this way, the ideas can be understood clearly and accurately by the design team and other designers, engineers, fabricators, suppliers, and machinists. It is in this phase of the design that the nitty gritty details have to be worked out. Should the device be 30 mm long or should it be 35 mm long? How will one part fit with another? What size hole should be used? What material should be used? What manufacturing process will be used to make the part? The number of individual decisions that need to be made can be very large, even for a relatively simple part. Once the engineering drawings have been created, the product can be manufactured and eventually sold.

The use of CAD has had a great impact on the design process. For example, a part may be modified several times to meet the design specification or to mate with another part. Before the advent of CAD, these modifications were very tedious, time-consuming, and prone to error. However, CAD has made it possible to make these changes relatively easily and quickly. The connectivity of computers using local area networks then makes the revised electronic drawings available to a team of engineers at an instant. This is crucial as engineering systems become more complex and operational requirements become more stringent. For example, a modern jet aircraft has several million individual parts that must all fit together and perform safely for several decades.

Although CAD had a great impact on making the design process speedier and more accurate, the capabilities of the first few generations of CAD were still limited. Early CAD systems only provided a means of automating the drafting process to create orthographic engineering drawings. The designer or engineer would simply generate a line on the computer screen rather than drawing the line on paper. Current computer graphics software such as "paint" or "draw" programs for personal computers work this way. As CAD became more sophisticated, it helped automate the drafting process based on the "intelligence" of the software. CAD software lacking such intelligence required an engineer to draw a pair of parallel lines an exact distance apart by specifying coordinates of the endpoints of the lines. More advanced generations of CAD software permitted an engineer to draw approximately parallel lines using a mouse. Then the engineer would specify a particular distance between the lines and that the lines should be parallel. The CAD software then automatically placed these lines the specified distance apart and made them parallel. However, the major problem with the early generations of CAD software was that the designer or engineer was simply creating two-dimensional orthographic views of a three-dimensional part using a computer instead of a pencil and paper. From these two-dimensional views, the engineer still needed to reconstruct the mind's eye view of the three-dimensional image in the same way as if the drawings were created by hand.

The current generation of CAD software has had a very profound effect on the design process, because it is now possible to create a virtual prototype of a part or assembly on a computer. For example, the solids model of a pizza cutter is shown in Figure 1.7. Rather than translating a three-dimensional image from the mind's eye to a two-dimensional orthographic projection of the object, current CAD software starts with generating a three-dimensional virtual model of the object directly on the computer. This virtual model can be rotated so that it can be viewed from different angles. Several parts can be virtually assembled on the computer to make sure that they fit together. The assembled parts can be viewed as an assembly or in an exploded view. All of this is done in a virtual environment on the computer before the two-dimensional orthographic engineering drawings are even produced. It is still usually necessary to produce the orthographic engineering drawings. But these drawings only to serve as a standard means of engineering graphics communication, rather than as a tedious, time-consuming task necessary to proceed with the design process.

Figure 1.7.

What Happened to Pencil and Paper Drawings?

CAD drawings have already replaced pencil and paper drawings. Through the 1970s and even into the 1980s many engineering and design facilities consisted of rows and rows of drafting tables with a designer or engineer hunched over a drawing on each table. Engineering colleges and universities required a full-year course in "engineering drafting" or "graphics communication" for all engineering students. Many of these students purchased a set of drawing instruments along with their first semester textbooks. They spent endless hours practicing lettering and drawing perfect circles.

Now nearly all of the drafting tables and drafting courses have been replaced by CAD. One can still find a drafting table here and there, but it is not for creating engineering drawings. Most often it is used for displaying a large CAD drawing to designers and engineers. They can make notes on the drawing or freehand sketch modifications on the drawing. The pencil is still an ideal means for generating ideas and quickly conveying those ideas to others. But eventually, all of the pencil markings are used as the basis for modifying the CAD drawing.

In some companies with traditional products that have not changed for decades (like a spoon or a chair), pencil and paper drawings are gradually being converted into electronic form. In some cases, the original drawing is simply scanned to create an electronic version. The scanned drawing cannot be modified, but the electronic version takes much less storage space than a hard copy. In other cases, the original pencil and paper drawings are being systematically converted to CAD drawings, so that they can be modified if necessary. In any case, though, the pencil and paper drawing is now just a part of the history of engineering.

KEY TERMS

CAD	Detail Design	Isometric view
Descriptive geometry	Engineering graphics	Orthographic projection
Design process	Exploded view	Pictorial perspective view
Design specification	Ideation	

Problems

1. Research and report on an important historical figure in engineering graphics such as Leonardo da Vinci, Albrecht Dürer, Gaspard Monge, René Descartes, William Farish, M. C. Escher, Frank Lloyd Wright, Ivan Sutherland, or Paolo Uccello.

2. Using the World Wide Web, search for computer-aided design web sites. Report on the variety of software available for CAD and its capabilities.

3. Trace the early development of CAD and report on your findings. A particularly useful starting point is an article by S. H. Clauser in the November 1981 issue of *Mechanical Engineering*.

4. Computer hardware and user interface development has had a profound effect on the evolution of CAD software. Research and report on the impact of the light pen, the graphics tablet, the direct view storage tube, raster graphics technology, the work-station computer, the personal computer, or the mouse on the capability and evolution of CAD. (Many textbooks on engineering graphics discuss these items.)

5. Outline the design process and indicate how the three steps in the design process would relate to:

   a. the design of a suspension system for a mountain bike.
   b. the design of an infant car seat.
   c. the design of headphones for a portable cassette player.
   d. the design of a squirrel-proof bird feeder.
   e. the design of a car-mounted bicycle carrier.
   f. the design of children's playground equipment.

6. Explain how "paint" or "draw" programs such as McDraw, Adobe Illustrator, MS Paint, or drawing tools in MS Word differ from CAD engineering graphics software.

2

Projections Used in Engineering Graphics

OVERVIEW

Engineering graphics is a highly stylized scheme to represent three-dimensional objects on a two-dimensional paper or computer screen. This can be accomplished by representing all three dimensions of an object in a single image or by presenting a collection of views of different sides of the object. Working drawings are the practical result of using engineering graphics to represent objects.

2.1 PROJECTIONS

The goal in engineering graphics, whether it is freehand sketching or CAD, is to represent a physical object or the mind's eye image of an object so that the image can be conveyed to other persons. Objects can be shown as *3-D projections* or *multiview projections*. Figure 2.1 shows the handle of a pizza cutter shown in both ways. The 3-D projection clearly suggests the three-dimensional character of the handle, even though it is displayed on a two-dimensional medium (the page). 3-D projections are useful in that they provide an image that is similar to the image in the designer's mind's eye. But 3-D projections are often weak in providing adequate details of the object, and there is often some distortion of the object. For instance, a circular hole at the right end of the handle becomes an ellipse in an isometric 3-D projection.

Multiview projections are used to overcome the weaknesses of 3-D projections. Multiview projections are a collection of flat 2-D drawings of the different sides of an object.

SECTIONS

OBJECTIVES

After reading this chapter, you should:

- Understand the spatial relation between 3-D projections and multiview projections
- Be able to differentiate isometric, trimetric, perspective, and oblique 3-D projections
- Understand how multiview projections are related to the views of the sides of an object
- Know the proper placement of orthographic views
- Know the difference between third-angle and first-angle orthographic projections
- Be able to differentiate the various kinds of working drawings

For instance, the side and bottom end of the pizza cutter handle are shown in the multi-view projection in Figure 2.1. Because there are two views, it is quite easy to depict details of the object. In addition, taken together, multiview projections provide a more accurate representation of the object than the 3-D projection—a circular hole appears as a circle in a multiview projection. On the other hand, multiview projections require substantial inter-pretation, and the overall shape of an object is often not obvious upon first glance. Conse-quently, the combination of the overall image provided by 3-D projections and details provided by multiview projections yield a representation of an object that is best. The shape of the object is immediately evident from the 3-D projection, and the detail needed for an accurate description of the object is available from the multiview projection.

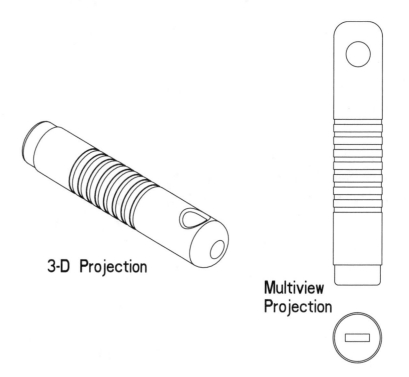

Figure 2.1.

2.2   3-D PROJECTIONS

Three different types of 3-D projections are available in most CAD software: isometric, trimetric, and perspective. These three views of a cube are shown in Figure 2.2. In all three cases, these 3-D projections represent all three dimensions of the cube in a single planar image. Although it is clear in all three cases that the object is a cube, each type of 3-D projection has its advantages and disadvantages.

The *isometric* projection has a standard orientation that makes it the typical projec-tion used in CAD. In an isometric projection, the width and depth dimensions are sketched at 30° above horizontal as shown in Figure 2.2a. This results in the three angles at the upper front corner of the cube being equal to 120°. The three sides of the cube are also equal, leading to the term iso (equal) -metric (measure). Isometric drawings work quite well for objects of limited depth. However, an isometric drawing distorts the object when the depth is significant. In this case, a pictorial perspective drawing is better.

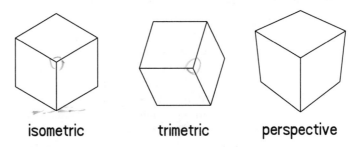

isometric   trimetric   perspective

Figure 2.2.

In general, the *trimetric* projection offers more flexibility in orienting the object in space. The width and depth dimensions are at arbitrary angles to the horizontal, and the three angles at the upper front corner of the cube are unequal. This makes the three sides of the cube each have a different length as measured in the plane of the drawing; hence the name tri-metric. In most CAD software, the trimetric projection fixes one side along a horizontal line and tips the cube forward as shown in Figure 2.2b. A *dimetric* projection sets two sides of the cube, usually those of the front face, equal.

A pictorial perspective, or simply *perspective*, projection is drawn so that parallel lines converge in the distance as shown in Figure 2.2c, unlike isometric or trimetric projections where parallel lines remain parallel. A perspective projection is quite useful in providing a realistic image of an object when the object spans a long distance, such as the view of a bridge or aircraft from one end. Generally, small manufactured objects are adequately represented by isometric or trimetric views.

Two types of pictorial sketches are used frequently in freehand sketching: isometric and oblique. The isometric projection was discussed with respect to 3-D CAD projections. The isometric projection is often used in freehand sketching because it is relatively easy to create a realistic sketch of an object. But the *oblique projection* is usually even easier to sketch. The oblique projection places the principal face of the object parallel to the plane of the paper with the axes in the plane of the paper perpendicular to one another. The axis into the paper is at an arbitrary angle with respect to the horizontal. Figure 2.3 compares an isometric projection and an oblique projection of a cube with a hole in it. The advantage of the oblique projection is that details in the front face of the object retain their true shape. For instance, the circle on the front face is circular in the oblique projection, while it is elliptical in the isometric projection. This feature often makes oblique freehand sketching somewhat easier than isometric sketching.

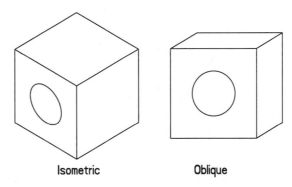

Isometric   Oblique

Figure 2.3.

2.3 MULTIVIEW PROJECTIONS

The standard means of multiview projection in engineering graphics is what we have referred to earlier as the *orthographic projection*. Although 3-D projections provide a readily identifiable visual image of an object, multiview projections are ideal for showing the details of an object. Dimensions can be shown easily and most features remain undistorted in multiview projections.

An orthographic projection is most easily thought of as a collection of views of different sides of an object—front, top, side, and so forth. For instance, two orthographic projections could be used for a coffee mug. The front view would show the sidewall of the mug along with the loop forming the handle. The top view would show what one would see looking down into the mug—a circular rim of the mug, the bottom of the inside of the mug, and the top of the handle that sticks out of the side of the mug. Dimensions of the mug could easily be added to the projections of each side of the mug to create an engineering drawing.

One useful way of looking at multiview projections is to imagine a glass box surrounding the object as shown in Figure 2.4. The image of each side of the object can be projected onto the wall of the glass box. Now an observer on the outside of the box can

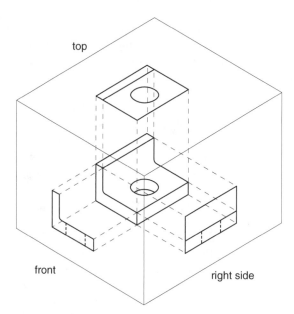

Figure 2.4.

see each side of the object as projected on each of the six walls of the box. Solid lines show the edges evident in the projection, and dashed lines show lines that are hidden by the object. Now imagine unfolding the glass box as if each of the edges of the glass box were a hinge, so that the front view is in the middle. Now the unfolded glass box represents all six sides of the object in a single plane as shown in Figure 2.5. In unfolding the glass box, the top view is positioned above the front view, the bottom view is below the front view, the right-side view is to the right of the front view, and so on. The dimensions of the object remain the same in all views. For example, the horizontal dimension (width of the object) in the front view is identical in that same dimension in the top view and bottom view. The views also remain aligned so that the bottom edge in the front

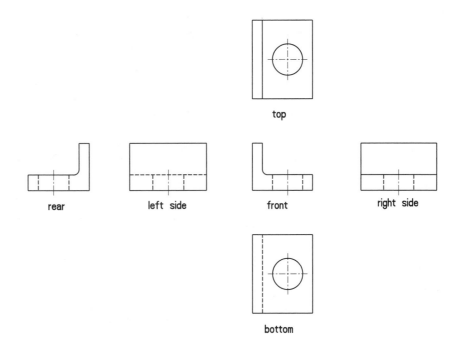

Figure 2.5.

view is even with the bottom edge in the right side, left side, and rear views. Likewise, the top edges remain aligned. Finally, the same edges in adjacent views are closest together. For instance, the same edge of the object is at the left-side of the front view and the right side of the left side view. This edge in the front view is closest to the same edge in the left-side view.

In many cases, three views are needed to represent an object accurately, although in some cases (like a coffee mug) only two views are necessary, and in other cases more than three views are needed to show complex features of the object. It is helpful to select the side of the object that is most descriptive of the object as the front view. Sometimes this may place an object so that what is normally thought of as the front of the object is not shown in the front view of the multiview projection. For example, what is usually described as being the side of a car should be chosen as the front view, because this view is probably most descriptive and easily recognizable as a car. A view of the front of a car (grille, bumper, and windshield) is not as descriptive or as obvious as the side of the car. Furthermore, the object should be properly oriented in the front view. For instance, a car should be shown with its wheels downward in their normal operating position for the front view. The other views that are shown in addition to the front view should be views that best represent features of the object. Normally the minimum number of views necessary to accurately represent the object is used. The standard practice is to use the front, top, and right-side views. But the choice of which views to use depends on the object and which details need to be shown most clearly.

A complication that arises in multiview projections is that two different standards are used for the placement of projections. In North America (and to some extent, in Great Britain) the unfolding of the glass box approach places the top view above the front view, the right-side view to the right of the front view, and so on. This placement of views is called *third-angle projection*. But in most of the rest of the world an alternative approach for the placement of views is used. In this case the placement of views is what would result if the object were laid on the paper with its front side up for the front view and then rolled on one edge for the other views. For instance, if the object were rolled to the right so that it rests on its right side, then the left side would be facing up. So the left-side view is placed to the right of the front view. Likewise, if the object were lying on the paper with the front view up and then rolled toward the bottom of the paper, it would be resting on its bottom side, so that the top side faces upward. Thus, the top view is placed below the front view. This placement of views, known as the *first-angle projection*, simply reverses the location of the top and bottom views and the location of the left-side and right-side views with respect to the front view compared to the third-angle projection. The views themselves remain the same in both projections.

Although, the difference between the two projections is only in the placement of the views, great potential for confusion and manufacturing errors can result in engineering drawings that are used globally. To avoid misunderstanding, international projection symbols, shown in Figure 2.6, have been developed to distinguish between third-angle and first-angle projections on drawings. The symbol shows two views of a truncated cone. In the first-angle projection symbol, the truncated end of the cone (two concentric circles) is placed on the base side of the cone, as it would be in a first-angle projection. In the third-angle projection symbol, the truncated end of the cone is placed on the truncated side of the cone, as it would be in a third-angle projection. Usually these symbols appear in or near the title block of the drawing when the possibility of confusion is anticipated. Most CAD software automatically uses the third-angle projection for engineering drawings.

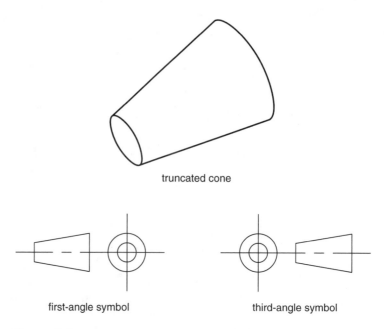

truncated cone

first-angle symbol   third-angle symbol

Figure 2.6.

A problem that frequently occurs in orthographic projections is that one of the faces of the object is at an angle to the orthographic planes that form the imaginary glass box. An example is the object shown in Figure 2.7. The circular hole with a keyway (rectangular cutout) that is perpendicular to the angled face appears in both the top view and the right-side view. However, it is distorted in both of these views, because it is on an angled plane of the object. An auxiliary view is used to avoid this distortion. In this case, a view of the object is drawn so that the angled face is parallel to the auxiliary view plane. The view is based on the viewer looking at the object along a line of sight that is perpendicular to the angled face. When viewed in this direction, the circular hole in the auxiliary view appears as a circle without any distortion. As suggested by the dash-dot lines in Figure 2.7, the auxiliary view is projected from the front view in the same way as the top and right-side views are projected. Thus, its position with respect to the front view depends on the orientation of the angled face. It is normal practice not to project hidden lines or other features that are not directly related to the angled surface.

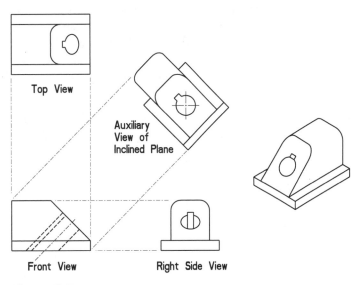

Figure 2.7.

2.4   WORKING DRAWINGS

Several types of *working drawings* are produced during the design process. Initially *freehand sketches* are used in the ideation phase of the design process. These are usually hand-drawn pictorial sketches of a concept that provide little detail, but enough visual information to convey the concept to other members of the design team. An example is the isometric sketch of a sheet metal piece that holds the blade of a pizza cutter, shown in Figure 2.8. The general shape of the object is clear, although details such as the thickness of the sheet metal and the radius of the bends in the sheet metal are not included. These conceptual sketches eventually evolve to final detailed drawings that define enough detail and information to support production.

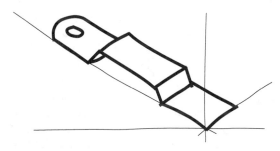

Figure 2.8.

Detail drawings document the detailed design of individual components using orthographic views. The detail drawing is the final representation of a design that is specific enough so that all of the information necessary for the manufacture of the part is provided. As a result, it is imperative that it includes the necessary views, dimensions, and specifications required for manufacturing the part. Figure 2.9 shows an example of a detail drawing of the part of the pizza cutter that was sketched in Figure 2.8. The detail drawing includes fully dimensioned orthographic views, notation of the material that the part is to be made from, information on the acceptable tolerances for the dimensions, and a title block that records important information about the drawing. Often an isometric view is included in the detail drawing to further clarify the shape of the part. Detail drawings provide sufficient detail so that the part can be manufactured based on the drawing alone.

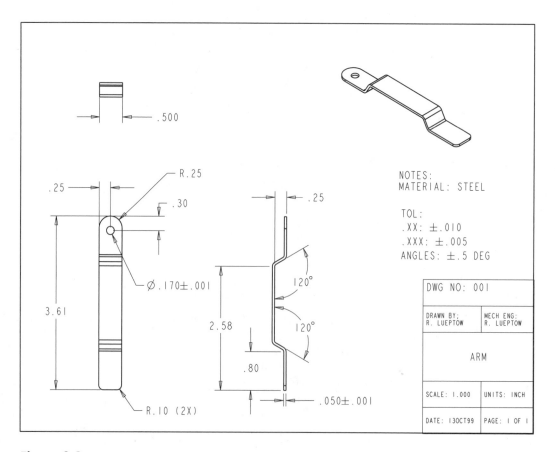

Figure 2.9.

Assembly drawings show how the components of a design fit together. Dimensions and other details are usually omitted in assembly drawings to enhance clarity. Several styles of assembly drawings are commonly used. Sometimes the assembly drawing is just an isometric view of the fully assembled device. But an exploded isometric view is often helpful to show the individual parts are assembled, as shown in Figure 2.10 for a pizza cutter. In some cases, a sectioned assembly, or cut-away view, shows how complicated devices are assembled. A cutting plane passes through the assembly and part of the device is removed to show the interior of the assembly. Numbers or letters can be assigned to individual parts of the assembly on the drawing and keyed to a parts list.

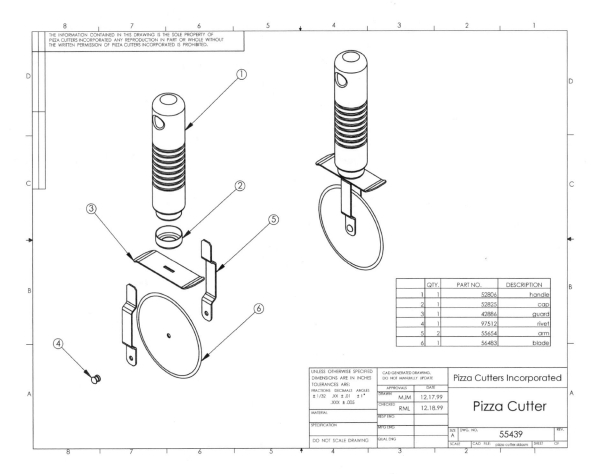

Figure 2.10.

Finally a *parts list*, or *bill of materials*, must be included with a set of working drawings. The parts list includes the part name, identification number, material, number required in the assembly, and other information (such as catalog number for standard parts such as threaded fasteners). An example is shown in Figure 2.11 for a pizza cutter. The parts list is used to ensure that all parts are ordered or manufactured and brought to the central assembly point.

	QTY.	PART NO.	DESCRIPTION
1	1	52806	handle
2	1	52825	cap
3	1	42886	guard
4	1	97512	rivet
5	2	55654	arm
6	1	56483	blade

Figure 2.11.

Taken together, the detail drawings of each individual part, the assembly drawing, and the bill of materials provide a complete set of working drawings for the manufacture of a part.

KEY TERMS

Assembly drawings
Bill of materials
Detail drawings
First-angle projection
Freehand sketches

Isometric projection
Multiview projection
Oblique projection
Orthographic projection
Perspective projection

3-D projections
Third-angle projection
Trimetric projection
Working drawings

Problems

1. Describe or sketch the front view that should be used in an orthographic projection of:

   a. a stapler.
   b. a television set.
   c. a cooking pot.
   d. a hammer.
   e. a pencil.
   f. a bicycle.
   g. an evergreen tree.
   h. a paper clip.
   i. a coffee mug.
   j. a padlock.

2. Identify the views shown in Figure 2.12 as isometric, trimetric, or perspective.

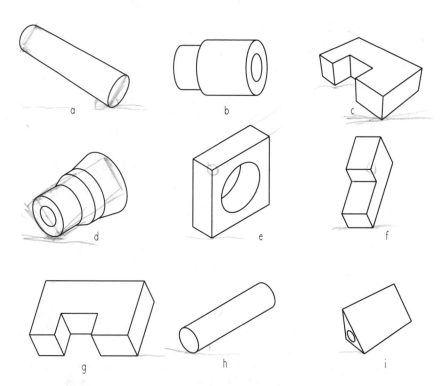

Figure 2.12.

3.   For the drawings shown in Figure 2.13, determine whether the multiview projection is first-angle or third-angle.

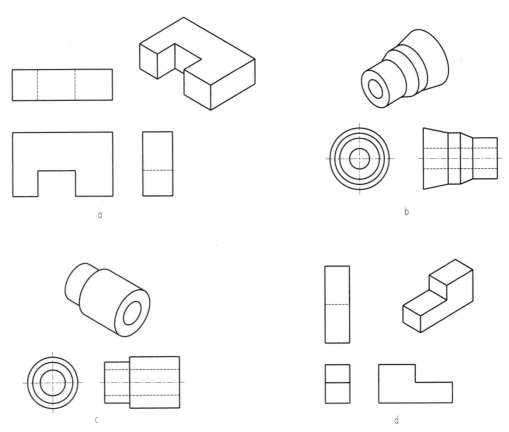

Figure 2.13.

4.   Develop a bill of materials for:

    a.   a pencil.

    b.   a squirt gun.

    c.   a click-type ball point pen.

    d.   a videocassette (take an old one apart).

    e.   an audio cassette (take an old one apart).

    f.   a disposable camera (ask a local photo developer for a used one to take apart).

    g.   eyeglasses.

    h.   a household cleaner pump bottle.

    i.   a claw-type staple remover.

    j.   an adhesive tape dispenser.

    k.   a bicycle caliper brake.

    l.   a floppy disk (take an old one apart).

    m.   a utility knife.

    n.   a Vise-Grip wrench.

3

Freehand Sketching

OVERVIEW

In this chapter you will learn useful techniques for freehand sketching to create both two-dimensional orthographic sketches and three-dimensional pictorial sketches. You will learn how to quickly make rough sketches to convey a concept and how to make more refined sketches of objects that are more complex.

3.1 WHY FREEHAND SKETCHES?

An integral part of the creative design process is *ideation*, the generation of concepts or ideas to solve a design problem. Often freehand sketching can be used to explore and communicate mental concepts that come about in the mind's eye. The process of sketching can solidify and fill out rough concepts. Furthermore, sketching captures the ideas in a permanent form that can be used to communicate the concept to others. In this way, sketches often act as stepping stones to refine and detail the original concept or generate new ideas. Many great design ideas are first sketched on the back of an envelope or in a lab notebook, such as the freehand sketch of one of helicopter inventor Igor Sikorsky's designs (Figure 3.1.)

While computers are the workhorses for engineering graphics, initially generating ideas on a computer screen is very rare. A more common scenario is sketching an idea on paper and subsequently refining the concept on paper using more rough sketches. This often occurs simply because all

OBJECTIVES

After reading this chapter, you should be able to:

- Explain why freehand sketching is important in design
- Freehand sketch lines and circles
- Sketch an oblique 3-D projection
- Sketch an isometric 3-D projection
- Sketch an orthographic multiview projection

that is needed for a freehand sketch is a pencil and a paper. Freehand sketching *quickly* translates the image of the concept in the mind's eye to paper. Engineers often communicate via rough freehand sketches to refine and improve the design. Sketches are much more useful than detailed CAD drawings early in the design process, because they are informal, quickly and easily changed, and less restrictive. It is only after clarifying the design concept by iterating through several freehand sketches that it is possible to draw the object using computer graphics. In fact, often an engineer will sit down to create a CAD drawing of an object using a freehand sketch as a guide.

This chapter focuses on the rudimentary elements of freehand technical sketching, because in many ways freehand sketching is the first step in CAD.

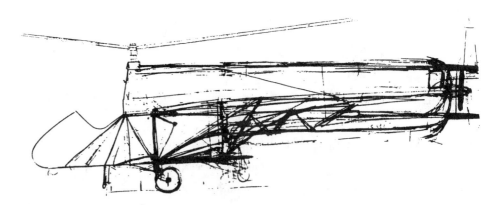

Figure 3.1.   Helicopter inventor Igor Sikorsky's sketch of an early helicopter prototype demonstrates the visual impact of freehand sketching. (Used with permission of the Sikorsky Aircraft Corporation, Stratford, CT. ["Straight Up," by Curt Wohleber, *American Heritage of Invention and Technology,* Winter, 1993, pp. 26–39.])

3.2   FREEHAND SKETCHING FUNDAMENTALS

Freehand sketching requires few tools: just a pencil and paper. It may be tempting to use straight-edged triangles or rulers for drawing straight lines and a compass to draw circles. But these instruments often slow down the process and distract from the purpose of sketching, which is to create a quick, rough graphical representation of the image in the mind's eye. Generally sketching has three steps, although the steps are usually subconscious. First, the sketch is planned by visualizing it in the mind including the size of the sketch on the paper, the orientation of the object, and the amount of detail to be included in the sketch. Second, the sketch is outlined using very light lines to establish the orientation, proportion, and major features of the sketch. Finally, sharpening and darkening object lines and adding details develops the sketch.

All sketches are made up of a series of arcs and lines, so the ability to draw circles and straight lines is necessary. A straight line is sketched in the following way. First, sketch the endpoints of the line as dots or small crosses. Then place your pencil on the starting endpoint. Keeping your eyes on the terminal point, use a smooth continuous stroke to draw the line between the points as shown in Figure 3.2. Nearly horizontal or vertical lines are frequently easier to draw than inclined lines, so it may be helpful to shift the paper to draw the line horizontally or vertically. For long lines, it may be helpful to mark two or three points along the line and use the procedure between consecutive points or to make two or three shorter passes lightly with the pencil before a final darker line.

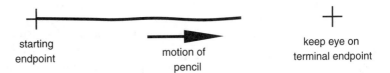

starting
endpoint

motion of
pencil

keep eye on
terminal endpoint

Figure 3.2.

A circle can be sketched using the following steps, illustrated in Figure 3.3a. First, draw light horizontal and vertical lines crossing at the center of the circle. Second, lightly mark the radius of the circle on each line. Finally, connect the radius marks with a curved line to form a circle. Another technique is to lightly draw a square box the same size as the circle diameter as shown in Figure 3.3b. Then lightly draw diagonals of the box and centerlines between midpoints of the sides of the box. The diagonals and centerlines should intersect at the center of the circle. Mark the radius on these lines, and sketch the circle within the box. It is sometimes helpful to mark the radius on the edge of a scrap paper and mark the radius at as many points as desired in addition to the marks on the centerlines and diagonals. Arcs are sketched in much the same way as circles, except that only a portion of the circle is sketched. It is generally easier to sketch an arc with your hand and pencil on the concave side of the arc.

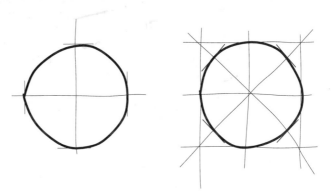

Figure 3.3.

3.3 BASIC FREEHAND SKETCHING

Many times, particularly during the conceptual stage of design, it is necessary to immediately communicate a graphical image to others. It has been said that some of the best design engineers are the ones who can sketch an idea clearly in a minute or so. The goal of the sketch in this case is not to show the details of the part, but to provide another person with a clear concept of the idea. For example, a design engineer may need to show a sketch to a manufacturing engineer to get input on the manufacturability of a part. If the concept is at an early phase, CAD drawings would not have been created yet. So the design engineer needs to use a freehand sketch of the part.

The sketch of Sikorsky's helicopter in Figure 3.1 exemplifies the power of freehand sketching. A brief glance at this sketch provides immediate insight to the concept that is being shown. One does not need to study the sketch to know what is being sketched, even if the viewer has never seen the concept before. These quick ideation sketches are not difficult to draw and require no artistic talent, just some practice.

Two types of pictorial sketches are used frequently in freehand sketching: oblique and isometric. The *oblique projection* places the principal face of the object parallel to the plane of the paper. The *isometric projection* tilts the part so that no surface of the part is in the plane of the paper. The advantage of the oblique projection is that details in the front face of the object retain their true shape. This often makes oblique freehand sketching easier than isometric sketching, where no plane is parallel to the paper. The disadvantage of the oblique projection is that it does not appear as "photorealistic" as an isometric projection. In other words, an isometric projection is similar to what a photograph of the object would look like.

3.3.1   Oblique Sketching

Often freehand sketching begins with light thin lines called *construction lines* that define enclosing boxes for the shape that is being sketched. Construction lines are used in several ways. First, the construction lines become the path for the final straight lines of the sketch. Second, the intersection of construction lines specify the length of the final lines. Third, points marked by the intersection of construction lines guide the sketching of circles and arcs. And finally, construction lines guide the proportions of the sketch. This last item is of crucial importance if the sketch is to clearly represent the object. For example, if an object is twice as wide as it is high, the proportions in the sketch must reflect this. Proper proportions of the boxes defined by the construction lines will result in proper proportions of the sketch.

An oblique freehand sketch is easy, since it begins with a two-dimensional representation of the face of the object. Figure 3.4 shows the steps in quickly sketching a part with a circular hole.

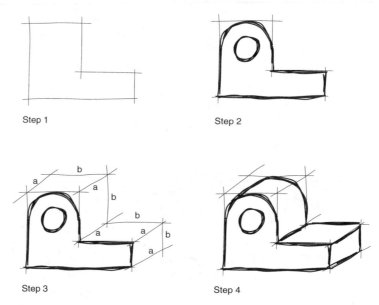

Step 1   Step 2

Step 3   Step 4

Figure 3.4.

Step 1: Horizontal and vertical construction lines are lightly drawn to outline the basic shape of the main face of the part. This is known as *blocking-in* the sketch. If you are using a pencil or felt-tip marker, press lightly when drawing the construction lines to produce a thin or light line. If you are using a ball-point pen, draw a single, light line.

Step 2: Sketch in the face of the part using the construction lines as a guide. How you sketch the outline of the part depends on the type of pen or pencil that you are using. The idea is to thicken the lines of the part compared to the construction lines. If you are using a pencil or a felt-tip marker, pressing hard for the outline of the part will result in heavy or dark lines. If you are using a ball-point pen, the line width does not depend much on how hard you press. In this case, the outline of the part is sketched with a back and forth motion of the pen to thicken the lines of the part compared to the construction lines as shown in Figure 3.4. The straight lines are usually sketched first, followed by the arcs. The circle for the hole in the part is added last to complete the face of the part.

Step 3: Sketch *receding construction lines* (lines into the plane of the paper labeled *a*) at a convenient angle. All of the receding lines must be parallel to each other and are usually at an angle of 30° to 45°. The receding lines end at the appropriate depth for the object. Then vertical and horizontal lines at the back plane of the part are added (lines labeled *b*). This blocks in the three-dimensional box enclosing the object.

Step 4: Sketch in and darken the lines outlining the part. Again it is usually easiest to sketch in the straight lines first, then the arcs, and finally any details. Because the construction lines are light compared to the outline of the part, they are not erased.

The final sketch, while rough and lacking detail, clearly shows the design intent for the part.

3.3.2 Isometric Sketching

Isometric freehand sketches are somewhat more difficult to master than oblique sketches because no face is in the plane of the paper in an isometric view. The steps to construct a simple freehand isometric sketch are shown in Figure 3.5.

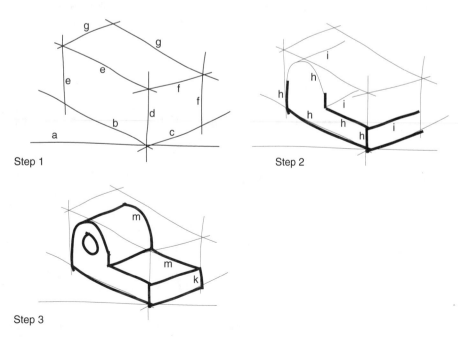

Step 1   Step 2   Step 3

Figure 3.5.

Step 1: Sketch a light horizontal line (*a*). From this line draw two intersecting lines at an angle of approximately 30° to the horizontal (*b* and *c*). Then draw a vertical line (*d*) through the intersection of the previous three lines. The three lines labeled *b*, *c*, and *d* form the isometric axes of the sketch. Next sketch the box to block in the front face of the part (*e*). These lines should be parallel to axes *b* and *d*. Similarly, sketch the lines to block in the right face (*f*) making sure that the lines are parallel to axes *c* and *d*. Finish this step by sketching lines parallel to the axes to complete the box that encloses the part (*g*).

Step 2: The outline for the front face is added by sketching in lines and curves (*h*). Then outline the front face using heavy lines. In this case, a single heavy line such as might be produced from pressing hard on a pencil or felt-tip marker is used. Next, lines are sketched to indicate the depth of the features of the front view (*i*). These lines should be parallel to axis *c*. They can be darkened after they are drawn lightly.

Step 3: Finally, a line is added to complete the back corner of the part (*k*). Lines and arcs are added to complete the back face of the part (*m*). Then the hole detail is added. Circular holes appear as ellipses in isometric views, as discussed in the next section.

The choice of whether to use an oblique projection or an isometric projection is often arbitrary. Because the oblique projection is easier to sketch, it is sometimes preferred. On the other hand, an isometric projection provides a more photorealistic image of the object.

3.4   ADVANCED FREEHAND SKETCHING

The sketching methods described in the previous section were focused on sketches in which the face of the object is in a single plane. Freehand sketching is somewhat more difficult when the face of the object is not in a single plane. The difficulty here is accurately depicting the depth of the object. Oblique and isometric projections are still useful, though somewhat more complicated than those in the previous section. In addition, orthographic projections are also valuable.

3.4.1   Freehand Oblique Sketching

An example of the steps leading to an oblique freehand sketch of a complicated object are shown in Figure 3.6. Because the face of the base of the object and the face of the upper portion of the object are in different planes, it is necessary to begin with a box that encloses the entire object before sketching either face. Some of the construction lines are removed after they are used in this example. This was done here to make the sketch more clear. However, this is not necessary in practice, if the construction lines are drawn as light lines.

Step 1: To begin, construction lines to form a box that encloses the object are drawn to block-in the sketch. Notice that the front and back faces of the box are rectangular with horizontal and vertical sides. The receding construction lines are parallel and at an angle of 30° to 45° to horizontal. The easiest way to draw this box is to first draw the front rectangle (*a*). Then draw an identical second rectangle above and to the right of the first rectangle (*b*). Finally connect the corners with receding construction lines (*c*).

Step 2: Now the front face of the base of the object can be sketched in the front rectangle. The lines are appropriately darkened.

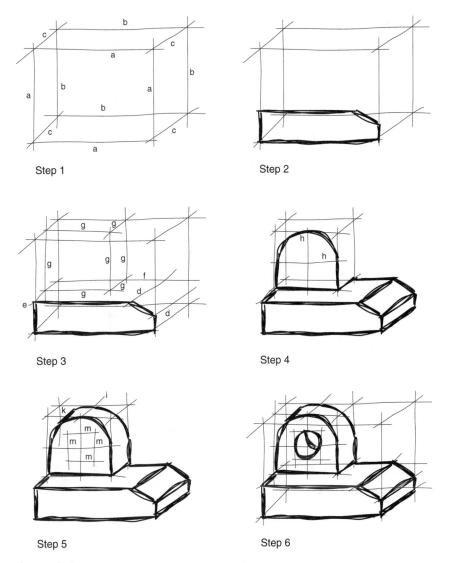

Figure 3.6.

Step 3: Certain features of the front face of the base extend backward along or parallel to the receding construction lines. For example, the lines (*d*) forming the chamfer (angled cut on the right side of the base) can be sketched parallel to receding lines. Likewise the receding line for the upper left corner of the base can be sketched (*e*). Then the base can be finished with a horizontal line on the back face (*f*). Now it is possible to block in the upper rounded portion of the object to create a box (*g*) that encloses the upper protrusion within the larger box that encloses the entire object.

Step 4: The front face of the upper portion of the object can be sketched in this box. Then receding lines corresponding to the chamfer and the left edge of the base can be darkened. In addition, the lines forming the back face can be sketched. Note that the line forming the back edge of the chamfer is parallel to the line forming the front edge of the chamfer. Construction lines (*h*) on the front face of the upper portion are drawn to center of the circle for the hole.

Step 5: A receding construction line (*i*) extending from the peak of the front face to the plane of the back face is sketched to aid in aligning the curved outline of the back of the upper portion. The back face is identical to the front face except that it is shifted upward and to the right. This results in the left side of the back face being hidden. A darkened receding line (*k*) finishes the left side of the upper portion of the object. Finally, four construction lines (*m*) are sketched to block in the circle for the hole.

Step 6: Now the hole can be sketched in and darkened. The back edge of the hole is also added to complete the sketch. The construction lines may be erased, but usually the construction lines are retained if they are made properly as light lines.

Oblique sketching is often aided by the use of graph paper with a light, square grid. The process is identical to that shown in Figure 3.6, but it is easier to keep the proportions correct by counting the number of boxes in the grid to correspond to the approximate dimensions of the part. Graph paper further improves the sketch by helping keep lines straight as well as more accurately horizontal or vertical.

3.4.2 Isometric Sketching

Isometric freehand sketches of more complex objects start with an isometric box to block in the sketch. Then faces are sketched and additional features are blocked in. Finally details are added. The steps to construct an isometric sketch are shown in Figure 3.7. Some of the construction lines are removed after they are used, to make the sketch more clear in this figure. Normally, removing construction lines is not necessary.

Step 1: To begin, sketch a light horizontal line (*a*). From this line draw two intersecting lines at an angle of approximately 30° to the horizontal (*b* and *c*) and a vertical line (*d*) through the intersection of the previous three lines to form the isometric axes of the sketch. Finish blocking in by sketching lines (*e*) to complete the box so that it will completely enclose the object. Unlike the oblique sketch, it is often better not to sketch hidden construction lines when blocking in.

Step 2: Block in the front face of the part (*f*) so that the construction line is parallel to the isometric axis. Similarly, sketch the line to block in the right face (*g*).

Step 3: Sketch the left face and the right face and darken the lines. This completes the faces that are in the front planes of the box. Now sketch in three lines (*h*) parallel to the isometric axis (*c*). The left line (*h*) is the top edge of the base. The middle line (*h*) finishes the chamfer. The right line (*h*) is used to aid in sketching a construction line for the back edge of the base (*i*), which is sketched next.

Step 4: Now the face of the chamfer can be darkened and the angled line at the back edge of the chamfer can be added. This completes the angled face of the chamfer. Next the protrusion above the base can be blocked in with seven lines (*k*).

Step 5: The front face of the upper protrusion is sketched first using light lines. Construction lines (*m*) are added to help identify the location of the endpoints of the arc of the front and back faces of the protrusion. The rounded rear face (*n*) is sketched lightly to be identical to the front face, except that part of it is not visible. The line at the top left edge of protrusion (*o*) is added. Then all lines forming the upper portion of the object are darkened In addition, the line forming the top edge of the base on the back side is darkened.

Step 6: The details related to the hole are added next. Circles in isometric projections are difficult to draw because they appear as ellipses with their major axes at an angle to horizontal. The center of the hole is where two lines (m) intersect on the front face of the upper portion of the object. The lines (p) forming the parallelogram to enclose the ellipse for the hole are added. Each side of the parallelo-

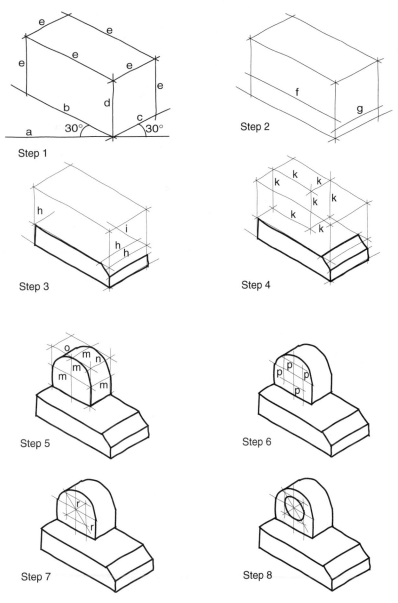

Figure 3.7.

gram should be parallel to one of the isometric axes. The sides should be equal in length to one another.

Step 7: To help in sketching the ellipse, construction lines forming the diagonals of the parallelogram (*r*) are added.

Step 8: Now the ellipse that represents the circular hole can be sketched. A few simple points help in sketching ellipses more easily. The major axis and minor axis of the ellipse are perpendicular to one another. The major and minor axes also coincide with the diagonals of the parallelogram enclosing the ellipse (*r*). The ellipse touches the parallelogram at the midpoints of the sides of the parallelogram. Start drawing the hole by sketching short elliptical arcs between the midpoints of the parallelogram on either side of the minor axis. Finish the hole by sketching sharply curved elliptical arcs between the midpoints of the parallelogram on either side of the major axis of the hole. Finally, darken and make heavy the lines outlining the hole and any remaining edges of the part.

Isometric sketching is made substantially easier by the use of isometric grid paper. This paper has a grid of lines at horizontal and 30° to horizontal (corresponding to lines b, c, and d in Figure 3.7). The procedure for using isometric grid paper is the same as that described above, but using the isometric grid paper keeps proportions of the part consistent. One simply counts grid boxes to approximate the dimensions of the object. The grid paper also aids in sketching straight lines parallel to the isometric axes.

3.4.3 Orthographic Sketching

In some cases it is necessary to sketch orthographic projection views rather than oblique or isometric pictorial views. Because orthographic views are two-dimensional representations, they are not as difficult to sketch as pictorial views. But there are several techniques that make freehand sketching of orthographic views easier and more efficient. The process for sketching three orthographic views of the object in the previous two figures is shown in Figure 3.8.

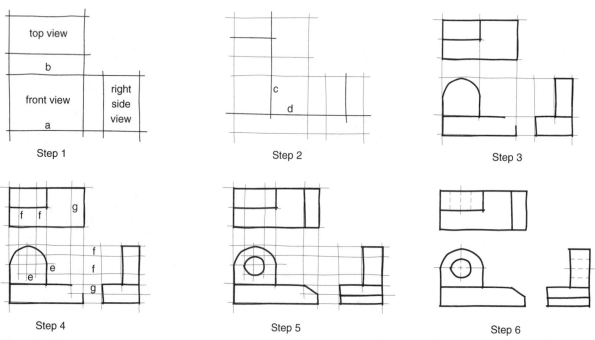

Figure 3.8.

Step 1: Begin by blocking in the front, top, and side views of the object using the overall width, height, and depth. The construction lines extend between views to properly align the views and maintain the same dimension in different views. For instance, line (*a*) represents the bottom edge and line (*b*) represents the top edge in both the front view and the right-side view. The distance between lines (*a*) and (*b*) is the height dimension in both views. The space between the views should be large enough so that the drawing does not look crowded and should be the same between all views.

Step 2: The upper protrusion is blocked in. Note that line (c) extends across the top and front views, to assure that the width of the protrusion is consistent in both views. Likewise, line (d) extends across the front and right-side views.

Step 3: The outline of the object is darkened to clearly show the shape of the object in all three views. Care must be taken in darkening lines. For instance, the right corner of the front view should not be darkened, because the detail of the chamfer has not yet been added.

Step 4: Construction lines for the holes and other details are added next. The center of the hole is positioned with construction lines (e). Then construction lines that block in the hole (f) are drawn. These construction lines extend between views to project the hole to the top view and to the right-side view. Construction lines extending between views (g) are also added for the chamfer.

Step 5: Now the hole and chamfer are sketched and darkened to show the completed object.

Step 6: Finally, centerlines (long-dash, short-dash) that indicate the center of the hole are added. Hidden lines (dashed lines) that indicate lines hidden behind a surface are also added. Construction lines may be erased as was done in this figure, but this is not usually necessary.

The quality of the sketch can often be improved by using square grid graph paper to keep proportions and act as a guide for horizontal and vertical lines. Some engineers prefer to use a straight-edge to produce a nicer sketch, but this is usually not necessary with practice and sufficient care in sketching.

PROFESSIONAL SUCCESS

Will Freehand Sketching Ever Become Obsolete?

CAD has almost totally eliminated pencil and paper drawings. But what about pencil and paper freehand sketching? Although many computers and palm-tops offer sketching programs, it is unlikely that freehand sketching will disappear soon. Just as it is easier to do a calculation in your head or on a piece of scratch paper rather than finding a calculator and punching in the numbers, it is easier to sketch an image on a piece of paper (or a napkin!) than to find a computer, log in, and start the appropriate "paint" program. Pencil and paper freehand sketches are quick, efficient, easily modified, and easily conveyed to others. And all that is needed is a pencil and a scrap of paper.

Even if the pencil and paper are totally replaced by palm-top computers some day, freehand sketching skills will still be useful. Instead of using a pencil on a piece of paper, we will use a stylus on a touch screen. The only difference is the medium. The freehand sketching techniques themselves are unlikely to change much. Perhaps one could imagine sketching software that assists in generating oblique or isometric sketches as they are drawn at some time in the future.

KEY TERMS

Blocking-in
Construction lines

Ideation
Receding construction lines

Problems

For all of the problems, the items shown in Figure 3.9, 3.10, and 3.11 are 2 inches wide, 1.5 inches high, and 1 inch deep. The holes in Figure 3.9b, 3.9c, 3.9d, 3.10c, and 3.10d are through holes. The hole in Figure 3.10b is through the front face only.

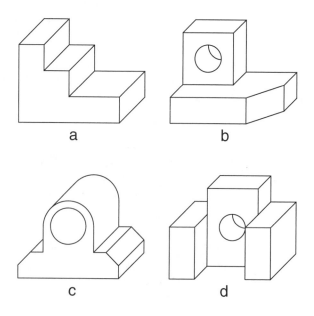

a   b

c   d

Figure 3.9.

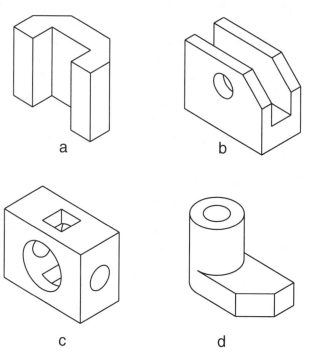

a   b

c   d

Figure 3.10.

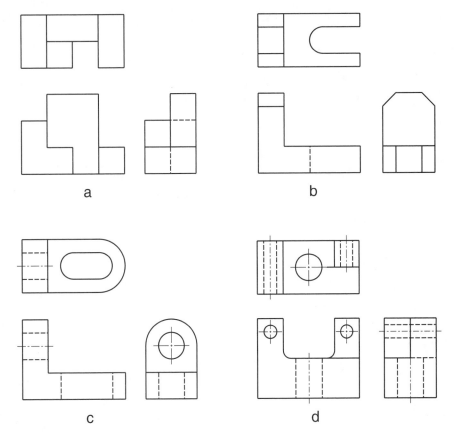

Figure 3.11.

1. Create freehand oblique sketches of the objects in Figure 3.9. (The objects are shown as oblique projections, so you must simply recreate the drawing by freehand sketching.)

2. Create freehand oblique sketches of the objects in Figure 3.10. (The objects are shown as isometric projections.)

3. Create freehand oblique sketches of the objects in Figure 3.11. (The objects are shown as orthographic projections.)

4. Create freehand isometric sketches of the objects in Figure 3.10. (The objects are shown as isometric projections, so you must simply recreate the drawing by freehand sketching.)

5. Create freehand isometric sketches of the objects in Figure 3.9. (The objects are shown as oblique projections.)

6. Create freehand isometric sketches of the objects in Figure 3.11. (The objects are shown as orthographic projections.)

7. Create freehand orthographic sketches of the objects in Figure 3.11. (The objects are shown as orthographic projections, so you must simply recreate the drawing by freehand sketching.)

8. Create freehand orthographic sketches of the objects in Figure 3.9. (The objects are shown as oblique projections.)

9. Create freehand orthographic sketches of the objects in Figure 3.10. (The objects are shown as isometric projections.)

4

Computer Aided Design and Drafting

OVERVIEW

Several different models for representing a part's geometry have been used in CAD, including 2-D models and 3-D wireframe and surface models. However, solids modeling is the current state-of-the-art in CAD. Solids modeling has the inherent advantage of more accurately representing the "design intent" of the part that modeled.

4.1 CAD MODELS

A CAD *model* is a computer representation of an object or part. It can be thought of as a "virtual" part in that it exists only as a computer image. The model is an engineering document of record. It contains all of the design information including geometry, dimensions, tolerances, materials, and manufacturing information. A CAD model replaces the paper blueprints and engineering drawings of just a few decades ago.

The simplest model used in CAD is a *2-D model*. This model is essentially the computer graphics equivalent to an orthographic projection created using a pencil and paper as shown in Figure 4.1. A 2-D model represents a three-dimensional object with several views, each showing the view of one side of the object projected onto a plane. On the computer, a 2-D model appears as lines and curves on a flat surface, and it is up to the engineer or designer to interpret several views to create a mind's eye image of the three-dimensional object. The CAD software electronically stores

SECTIONS

- 4.1 CAD Models
- 4.2 CAD and Solids Modeling
- 4.3 The Nature of Solids Modeling

OBJECTIVES

After reading this chapter, you should be able to:

- Differentiate 2-D, 2 1/2-D, and 3-D models
- Differentiate wireframe, surface, and solids models
- Explain how a cross-section is extruded or revolved to create a solids model
- Explain the analogy between creating a solids model of a part and machining the part
- Explain feature-based modeling
- Explain constraint-based modeling
- Explain associative modeling

the 2-D model as several views but does not inherently "know" that the views can be connected to one another to form a three-dimensional object.

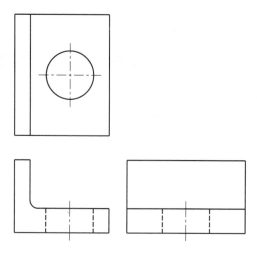

Figure 4.1.

A *2 1/2-D model* has a third dimension that is recognized by the CAD software, but the third dimension is simply an extrusion of a two-dimensional shape. In this case, the CAD software electronically stores the cross-section shape of the object and the depth that it is *extruded*, or stretched, in the third dimension. Thus, the only objects that can be represented using a 2 1/2-D model model are those that have a constant cross-section. For instance, the simple shape shown in Figure 4.2 is the 2 1/2-D model of the object shown using a 2-D model in Figure 4.1 without the hole. The object, including the hole, cannot be represented as a 2 1/2-D model because the hole results in a change in the cross-section. A 2 1/2-D model could be used to represent a shape such as an I-beam or C-channel.

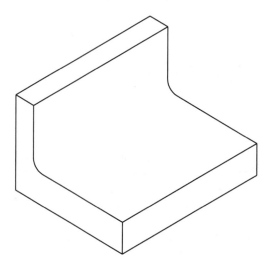

Figure 4.2.

A *3-D model* is the most general model used in CAD software. In this case, the CAD software electronically stores the entire three-dimensional shape of the object. Most simply, one can think of the software storing the three-dimensional coordinates of various points on the object and then defining how these points are connected. Of course, a two-dimensional drawing representing the orthographic views of the object can be automatically created from the 3-D model. The current generation of CAD software is based on 3-D models.

The simplest 3-D model is a *wireframe model*. Figure 4.3a shows a wireframe representation of the object that we have been considering. In a wireframe model, only edges of the object are represented. Thus, the CAD software needs to store the locations of the vertices (intersections of lines) and which vertices are to be connected to each other by lines. A circle or curved section can be represented by a series of closely spaced vertices with linear edges connecting them or as an arc defined by a center, radius, and end points. Before more powerful computers were available, the low storage requirements of a wireframe model made it quite popular. The problem inherent in a wireframe representation is quite clear in Figure 4.3a—it is difficult to interpret the drawing because all of the edges are visible. In fact, there are many situations where a wireframe representation cannot be unambiguously interpreted because it is not clear which lines would remain hidden if the surfaces of the part were filled in. This problem can be solved using various methods to remove "hidden lines" from the wireframe. This is tricky because the CAD software has to first determine how the edges of the wireframe form a surface and then determine if that surface hides any lines. Figure 4.3b shows the object with the hidden lines shown as dashed lines to indicate that they are behind a surface. 3-D models other than wireframes are able to deal with hidden lines more effectively and offer other advantages.

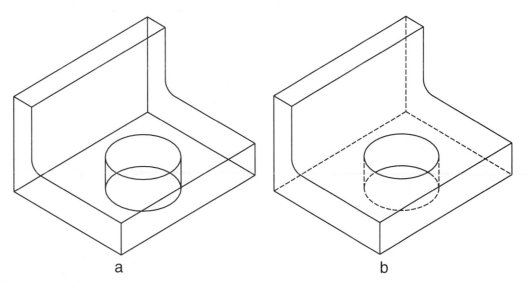

a   b

Figure 4.3.

A 3-D *surface model* defines the object in terms of surfaces such as plates (flat) and shells (curved) in addition to edges. This makes it easy to determine whether a line or surface is hidden, because the surfaces are defined. Using a surface model also permits the construction of smoothly curved surfaces, such as a circular hole, rather than using many line segments to form a curved line as with some wireframe models. It is also possible to "fair" or smooth one surface into another surface to provide a sculpted shape.

Figure 4.4a shows the simple object with hidden lines removed altogether. Although a surface model can be displayed to look like a wireframe, either with or without hidden lines, it can also be displayed by assigning different degrees of shading to the surfaces. A virtual light source is assumed to be near the object to provide a three-dimensional lighting effect as shown in Figure 4.4b. This is known as *shading* or *rendering*. Although a variety of shading techniques are available, all depend on determining how much light from a virtual light source strikes each portion of the virtual object. The use of shading provides a very realistic image of the object, which permits a much more vivid communication of the nature of the object. However, the problem that remains with a surface model is that the interior of the object remains undefined. The surface model just represents the shell of the object.

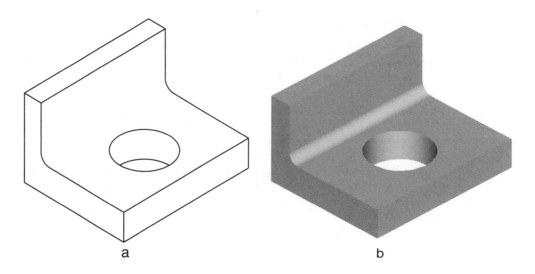

a   b

Figure 4.4.

4.2   CAD AND SOLIDS MODELING

Solids modeling, the current state-of-the-art in CAD, is the most sophisticated method of representing an object. Unlike wireframe or surface models, a solids model represents an object in the virtual environment just as it exists in reality, having volume as well as surfaces and edges. In this way, the interior of the object is represented in the model as well as the outer surfaces.

The first attempt at solids modeling was a technique known as *constructive solid geometry* or *primitive modeling*, which is based on the combination of geometric primitives such as right rectangular prisms (blocks), right triangular prisms (wedges), spheres, cones, and cylinders. Each primitive could be scaled to the desired size, translated to the desired position, and rotated to the desired orientation. Then one primitive could be added to or subtracted from other primitives to make up a complex object. It is easy to see how two blocks plus a negative cylinder (hole), as shown in Figure 4.5, could represent an object similar to the one shown in Figure 4.4. (The rounded surface, or fillet, at the corner between the horizontal and vertical surfaces has been omitted.) The problem with constructive solid geometry was that the mental process of creating a solid model based on geometric primitives was much more abstract than the mental processes required for designing real world objects.

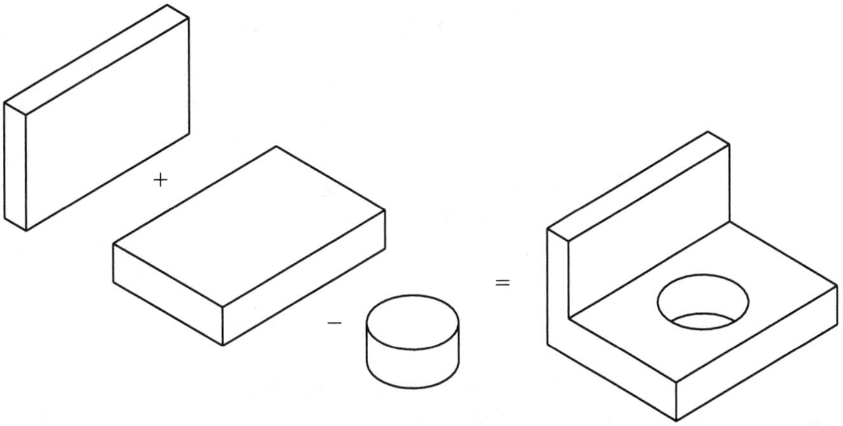

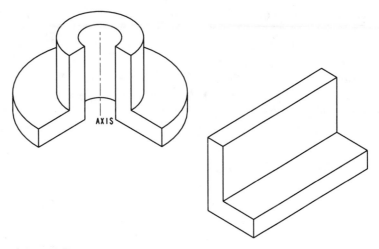

Figure 4.5.

Constraint-based solids modeling overcomes the weakness of constructive solid geometry modeling by making the modeling process more intuitive. Instead of piecing together geometric primitives, the constraint-based modeling process begins with the creation of a 2-D sketch of the profile for the cross-section of the part. Here, "sketch" is the operative word. The sketch of the cross-section begins much like the freehand sketch of the face of an object in an oblique view. The only difference is that CAD software draws straight lines and perfect arcs. The initial sketch need not be particularly accurate; it need only reflect the basic geometry of the part's cross-sectional shape. Details of the cross-section are added later. The next step is to constrain the 2-D sketch by adding enough dimensions and parameters to completely define the shape and size of the 2-D profile. The name *constraint-based modeling* arises because the shape of the initial 2-D sketch is "constrained" by adding dimensions to the sketch. Finally, a three-dimensional object is created by *revolving* or *extruding* the 2-D sketched profile. Figure 4.6 shows the result of revolving a simple L-shaped cross-section by 270° about an axis and extruding the same L-shaped cross-section along an axis. In either case, these solid bodies form the basic geometric solid shapes of the part. Other features can be subsequently added to modify the basic solid shape.

Figure 4.6.

Once the solids model is generated, all of the surfaces are automatically defined, so it is possible to shade it in the same way as a surface model is shaded. It is also easy to generate 2-D orthographic views of the object. This is a major advancement from other modeling schemes. With solids modeling, the two-dimensional drawings are produced as views of the three-dimensional virtual model of the object. In traditional CAD, the three-dimensional model is derived from the two-dimensional drawings. One might look at solids modeling as the sculpting of a virtual solid volume of material. Because the volume of the object is properly represented in a solids model, it is possible to slice through the object and show a view of the object that displays the interior detail. Once several solid objects have been created, they can be assembled in a virtual environment to make sure that they fit together and to visualize the assembled product.

PROFESSIONAL SUCCESS

How Solids Models are Used

Solids models are useful for purposes other than visualization. The solids model contains a complete mathematical representation of the object, inside and out. This mathematical representation is converted easily into specialized computer code that can be used for stress analysis, heat transfer analysis, fluid flow analysis, and computer-aided manufacturing.

Finite Element Analysis (FEA) is a method to subdivide the object under study into many small, simply shaped elements. The simple geometry of the finite elements allows the relatively simple application of the appropriate equations for the stress and deformation of the elements or for the heat transfer between elements. By properly relating nearby elements to one another, all of these equations for each element can be solved simultaneously. The final result is the stress, deformation (strain), or temperature throughout the object for a given applied load or thermal condition. The stress, deformation, or temperature is often displayed as a color map on the solid model, visually displaying the regions of high stress or temperature. From these results, the engineer can redesign the object to avoid stress concentrations, large deformations, or undesirable temperatures. Likewise, the fluid flow through or around an object can be calculated by applying similar FEA techniques using the equations of fluid flow to the regions bounded by the object. These analysis tools have greatly improved and enhanced the design of many products.

Solids models can also be used in the manufacturing process. Software is available to automatically generate machine tool paths to machine the object based on the solids model. Then the software simulates the removal of material from an initial block of material on the computer. This allows the engineer to optimize the machining operation. These tool paths can be downloaded onto Computer Numerical Control (CNC) machine tools. The CNC machine tool automatically removes the desired surfaces from a block of material with high precision, allowing many identical parts to be machined automatically based directly on the solids model. Alternatively, the solids model can be downloaded onto a rapid prototyping machine. This machine automatically drives lasers that solidify liquid plastic resin, drives a robotic system to dispense a fine bead of molten plastic, or drives a laser that cuts layers of paper. In all three cases, layers are built up to become a physical model of the computer solids model, often within just a few hours. These manufacturing tools have made it possible to obtain parts from CAD models in several hours instead of several weeks.

4.3   THE NATURE OF SOLIDS MODELING

Solids modeling grew steadily in the 1980s, but it was not until Pro/ENGINEER® was introduced in 1988 and SolidWorks® was introduced in the 1990s that solids modeling delivered on its promised gains in productivity. These gains result from three characteristics of the software: feature-based, constraint-based, and associative modeling.

Feature-based modeling attempts to make the modeling process more efficient by creating and modifying geometric *features* of a solid model in a way that represents how geometries are created using common manufacturing processes. Features in a part have a direct analogy to geometries that can be manufactured or machined. A *base feature* is a solid model that is roughly the size and shape of the part that is to be modeled. The base feature is the 3-D solid created by revolving or extruding a cross-section, such as those shown in Figure 4.6. It can be thought of as the initial work block. All subsequent features reference the base feature either directly or indirectly. Additional features shape or refine the base feature. Examples of additional features include holes or cuts in the initial work block.

The analogy between feature-based modeling and common manufacturing processes is demonstrated in Figure 4.7 for making a handle for a pizza cutter. Beginning at the top of the figure we follow the steps that an engineer would use to create a solid model, or virtual part, on the left and the steps that a machinist would take to create the same physical part in a machine shop on the right. The engineer using solids modeling software begins by creating a two-dimensional profile, or *cross-section*, of a part, in this case a circle (shown in isometric projection). The analogous step by a machinist is to choose a circular bar stock of material with the correct diameter. Next the engineer *extrudes*, or stretches, the circular cross-section along the axis perpendicular to the plane of the circle to create a three-dimensional base feature (a cylinder in this case). The equivalent action by a machinist is to cut off a length of bar stock to create an initial work block. Now the engineer adds features by cutting away material on the left end to reduce the diameter and by rounding the right end of the cylinder. The machinist performs similar operations on a lathe to remove material from the cylinder. Next the engineer creates a circular cut to form a hole through the cylinder on the right end. The machinist drills a hole in the right end of the cylinder. Finally, the engineer creates a pattern of groove cuts around the handle. Likewise the machinist cuts a series of grooves using a lathe. In similar fashion a geometric shape could be added to the base feature in the solids model, analogous to a machinist welding a piece of metal to the work block. Feature-based techniques give the engineer the ability to easily create and modify common manufactured features. As a result, planning the manufacture of a part is facilitated by the correspondence between the features and the processes required to make them.

Constraint-based modeling permits the engineer or designer to incorporate "intelligence" into the design. Often this is referred to as *design intent*. Unlike traditional CAD software, the initial sketch of a two-dimensional profile in constraint-based solids modeling does not need to be created with a great deal of accuracy. It just needs to represent the basic geometry of the cross-section. The exact size and shape of the profile is defined through assigning enough parameters to fully "constrain" it. Some of this happens automatically. For example, if two nearly parallel edges are within some preset tolerance range of parallel (say 5 degrees), then the edges are automatically constrained to be parallel. As the part is resized, these edges will always remain parallel no matter what other changes are made. Likewise, if a hole is constrained to be at a certain distance from an edge, it will automatically remain at that distance from the edge, even if the edge is moved. This differs from traditional CAD where both the hole and the edge would each be fixed at a particular coordinate location. If the edge were moved, the hole location would need to be respecified so that the hole will remain the same distance from the edge. The advantage of constraint-based modeling is that the design intent of the engineer remains intact as the part is modified.

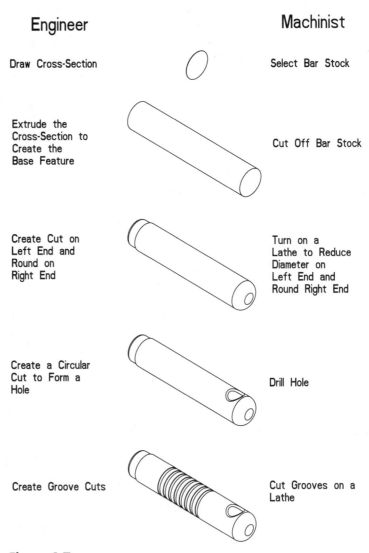

Engineer

Draw Cross-Section

Extrude the
Cross-Section to
Create the
Base Feature

Create Cut on
Left End and
Round on
Right End

Create a Circular
Cut to Form a
Hole

Create Groove Cuts

Machinist

Select Bar Stock

Cut Off Bar Stock

Turn on a
Lathe to Reduce
Diameter on
Left End and
Round Right End

Drill Hole

Cut Grooves on a
Lathe

Figure 4.7.

Another aspect of constraint-based modeling is that the model is *parametric*. This means that parameters of the model may be modified to change the geometry of the model. A dimension is a simple example of a parameter. When a dimension is changed, the geometry of the part is updated. Thus, the *parameter drives the geometry*. This is in contrast to other modeling systems in which the geometry is changed, say by stretching a part, and the dimension updates itself to reflect the stretched part. An additional feature of parametric modeling is that parameters can reference other parameters through relations or equations. For example, the position of the hole in Figure 4.4 could be specified with numerical values, say 40 mm from the right side of the part. Or the position of the hole could be specified parametrically, so that the center of the hole is located at a position that is one-half of the total length of the part. If the total length was specified as 80 mm, then the hole would be 40 mm from either side. However, if the length was changed to 100 mm, then the hole would automatically be positioned at half of this distance, or 50 mm from either side. Thus, no matter what the length of the part is, the hole stays in the middle of its length. The power of this approach is that when one dimension is modified, all linked dimensions are updated according to specified mathematical relations, instead of having to update all related dimensions individually.

The last aspect of constraint-based modeling is that the order in which parts are created is critical. This is known as *history-based modeling*. For example, a hole should not be created before a solid volume of material in which the hole occurs has been modeled. If the solid volume is deleted, then the hole should be deleted with it. This is known as a *parent-child relation*. The child (hole) cannot exist without the parent (solid volume) existing first. Parent-child relations are critical to maintaining design intent in a part. Most solids modeling software recognizes that if you delete a feature with a hole in it, you do not want the hole to remain floating around without being attached to a feature. Consequently, careful thought and planning of the base feature and initial additional features can have a significant effect on the ease of adding subsequent features and making modifications.

The *associative* character of solids modeling software causes modifications in one object to "ripple through" all associated objects. For instance, suppose that you change the diameter of a hole on the engineering drawing that was created based on your original solid model. The diameter of the hole will be automatically changed in the solid model of the part, too. In addition, the diameter of the hole will be updated on any assembly that includes that part. Similarly, changing the dimension in the part model will automatically result in updated values of that dimension in the drawing or assembly incorporating the part. This aspect of solids modeling software makes the modification of parts much easier and less prone to error.

As a result of being feature-based, constraint-based, and associative, solids modeling captures "design intent," not just the design. This comes about because solids modeling software incorporates engineering knowledge into the solid model with features, constraints, and relationships that preserve the intended geometrical relationships in the model.

PROFESSIONAL SUCCESS

Has CAD Impacted Design?

CAD has not only automated and provided a more accurate means of creating engineering drawings, it has created a new paradigm for design. Parts can be modeled, visualized, revised, and improved on the computer screen before any engineering drawings have even been created. Parts that have been modeled can be assembled in the virtual environment of the computer. The relative motion of moving parts can be animated on the computer. The stresses in the parts can be assessed computationally and the part redesigned to minimize stress concentrations. The flow of fluids through the part or around the part can be modeled computationally. The machine tool path

or mold-filling flow to fabricate the part can be modeled on the computer. The part model can be downloaded to a rapid prototyping system that can create a physical model of the part in a few hours with virtually no human intervention.

Although some of the analyses described above are outside of the capability of the CAD software itself, the ability to produce a CAD model makes these analyses possible. Without the ability to create a complex solid geometry computationally using CAD, much of the engineering analysis that is used to design, improve, and evaluate a new design would be much more difficult.

KEY TERMS

Associative modeling	Feature	Revolve
Base Feature	Feature-based modeling	Solids modeling
Constraint-based modeling	History-based modeling	Surface model
Design intent	Parametric modeling	Wireframe model
Extrude	Parent-child relation	

Problems

1.   The wireframe model shown in Figure 4.8 is a small cube centered within a large cube. The nearest corners of the two cubes are connected. For instance, the lower left front corners of both cubes are connected with a line. This wireframe model is ambiguous; that is, it could represent several different solid bodies. Freehand sketch or trace the figure. Then use dashed lines to indicate hidden lines to show two different solids model configurations that are possible for this wireframe model.

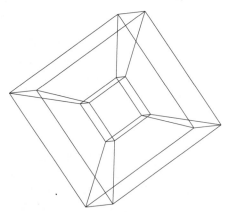

Figure 4.8.

2.   Using a technique similar to that shown in Figure 4.5, freehand sketch the geometric primitives that could be added or subtracted to form the objects shown in Figure 4.9. (The hole in Figure 4.9b is only through the face shown, not the back face. The holes in Figures 4.9c and 4.9d are through holes.)

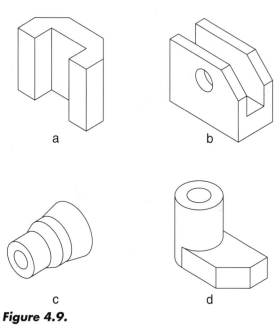

Figure 4.9.

3.   Sketch the cross-section that should be revolved to create the objects shown in Figure 4.10. Include the axis about which the cross-section is revolved in the sketch.

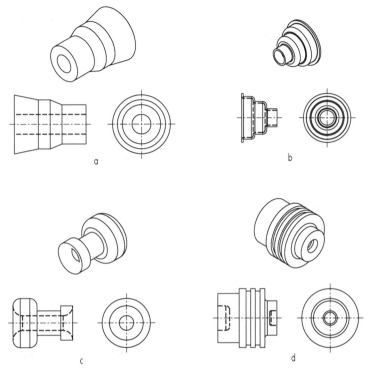

Figure 4.10.

4.   Sketch at least two cross-sections that could be extruded to form a base feature for the objects shown in Figure 4.11. Use cross-sections that can be extruded into a base feature from which material is only removed, not added. Make sure that the cross-sections that you propose minimize the number of additional features necessary to modify the base feature. (The hole in Figure 4.11a is only through the face shown, not the back face. The holes in Figure 4.11b, 4.11c, and 4.11e are through holes.)

5.   Consider the following objects. Sketch what the base feature would look like. List what features would be added to model the object. The type of base feature to be used (extrude, revolve, or both) is noted.

   a.   hexagonal cross-section wooden pencil that is sharpened to a point (do not include eraser)—extrude.

   b.   plastic 35 mm film container and cap—extrude and revolve.

   c.   nail—extrude and revolve.

   d.   push pin—revolve.

   e.   baseball bat—revolve.

   f.   broom handle—revolve and extrude.

   g.   ceiling fan blade—extrude.

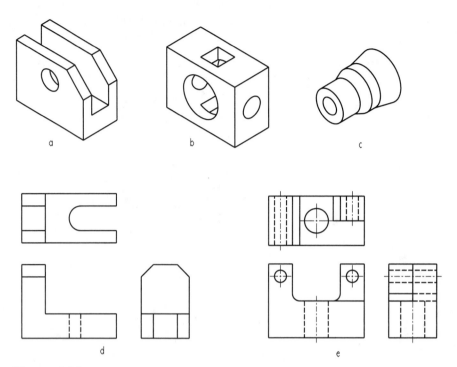

Figure 4.11.

     h.   cinder block—extrude.

     i.   compact disk—revolve and extrude.

     j.   single staple (before being deformed)—extrude.

     k.   automobile tire—revolve.

     l.   gear—extrude.

     m.   round toothpick—revolve.

6.   Describe parametric modeling and give an example of a family of parts where parametric modeling would be useful.

7.   Describe constraint-based modeling and explain how it relates to design intent.

5

Standard Practice
for Engineering Drawings

OVERVIEW

Drawing standards and conventions are used to clarify engineering drawings and simplify their creation. For example, standard sizes for drawings are used, and standard types and weights of lines designate different items on a drawing. The proper placement of dimensions on drawings is helpful in making the drawing more readable. In addition, internal or small details of the part can be displayed using special views. Screw threads are difficult to draw, so standard representations are used for screw threads.

5.1 INTRODUCTION TO DRAWING STANDARDS

Not only is the accurate and clear depiction of details of a part necessary in an engineering drawing, but it is also necessary that the drawing conforms to commonly accepted standards, or conventions. There are two reasons for the existence of standards and conventions. First, using standard symbols and projections ensures clear interpretation of the drawing by the viewer. An example of the problem of differing presentations is the use of the third-angle orthographic projection in North America and the first-angle orthographic projection elsewhere in the world. (Recall that the top and bottom views and the right and left views are reversed in third-angle and first-angle projections.) This can bring about confusion if, for example, a U. S. engineer tries

SECTIONS

- •5.1   Introduction to Drawing Standards
- •5.2   Sheet Layouts
- •5.3   Lines
- •5.4   Dimension Placement and Conventions
- •5.5   Section and Detail Views
- •5.6   Fasteners and Screw Threads
- •5.7   Assembly Drawings

OBJECTIVES

After reading this chapter, you should be able to:

- Explain why drawing standards are used
- Choose the proper sheet layout
- Read and understand the scale of a drawing
- Differentiate linetypes used in engineering drawings
- Properly place dimensions on a drawing
- Read and understand section and detail views on a drawing
- Read and understand screw thread designations on a drawing
- Read an assembly drawing

to interpret a German drawing. If a single standard existed in the world, there would be no confusion. A second reason for using conventions is to simplify the task of creating engineering drawings. For example, the symbol Ø associated with a dimension indicates that the dimension is a diameter of a circular feature. Without this convention, it would be more difficult to unambiguously represent diameter dimensions on a drawing.

Most CAD programs automatically use a standardized presentation of drawings, usually based on standards from the American National Standards Institute (ANSI) in the United States and the International Standards Organization (ISO) in the rest of the world. Even with the use of CAD software to assure standard presentation in drawings, it is up to the engineer to implement drawing standards in some cases. An example is in the placement of dimensions in a drawing. The user controls where dimensions appear on the drawing. Even in cases where the CAD software automatically implements drawing standards, it is still necessary to understand what the conventions mean so they are properly interpreted.

5.2   SHEET LAYOUTS

Engineering drawings are created on standard size sheets that are designated by the code indicated in Table 5.1. The ISO drawing sizes are just slightly smaller than ANSI sizes. Engineering drawings are almost always done in "landscape" orientation so that the long side of the drawing is horizontal. The choice of drawing size depends upon the complexity of the object depicted in the drawing. The drawing should be sized so that the projections of the part, dimensions, and notes all fall within the borders of the drawing with adequate spacing so that the drawing is not cluttered. The drawing should be large enough so that all details are readily evident and readable. As a result, regardless of the physical size of the part, simple parts are usually drawn on smaller sheets because it is not necessary to show much detail. Complex parts are usually drawn on larger sheets to readily show adequate detail. When using CAD software, it is necessary to consider the printed drawing size in addition to the drawing size on the computer screen. On the computer screen, it is possible to Zoom In or Zoom Out to read detail, but this cannot be done for a printed drawing. Consequently, the sheet size should be chosen carefully.

TABLE 5-1 Standard Sheet Sizes

ANSI	ISO
A—8.50″ × 11.00″	A4—210 mm × 297 mm
B—11.00″ × 17.00″	A3—297 mm × 420 mm
C—17.00″ × 22.00″	A2—420 mm × 594 mm
D—22.00″ × 34.00″	A1—594 mm × 841 mm
E—34.00″ × 44.00″	A0—841 mm × 1189 mm

The *title block* on a drawing records important information about the working drawing. Normally the title block of a drawing is in the lower right corner of the drawing. ANSI standard title blocks can be used, but often individual companies use their own standard title block. The title block, such as the one shown in Figure 5.1, is used primarily for drawing control within a company. The title block includes information regarding the part depicted in the drawing, such as its name and part number; the person who created the drawing; persons who checked or approved the drawing; dates the drawing was created, revised, checked, and approved; the drawing number; and the name of the company. This information allows the company to track the drawing within the company if questions arise about the design.

UNLESS OTHERWISE SPECIFIED DIMENSIONS ARE IN INCHES TOLERANCES ARE: FRACTIONS DECIMALS ANGLES ± 1/32 .XX ± .01 ± 1° .XXX ± .005	CAD GENERATED DRAWING, DO NOT MANUALLY UPDATE		PIZZA CUTTERS INCORPORATED	
	APPROVALS	DATE		A
	DRAWN MJM	10.10.99		
	CHECKED RML	10.12.99	PIZZA CUTTER ASSEMBLY	
MATERIAL --	RESP ENG LDV	10.13.99		
FINISH --	MFG ENG AA	10.15.99	SIZE A / DWG. NO. 554391	REV. C
DO NOT SCALE DRAWING	QUAL ENG DM	10.15.99	SCALE 1:2 / CAD FILE: pizza cutter.sldasm / SHEET 1 OF 1	

Figure 5.1.

Other information can appear in the title block to provide details about the manufacture of the part, such as the material for the part, the general tolerances, the surface finish specifications, and general instructions about manufacturing the part (such as "remove all burrs"). Many times, though, this information is shown as notes on the drawing rather than in the title block.

Finally the title block provides information about the drawing itself, such as the units used in dimensioning (typically inches or millimeters) and the scale of the drawing. The *scale* of the drawing indicates the ratio of the size on the drawing to the size of the actual object. It can be thought of as the degree to which the object is enlarged or shrunk in the drawing. Scales on drawings are denoted in several ways. For instance, consider an object that is represented in the drawing as half of its actual size. Then the drawing is created such that 1 inch on the drawing represents 2 inches on the physical object. This can be reported in the Scale box in the title block as HALF SCALE, HALF SIZE, 1 = 2, 1:2, or 1/2″ = 1″. In the numerical representations, the left number is the length on the drawing and the right number is the length of the actual object. A part that is drawn twice as large as its physical size would be denoted as DOUBLE, 2× (denoting "2 times"), 2 = 1, or 2:1. In some cases, such as architectural drawings, the scale can be quite large. For instance 1/4″ = 1′-0″ corresponds to a scale of 1:48, where ″ denotes inches and ′ denotes feet. Common scales used in engineering drawing are 1 = 1, 1 = 2, 1 = 4, 1 = 8, and 1 = 10 for English units and 1:1, 1:2, 1:5, 1:10, 1:20, 1:50, and 1:100 for metric units. A 1:1 scale is often specified as FULL SCALE or FULL SIZE.

5.3 LINES

The types of lines used in engineering drawing are standardized. Different linetypes have different meanings and a knowledge of linetypes makes interpreting drawings easier. The linetypes vary in thickness and in the length and number of dashes in dashed lines. Most CAD software automatically produces linetypes that correspond correctly to the application. Figure 5.2 shows some of the more commonly used linetypes, each of which is described below:

> *Visible lines* (thick, solid lines) represent the outline of the object that can be seen in the current view.
> *Hidden lines* (thin, dashed lines) represent features that are hidden behind surfaces in the current view.

Centerlines or *symmetry lines* (thin, long-dash/short-dash lines) mark axes of rotationally symmetric parts or features.

Dimension lines (thin lines with arrowheads at each end) indicate sizes in the drawing.

Extension lines or *witness lines* (thin lines) extend from the object to the dimension line to indicate which feature is associated with the dimension.

Leader lines (thin, solid lines terminated with arrowheads) are used to indicate a feature with which a dimension or note is associated.

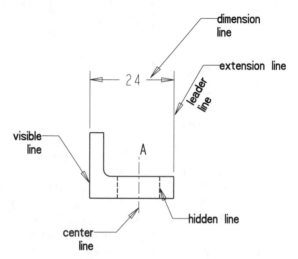

Figure 5.2.

Other linetypes are used for break lines (lines with zigzags) that show where an object is "broken" in the drawing to save drawing space or reveal interior features and cutting plane lines (thick lines with double short dashes and perpendicular arrows at each end) that show the location of cutting planes for section views.

The arrowheads for dimension lines, leader lines, and other types of lines may be filled or not filled. Most CAD software uses unfilled arrowheads as a default, although many engineering graphics textbooks prefer filled arrowheads.

It is common in technical drawings that two lines in a particular view coincide. When this happens, a convention called the *precedence of lines* dictates which line is shown. Visible lines have precedence over hidden lines, which have precedence over centerlines, which have precedence over extension lines.

Conventions also exist for the intersection of lines in a drawing. For instance, an extension line is always drawn so that there is a slight, visible gap between its end and the outline of the object as shown in Figure 5.2. Similarly, perpendicular centerlines that cross are drawn so that the short dashes of each line intersect to form a small cross. Fortunately, most CAD software takes care of all of the details related to linetypes automatically. The engineer or designer need only know how to properly interpret the various linetypes.

5.4 DIMENSION PLACEMENT AND CONVENTIONS

Engineering drawings are usually drawn to scale, but it is still necessary to specify numerical dimensions for convenience and to ensure accuracy. In general, sufficient dimensions must be provided to define precisely the geometry of the part, but redundant dimensions should be avoided. Furthermore, dimensions on the drawing should reflect the way the part is made or the critical dimensions of the part. For example, consider the three drawings of a plate with two holes shown in Figure 5.3. The left drawing is over-dimensioned, having one redundant dimension. It is clear that given the distances from the left edge to the left hole, the distance from the right edge to the right hole, and the overall width of the plate, the distance between the holes has to be 6-mm. Thus, the 6-mm dimension could be omitted, suggesting that the distance between each hole and the nearest edge of the plate is most important. But suppose that the distance between the holes is critical. This might be necessary if the holes in the plate are supposed to align with another part. Then the dimensions on the middle drawing would clearly show that the distance between the holes is most important by omitting the dimension from the right hole to the right edge. The right drawing indicates that the distance from the left edge to each hole, not the distance between the holes, is critical. The engineer or designer must consider the optimal way to display dimensions to clearly show which dimensions are most important.

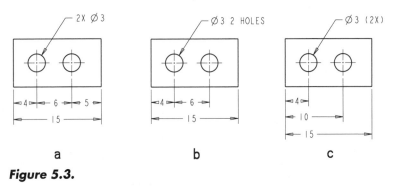

a   b   c

Figure 5.3.

It is natural for a person reading the drawings to look for the dimensions of a feature in the view where the feature occurs in its most characteristic shape and where it is visible (as opposed to hidden). This is known as *contour dimensioning*. For example, the location and size of a hole should be dimensioned in the view where the hole appears as a circle. Likewise, it is best to show the overall dimensions of the object in a view that is most descriptive of the object. If possible both the horizontal and vertical location of a feature should be dimensioned in the same view. The upper part of Figure 5.4 shows an object properly dimensioned in millimeters to show the relation of the dimensions to the features in the most obvious manner. In the lower part of Figure 5.4, the dimensioning has several problems. The overall dimensions of the L-shaped profile are shown on the view where it is not clear that the object is L-shaped. The diameter of the hole is shown in a view where the hole is shown only as a pair of parallel hidden lines, not as a circle. And the vertical location of the hole is shown in one view, while the horizontal location is shown in another view.

The conventions for millimeter and inch dimensioning are different. For millimeter dimensioning, dimensions less than 1 mm have a zero preceding the decimal point, and integer dimensions may or may not include a decimal point and following zeros. Thus, legitimate millimeter dimensions are 0.8, 6, 8.00, and 1.5. Inch dimensions do not include a zero before the decimal point for values less than 1 inch. Zeros to the right of the decimal point are usually included. Legitimate inch dimensions are .800, 6.00, 8.00, and 1.500. For both millimeter and inch dimensions, the number of digits to the right of the decimal point may be used to indicate the tolerance (acceptable variation). It is standard practice to omit the units for dimensions. However, it is wise to note the units in the title block or as a note on the drawing.

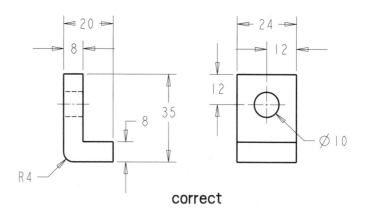

correct

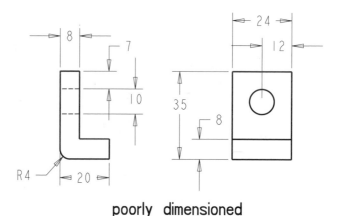

poorly dimensioned

Figure 5.4.

Circles and arcs are dimensioned using special symbols and rules. A radius is denoted using a leader line with an arrow pointing at the arc as shown in Figure 5.4. Sometimes a small cross is placed at the center of the radius. The position of the center should be dimensioned unless the radius is for a rounded edge, in which case the arc is positioned by virtue of being tangent at its ends to the sides forming the corner that is rounded, as shown in Figure 5.4. The dimension for a radius begins with a capital letter R to indicate radius. Full circles are dimensioned using the diameter with a leader line having an arrow pointing at the circle, as shown in Figure 5.4. If space permits, the leader line extends across a diameter of the circle with arrows at each end of the diameter. The dimension for a diameter begins with the Greek letter phi (Ø) to indicate diameter. The location of the center of the circle must also be dimensioned. Sometimes maintaining clarity makes it necessary to dimension several concentric circles from a side view, where the circle does not appear as a circle, thus violating the rule to dimension a feature in its most characteristic shape.

Angles are dimensioned as decimals or in degrees and minutes (60 minutes is one degree), so that 32.5° and 32°30′ are equivalent, where ′ indicates minutes. The dimension line for an angle is drawn as an arc with its center at the apex of the angle. When lines are drawn at right angles, a 90° angle is implied.

Multiple features that are identical need not be individually dimensioned. For example, the diameter of the two 3-mm holes in Figure 5.3 could be dimensioned with a leader line to one hole with the dimension 2× Ø3. The 2× indicates "two times." Alternative dimensions are Ø3 (2×), Ø3 2 PLACES, or Ø3 2 HOLES.

There are several other "rules" for dimensioning:

- Dimension lines should be outside of the outline of a part whenever possible.

- Dimension lines should not cross one another.

- Dimensions should be indicated on a view that shows the true length of the feature. This is particularly important when dimensioning features on a surface that is at an angle to the plane of the orthographic view.

- Each feature should be dimensioned only once. Do not duplicate the same dimension in different views.

- Dimension lines should be aligned and grouped when possible to promote clarity and uniform appearance. See for example the placement of the horizontal dimensions in Figure 5.3c.

- The numerical dimension and arrows should be placed between the extension lines where space permits. If there is space only for the dimension, but not the arrows, place the arrows outside of the extension lines. When the space is too small for either the arrows or the numerical value, place both outside of the extension lines. See Figure 5.4 for examples.

- Place the dimension no closer than about 10 mm (3/8 inch) from the object's outline.

- Dimensions should be placed in clear spaces, as close as possible to the feature they describe.

- When dimensions are nested (such as the horizontal dimensions in Figure 5.3c) the smallest dimensions should be closest to the object.

- Avoid crowding dimensions. Leave at least 6 mm (1/4 inch) between parallel dimension lines.

- Extension lines may cross visible lines of the object.

- Dimensions that apply to two adjacent views should be placed between the views, unless clarity is enhanced by placing them elsewhere. The dimension should be attached to only one view. Extension lines should not connect two views.

- Dimension lines and extension lines should not cross, if possible. Extension lines may cross other extension lines.

- A centerline may be extended to serve as an extension line, in which case it is still drawn as a centerline.

- Centerlines should not extend from view to view.

- Leader lines are usually sloped at about 30°, 45°, or 60° and are never horizontal or vertical.

- Numerical values for dimensions should be centered between arrowheads, except in a stack of dimensions (like Figure 5.3c).

- When a rough, noncritical dimension (such as a round) is indicated on a drawing, add the note TYP to the dimension to indicate that the dimension is "typical" or approximate.

5.5 SECTION AND DETAIL VIEWS

The cutaway view of a device appeared first in various forms in the 15th and 16th centuries to show details of parts hidden by other elements. These cutaway views have evolved to *section views* in which interior features that cannot be effectively displayed by hidden lines are exposed by slicing through a section of the object. To create a section view, a cutting plane is passed through the part and the portion of the part on one side of the cutting plane is imagined to be removed. In a section view, all visible edges and contours behind the cutting plane are shown. Hidden lines are usually omitted. The portion of the object that is sliced through is designated with angled crosshatch lines known as section-lining.

Key to the interpretation of a section view is the clear representation of where the cutting plane is and from which direction it is viewed. This is accomplished using a *cutting plane line* (long dash - short dash - short dash - long dash with perpendicular arrows at each end). The cutting plane line shows where the cutting plane passes through the object. The arrows on either end of the cutting plane line show the direction of the line of sight for the section view. An example of a block with a hole that has a large diameter partway into it and a smaller diameter through it is shown in Figure 5.5. In this case, the object is sectioned along a plane parallel to the right and left edges of the front view and through the center of the hole, as indicated by the position of cutting plane line A-A. The arrows indicate that the section view will be shown as if we are looking in the direction of the arrows. Thus, the section view shown to the right of the front view (as if unfolding the glass box) shows what the viewer would see if the portion of the object to the right of the cutting plane line was removed. The viewer sees the two diameters of the hole with the material that has been "cut" shown as cross-hatched. This view is designated Section A-A to correspond to the cutting plane line A-A. This type of section in which a single plane goes completely through an object is known as a *full section*.

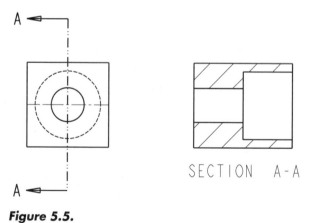

Figure 5.5.

A slightly more complicated example of a full section is shown in Figure 5.6. The whole object is shown in the upper left portion of the figure, and the sectioned object is shown with a portion removed just below it. The right side of the figure shows a top view of the object with the cutting plane displayed. Imagine that the material on the side of the cutting plane in the direction the arrows are pointing is retained, and the material behind the arrows is removed. Then the projection of the retained portion appears as SECTION B-B when viewed in the direction of the arrows.

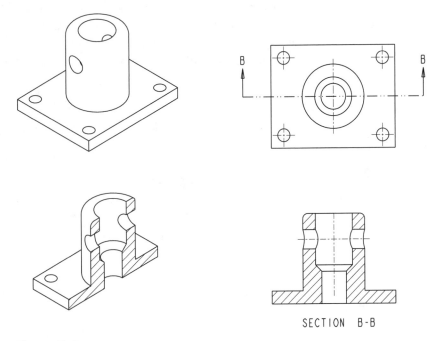

Figure 5.6.

Much more sophisticated section views can be created for complicated parts. In all cases, though, the clear definition of the cutting plane line and the direction of the line of sight for the view are critical. For example, Figure 5.7 shows a *half section* of the same part. The cutting plane extends halfway through the object to show the interior of one half of the object and the exterior of the other half. This type of section is ideal for

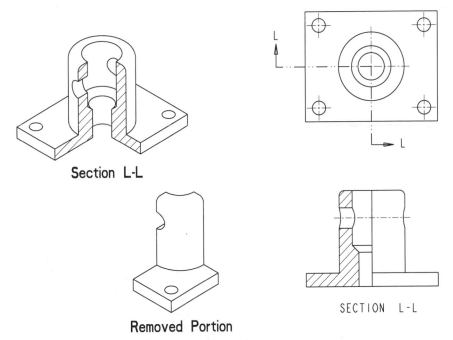

Figure 5.7.

symmetrical parts in which it is desired to show internal and external features in a single view. An *offset section* like that shown in Figure 5.8 is used to show internal details that are not in the same plane. The cutting plane for offset sections is bent at 90° angles to pass through important features. Note that the change of plane that occurs at the

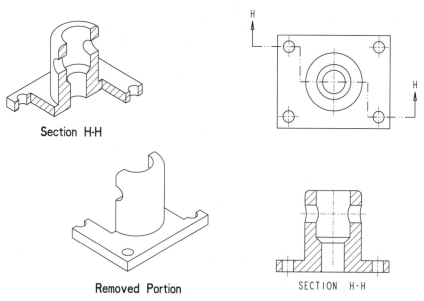

Figure 5.8.

90° bends is not represented with lines on the section view. When only a portion of the object needs to be sectioned to show a particular internal detail, a *broken-out section* like that shown in Figure 5.9 can be used. A break line separates the sectioned portion from the unsectioned portion, but no cutting plane line is drawn.

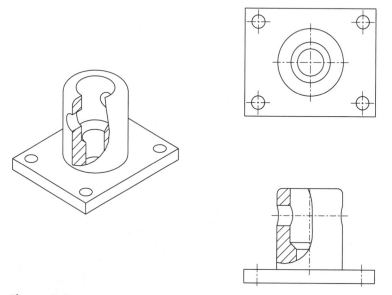

Figure 5.9.

In some cases it is necessary to clarify details of the part that may not be readily evident in the views normally shown in the drawing. For instance, a particular detail may be so small that it cannot be shown clearly on the same scale as the remainder of the part. This is done using an auxiliary *detail view* consisting of a small portion of the object magnified to make clear the small feature. An example is shown in Figure 5.10. In this case the small rivet holding the blade onto the arms of the pizza cutter is too small to see in the orthographic views. The region of interest near the rivet is circled in the left-most projection of the pizza cutter, and a note directs the reader to a magnified detail view in the upper right part of the drawing. The cross section of the rivet is clearly visible in this detail view.

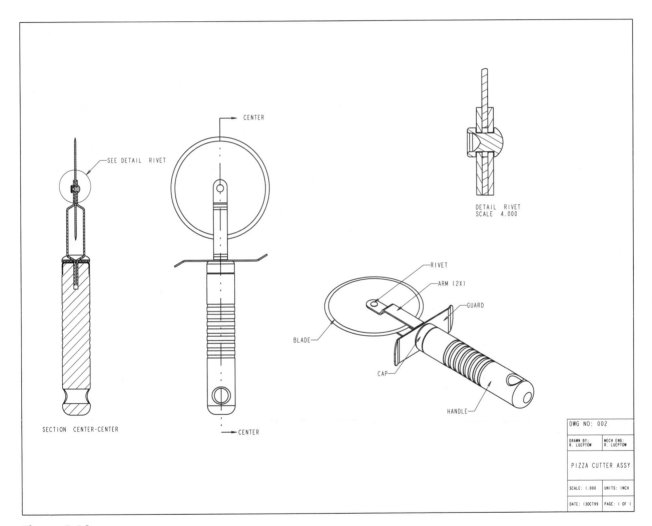

Figure 5.10.

5.6   FASTENERS AND SCREW THREADS

Fasteners include a broad range of items such as bolts, nuts, screws, and rivets used to "fasten" parts together. In most cases, fasteners are standard parts purchased from an outside vendor, so detail drawings of fasteners are rarely necessary. Nevertheless, threaded holes and threaded shafts must be represented on a drawing.

The geometry of screw threads is too complicated to draw exactly in an engineering drawing and screw threads are standard, so either of two simple conventions is used to indicate screw threads, as shown in Figure 5.11. The *schematic representation* is used when a realistic representation of the side view of a screw thread is desired. For an external thread, the lines that extend across the entire diameter represent the *crest*, or peak, of the thread, while the shorter lines in between represent the *root*, or valley, of the thread. The distance between crests or between roots is called the *pitch*. On a drawing, the crests and roots are shown perpendicular to the axis of the threaded section rather than helical as they actually appear on the physical thread. In the end view, threads are depicted with concentric circles. The outer circle is the largest diameter of the screw thread, known as the *major diameter*, and the inner circle is the smallest diameter of the screw thread, or *minor diameter*. In the end view of the external thread, both diameters are shown as solid circles. In the *simplified representation* of external screw threads, the threads are omitted altogether. The major diameter is represented as a solid line in the side view, and the minor diameter is represented with a dashed line.

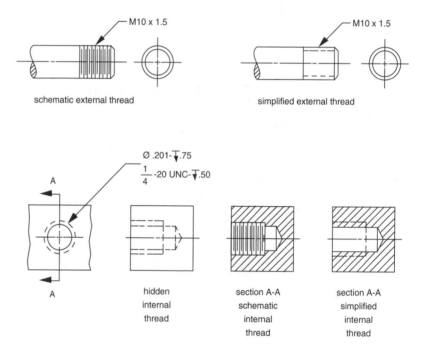

Figure 5.11.

The end view of an internal thread is shown as two concentric circles representing the major and minor diameter, but the major diameter is a hidden line. For a side view of a hidden internal screw thread, the major and minor diameters are both shown as hidden lines for both schematic and simplified screw thread representations. In a cross-section, internal threads can be shown in either the schematic or the simplified representation, as shown. For a hole that does not go completely through the part, called a *blind hole*, the lines in the side view representing the minor diameter continue deeper than the thread and come to a point. This represents the hole that is drilled prior to tapping, or cutting threads in the hole. The hole needs to be longer than the threaded section to permit the tool that is used to cut the threads, or tap, to penetrate deeply enough to fully cut the threads in the portion of the hole to be tapped.

Screw threads are specified in terms of the nominal (major) diameter, the pitch, and the thread series. For instance, the designations 1/4-20 UNC or .25-20 UNC or 1/4-20 NC all indicate a major diameter of .25 inches, a pitch of 20 threads per inch, and the United Course series. The diameter of the hole drilled before tapping an internal thread is specified in a wide variety of machinist and engineering handbooks. In this case the proper hole to be drilled has a diameter of .2010 inches, which corresponds to a number 7 drill. To make an internal thread of this size, a machinist would first drill a hole using a number 7 drill bit and then cut the threads using a 1/4-20 tap. For screw threads with a nominal diameter less than .25 inches, a number designation is used to specify the nominal diameter. For example, the designation 10-32 UNF indicates a nominal diameter of .1900 inches, 32 threads per inch, and the United Fine series. The pitch is equal to 1 divided by the number of threads per inch.

Metric threads are specified in a slightly different way. A designation M10 × 1.5 indicates a metric thread with a 10 mm major diameter and a pitch of 1.5 mm between crests of the thread. The number of threads per mm is 1 divided by the pitch. Other letters and numbers may follow the thread specification to denote tolerances and deviations of the thread, but for many cases these are not necessary. In addition, for a blind hole, the depth of the thread can be specified in several ways. Following the thread designation, the notation X .50 DEEP, THD .50 DP, or a downward arrow with a horizontal bar at its tail followed by .50 all indicate that the thread should extend .50 inches below the surface of the piece, as shown in Figure 5.11. (THD indicates "thread," and DP indicates "deep.") The threaded depth is usually 1.5 to 2 times the nominal diameter of the screw thread.

The dimensions for a threaded hole are indicated on a drawing using a leader line with the arrow pointing at the major diameter, as shown in Figure 5.11. Threaded holes are usually dimensioned in the view where they appear as circles, rather than in a side view of the threaded hole. Multiple threaded holes of the same specification are typically denoted in the same way as other multiple features using the notation (2X) or 2 TIMES at the end of the thread designation.

Nuts and bolts are usually only shown in a parts list and not on any drawings. They are specified in the same way as threaded holes, plus a bolt length and the type of head. For instance .25-28 UNF X 1.50 HEXAGON CAP SCREW or .25-28 NF X 1.50 HEX CAP SCR indicates a bolt that is 1.5 inches long with hexagonal head. Nuts are specified in terms of their thread and shape, such as M8 X 1.25 HEX NUT.

5.7 ASSEMBLY DRAWINGS

An assembly drawing shows all of the components of a design either assembled or in an exploded view. Many times assembly drawings include sections. Most dimensions are omitted in assembly drawings. Individual parts are not dimensioned, but some dimensions of the assembled mechanism may be included. Hidden lines are seldom necessary in assembly drawings, although they can be used where they clarify the design. Leader lines attached to a ballooned letter or detail number, as shown in Figure 5.12, reference the parts of the assembly. The leader lines should not cross and nearby leader lines should be approximately parallel. Sometimes parts are labeled by name rather than number. The parts list may be on the assembly drawing (usually on the right side or at the bottom) or it may be a separate sheet. The assembly drawing may also include machining or assembly information in the form of notes on the drawing.

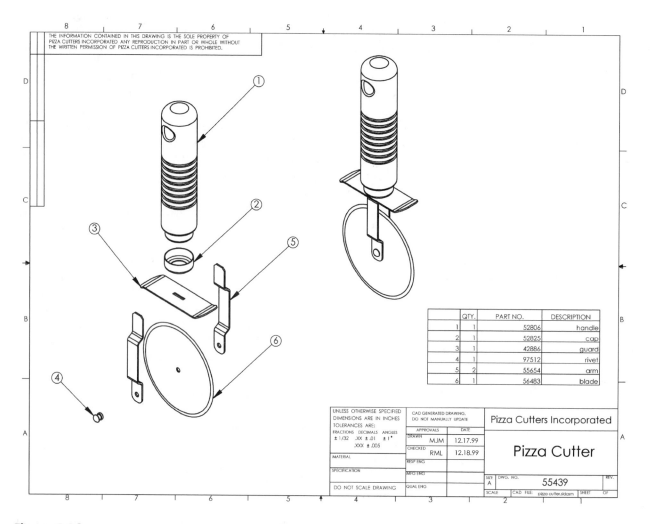

THE INFORMATION CONTAINED IN THIS DRAWING IS THE SOLE PROPERTY OF
PIZZA CUTTERS INCORPORATED ANY REPRODUCTION IN PART OR WHOLE WITHOUT
THE WRITTEN PERMISSION OF PIZZA CUTTERS INCORPORATED IS PROHIBITED.

	QTY.	PART NO.	DESCRIPTION
1	1	52806	handle
2	1	52825	cap
3	1	42886	guard
4	1	97512	rivet
5	2	55654	arm
6	1	56483	blade

UNLESS OTHERWISE SPECIFIED
DIMENSIONS ARE IN INCHES
TOLERANCES ARE:
FRACTIONS DECIMALS ANGLES
± 1/32 .XX ± .01 ± 1°
.XXX ± .005

CAD GENERATED DRAWING.
DO NOT MANUALLY UPDATE

APPROVALS		DATE
DRAWN	MJM	12.17.99
CHECKED	RML	12.18.99
RESP ENG		

MATERIAL

SPECIFICATION

MFG ENG

DO NOT SCALE DRAWING

QUAL ENG

Pizza Cutters Incorporated

Pizza Cutter

SIZE A | DWG. NO. 55439 | REV.

SCALE | CAD FILE: pizza cutter.sldasm | SHEET | OF

Figure 5.12.

Often assembly drawings include assembly sections. These are typically orthographic or pictorial section views of parts as put together in an assembly. Adjacent parts
in assembly drawings are cross-hatched at different angles to make the separate parts
clear. The assembly cross-section on the left side of Figure 5.10 shows the interior structure of the parts of a pizza cutter and how they fit together. The detail view in the upper
right of Figure 5.10 shows the cross-section through the rivet to indicate how the parts
are assembled. Usually standard parts such as fasteners, washers, springs, bearings, and
gears are not cross-hatched. But in the case of Figure 5.10, the rivet detail is integral to
the assembly, and it is helpful to show its cross-section with cross-hatching to indicate
how it fits with the other parts.

KEY TERMS

Centerlines

Contour dimensioning

Cutting plane lines

Detail view

Dimension lines

Extension lines

Hidden lines

Leader lines

Scale

Section views

Title block

Visible lines

Problems

1. Three orthographic views and an isometric view of an object that has overall dimensions of $4 \times 4 \times 4$ inches are to be shown in a drawing. Determine the best ANSI sheet size for an object of this size at the scales indicated below:

   a. Half Size.

   b. 2:1.

   c. 1 = 1.

2. Three orthographic views and an isometric view of an object that has overall dimensions of $200 \times 200 \times 200$ mm are to be shown in a drawing. Determine the optimal standard metric scale to be used for the ISO sheet sizes indicated below:

   a. A1.

   b. A3.

   c. A4.

3. The drawing shown in Figure 5.13 has many errors in the dimensioning. Sketch the orthographic views and show proper placement of dimensions.

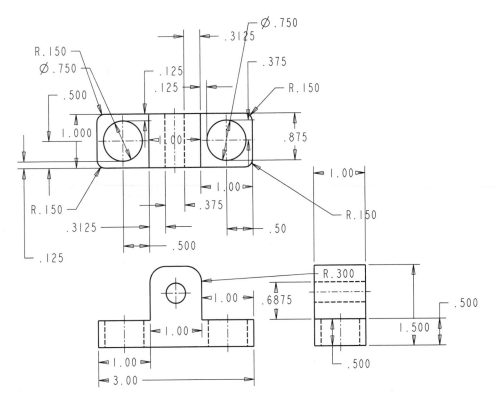

Figure 5.13.

4. The drawing shown in Figure 5.14 has many errors in the dimensioning. Sketch the orthographic views and show proper placement of dimensions. The M10 × 1.5 threaded hole requires a tap drill of 8.5 mm. Only two views are needed for this part.

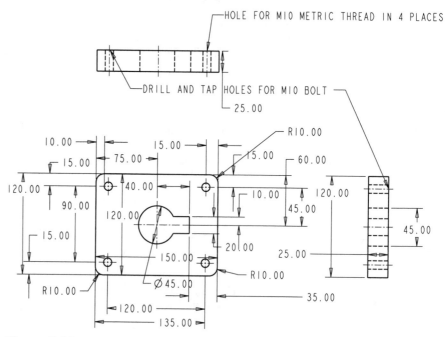

Figure 5.14.

5. Sketch the following section views for the object shown in Figure 5.15. The threaded holes extend from the top surface approximately halfway through the thickness of the part. The other holes extend through the part.

    a. A-A.
    b. B-B.

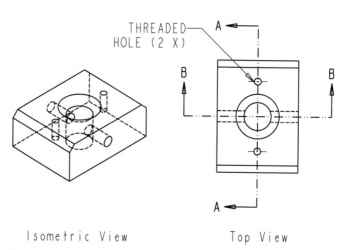

Isometric View   Top View

Figure 5.15.

6. Sketch the following section views for the object shown in Figure 5.16. All holes extend through the part.

    a. B-B.

    b. D-D.

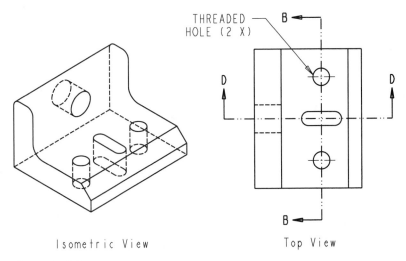

Figure 5.16.

7. Look up the following machine screw threads in an engineering graphics book (such as *Engineering Graphics* by Giesecke, et al), a machinists or engineering handbook (such as *Marks' Standard Handbook for Mechanical Engineers*), an industrial supply catalog (such as McMaster–Carr), or on the World Wide Web (search on "tap drill size"). Specify the series (UNC or UNF), tap drill size or number, number of threads per inch, pitch, and nominal diameter.

    a. 4-40.

    b. 6-32.

    c. 8-32.

    d. 3/8-24.

    e. 6-40.

    f. 1/4-28.

8. Look up the following machine screw threads in an engineering graphics book (such as *Engineering Graphics* by Giesecke, et al), a machinists or engineering handbook (such as *Marks' Standard Handbook for Mechanical Engineers*), an industrial supply catalog (such as McMaster–Carr), or on the World Wide Web (search on "tap drill size metric"). Specify the series (course or fine), tap drill size, number of threads per mm, and nominal size.

    a. M2 × 0.4.

    b. M12 × 1.75.

    c. M30 × 3.5.

    d. M30 × 2.

    e. M10 × 1.25.

6

Tolerances

OVERVIEW

Tolerances on dimensions are necessary to specify the acceptable variability in the dimension of a part. Tolerances can be indicated for all dimensions using a general note or they can be specified for each individual dimension. Tolerances are based on the function of the part or are used to assure that mating parts fit together. However, in many cases the manufacturing process determines the tolerance. The surface finish may also be specified on a drawing to indicate the roughness of the surface. To further minimize ambiguity in engineering drawings, geometric dimensioning and tolerancing is used to specify the form of a feature, such as flatness or roundness, or to indicate the ideal position of a feature.

SECTIONS

- 6.1 Why Tolerances?
- 6.2 Displaying Tolerances on Drawings
- 6.3 How to Determine Tolerances
- 6.4 Surface Finish
- 6.5 Geometric Dimensioning and Tolerancing

OBJECTIVES

After reading this chapter, you should be able to:

- Explain interchangeable parts
- Explain the necessity of tolerancing
- Read a general tolerance on a drawing
- Read limit dimensions and tolerances on individual dimensions
- Determine a tolerance stackup
- Determine the range of tolerances for manufacturing processes
- Read a surface finish specification
- Understand basic form tolerances
- Understand simple positional tolerances
- Read geometric dimensioning and tolerancing symbols

6.1 WHY TOLERANCES?

In 1815, it was hoped that muskets could be produced in a number of different U. S. Government and private armories so that the parts of the musket would be interchangeable. Before this time, muskets were individually handcrafted, so parts from one musket rarely fit another musket. Because engineering drawings were not commonly used, a number of "perfect" muskets were made according to master gages and jigs. *Gages* are devices used to check the individual dimensions of a part. For instance, the diameter of a shaft could be checked using a gage consisting of two holes: one of the maximum allowable diameter of the shaft and one of the minimum allowable diameter. If the shaft fit through the larger hole but not the smaller hole, then it was within the allowable dimensions for the shaft. *Jigs* are devices used to hold a workpiece and guide the tool to assure repeatable machining. The master gages and jigs were sent to the armories with the instruction that "no deviations from the pattern were to be allowed." In 1824, this concept of *interchangeable parts* was tested by disassembling a hundred rifles from several different armories, mixing the parts, and then reassembling at random. Most reassembled rifles worked as they should, proving the concept and value of interchangeable parts.

The interchangeability of parts is so common now that it is hard to imagine anything different. The concept allows parts made in various locations by different manufacturers to be successfully assembled and to function properly as an assembly. Although engineering drawings rather than "master parts" came into use in the mid-19th century, it was the two world wars in the 20th century that brought about the development of methods of showing the acceptable variation in a dimension on a drawing, or *tolerancing*.

The need to control precisely the geometry of a part arises from the part's function. For instance, the cross-sectional geometry of an airfoil, such as the wing of a jet aircraft or a turbine blade, must be accurately controlled to assure aerodynamic efficiency. The more commonplace need for controlling geometry results from the requirement for parts to fit together. But it is quite difficult to make every part the exact size that is specified in a dimension because of slight differences in tool size, machine tool wear, human operator error, and other factors. As a consequence, tolerances are used in engineering drawings to specify the limit in the variation between mating parts and to provide guidelines to control the manufacturing process. The *tolerance* is the amount that a specific dimension is permitted to vary, or the difference between the maximum and minimum limits of a dimension.

Consider a dimension on a drawing specified as 3.750 ± .003. This dimension indicates that the part has a *nominal size*, or general size, of 3 3/4 inches (usually expressed as a common fraction). The *basic size*, or theoretical size for the application of the tolerance, is 3.750 inches (expressed as a decimal). The tolerance of the dimension is .006 inches. Thus, an acceptable machined part can have an *actual size* ranging from 3.747 to 3.753 inches, which are the minimum and maximum limits of the dimension. If the actual size is smaller than 3.747 or larger than 3.753, then the part is not acceptable.

Of course, it is desirable to make the part as close as possible to the basic size, sometimes called the *target size*. But the more accuracy needed in a machined part, the higher the manufacturing cost. Furthermore, the method of machining a part limits the tolerance that can be specified. For instance, the tolerance in drilling a .500 inch hole is between .002 and .005 depending on the quality of the drill press and drill bit. To require a tolerance smaller than .002 would require an additional machining process, such as reaming. Consequently, tolerances can play a large role in the cost of manufacturing a part. Therefore, the tolerances should not be specified tighter than necessary for the product to function properly.

An increased awareness of the importance of tolerances in manufacturing has led to an approach in which the deviation of the actual size of a part from the target size has a cost in terms of reworking of the part, scrap, customer dissatisfaction, and poor reliability. An approach to handle this is to design a product so that it is less sensitive to manufacturing tolerances. The idea is to design the part intelligently so that easy-to-manufacture tolerances, rather than exceptionally tight tolerances, are necessary. Consequently, proper fit between mating parts comes about because of good design, instead of depending on tight tolerances. This approach is known as *robust design*.

6.2   DISPLAYING TOLERANCES ON DRAWINGS

Every dimension on a drawing should have a tolerance. Tolerances can be displayed on engineering drawings in several ways depending on the situation.

General tolerances can be given in a note on the drawing or in the title block. An example would be the note ALL DIMENIONS TO BE HELD TO ± .003″. Thus, a dimension of .375 would have a minimum limit of .372 and a maximum limit of .378. Often general tolerances are specified in terms of the number of digits following the decimal point in a dimension. In this case, a note would appear on the drawing such as:

$$\text{UNLESS OTHERWISE SPECIFIED}$$
$$\text{TOL:.XX} = \pm.010$$
$$\text{.XXX} = \pm.005$$
$$\text{HOLES} = \pm.002$$
$$\text{ANGLES} = \pm.5 \text{ DEG} \qquad\qquad (6\text{-}1)$$

Thus, a dimension of .50 on a drawing would indicate an actual size between .490 and .510. A dimension of .500 would indicate an actual size between .495 and .505. For metric dimension, a similar form for general tolerances would be X.X METRIC = ±.08.

Two other methods of displaying tolerances on a drawing are shown in Figure 6.1. The maximum and minimum sizes are specified directly when using *limit dimensions* to specify the tolerance. Usually the upper limit is placed above the lower limit. While this method clearly shows the limits of the dimension, many engineers, designers, and machinists think in terms of the nominal or basic size plus a tolerance, neither of which are immediately evident using limit dimensions. Thus, a more common approach is to use *plus and minus dimensions* where the basic size is shown followed by the tolerance values. If the plus and minus tolerance values are identical, then the basic dimension is followed by a plus/minus sign and half of the numerical value of the tolerance. Otherwise, the plus and minus tolerances are indicated separately with the plus above the minus. A *bilateral tolerance*, such as the tolerance for the 1.500 inch dimension in Figure 6.1, varies in both directions from the basic size. A *unilateral tolerance*, such as the tolerance on the shaft in Figure 6.1, varies in only one direction from the basic size. In both cases, the number of digits to the right of the decimal point for the dimension should be the same as the number of digits to the right of the decimal point for the tolerance.

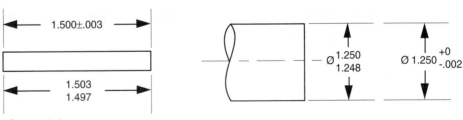

Figure 6.1.

Sometimes it is not necessary to specify both limits of a tolerance and only one limit dimension is needed. MIN or MAX is placed after a numerical dimension to indicate that it is a *single limit dimension*. The depth of holes, length of threads, and radii of corner rounds are often specified using single limit dimensions.

Many times several methods of representing tolerances are used on a single drawing. For instance, general tolerances may be listed in the title block and plus and minus dimensions or limit dimensions may be used for a few dimensions to which the general tolerances do not apply.

An important consideration in applying tolerances is the effect of one tolerance on another, especially because tolerances are cumulative. This is known as *tolerance accumulation* or *tolerance stackup* for a chain of dimensions. In the example shown in Figure 6.2, two dimensioning schemes are shown. Above the part, *chain dimensioning* shows the distance from one feature to the next. This would be an appropriate dimensioning scheme if the distance from one hole to the next were critical, because the distance between holes must be between .995 and 1.005. But if the distance of the holes from left edge of the part were critical, a large tolerance would accumulate. The third hole would be 2.985 from the left edge if all of the dimensions happened to be at the minimum limit of the dimension, or 3.015 from the left edge if all dimensions were at the maximum limit. Thus, the actual dimension of the third hole from the left edge using chain dimensioning is 3.000 ± .015. This tolerance accumulation could be avoided using *datum dimensioning*, where the dimensions are given with respect to a datum, in this case the left edge of the part as shown below the part in Figure 6.2. Using this scheme the third hole is specified to be between 2.995 and 3.005 from the left edge. Of course, the distance between the second and third holes could be as small as .990, if the second hole is at 2.005 and the third hole is at 2.995. The distance between the second and third holes could be as large as 1.010 if the holes are at 1.995 and 3.005. Consequently, the decision about which way to dimension the holes depends on whether the distance between holes is critical, or whether the distance from each hole to the left edge is critical.

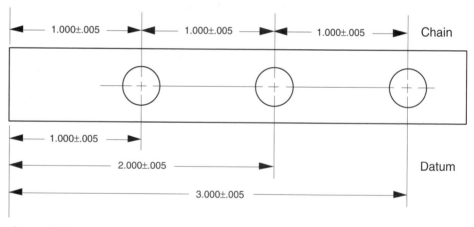

Figure 6.2.

6.3   HOW TO DETERMINE TOLERANCES

One of the most difficult aspects of dimensioning and tolerancing for inexperienced engineers and designers is to determine what tolerance to specify on a drawing. In some cases a specific tolerance is quite clear based on the function of the design. For instance, if a 3/4-inch shaft must rotate at moderate speed in a hole, the tolerances on the shaft and the hole can be determined based on standard classes of fits that are available in many engineering and machinist handbooks. In this particular case the hole could be between .7500 and .7512, while the shaft could have a diameter of .7484 to .7492. A shaft any bigger or a hole any smaller would result in too tight of a clearance for the shaft to rotate freely, or could result in the shaft being too big for the hole. A smaller shaft or larger hole than the specified limits would result in a sloppy fit between the shaft and the hole. The point here is not the details of how the tolerances are determined. That is too specific to individual cases for this discussion and is presented in many handbooks and texts. Instead, the point is that the function of the system that is being designed drives the tolerances. In this case, *the tolerances drive the manufacturing process* used to machine the hole and the shaft.

But more a more common situation is the opposite: *the manufacturing process drives the tolerance*. If the only machine tool that is available to form a hole is a drill press, the 3/4-inch hole that will result will be between .748 and .754 in diameter based on expected tolerances for the drilling operation. But this means that the hole in the example above would have too much variability to assure that the shaft rotates in it properly. Of course, if only one shaft-hole assembly was being made, the hole could be drilled first and measured. Then the shaft could be turned on a lathe to a diameter just slightly smaller to achieve the fit described above. But this approach will clearly not work for mass-produced, interchangeable parts. Either a more accurate machining method is needed to create the hole or the design must be altered to avoid drilling a tightly dimensioned hole altogether. (In this example, a standard-size, off-the-shelf bearing could be inserted into a larger drilled hole to mate with the shaft.)

When the manufacturing processes that are available drive the tolerances, the tolerances on the drawing must reflect the manufacturing process that is used to make the part, and the design must be altered to ensure that the part can be made with the available machining processes. Guidelines are available for the tolerance range of various common machining processes. These processes include the following:

Lapping: A process to produce a very smooth and accurate surface by rubbing the surface of the workpiece against a mating form, often using a fine abrasive between the surfaces.

Honing: A process in which a honing stone made of fine abrasive is used to form a surface on a workpiece.

Grinding: A process to remove a small amount of material from a workpiece with a rapidly rotating grinding wheel.

Broaching: A process similar to filing in which a cutting tool is reciprocated along its axis to remove a small amount of material from a workpiece.

Reaming: Removal of a small amount of material from a drilled hole using a rotating cutting tool (reamer).

Turning: Axisymmetric removal of material from a rotating workpiece by feeding a cutting tool into the workpiece using a lathe.

Boring: Axisymmetric removal of material from a workpiece using a tool with a single cutting surface. Either the workpiece or the tool may be rotating.

Milling: Removal of material by feeding workpiece into a rotating cutting tool.

Drilling: Creating a hole by feeding the end of a sharpened cylindrical cutting tool (drill bit) into the material.

Stamping and *Punching*: Cutting material using a punch and a die to shear the material, much like a paper hole-punch.

The tolerance typically depends on the size of the feature, as well as the quality of the machine tool, sharpness of the cutting tool, and skill of the operator. Figure 6.3 indicates the range of tolerances to be expected for various machining operations. To use this table, first consider the size of the feature in the left column. Then go below the sizes in the left column to the type of machining operation used. The bar associated with that process indicates the range of tolerances in the row associated with the feature size. For instance, consider a feature that has a dimension of 2 inches. If broaching were used to create that feature, the chart indicates that the total tolerance would be .0004 to .0015, depending on the machining conditions. Thus, this dimension could be specified as 2.0000 ± .0002 up to 2.0000 ± .0008 (rounding up). If the same piece was created on a milling machine, the tolerances would be .0025 to .010, indicating a dimension of 2.0000 ± .0013 up to 2.000 ± .005. If broaching were not available, we would have to be satisfied with the tolerances of a milling machine and adjust the design accordingly, if the milling tolerances are too large. If both broaching and milling were available, the criticality of the tolerance and the cost of manufacturing would drive the tolerance that would be specified on the drawing. (Broaching, a mass-production process, is usually more expensive than milling, so milling would be preferred if the milling tolerances are acceptable.) Tolerances for metric dimensioning can be determined by converting the values in Figure 6.3 to millimeters and rounding off the result to one less place to the right of the decimal point.

Size (in.)	Total Tolerance (in.)								
0.000-0.599	0.00015	0.0002	0.0003	0.0005	0.0008	0.0012	0.002	0.003	0.005
0.600-0.999	0.00015	0.00025	0.0004	0.0006	0.001	0.0015	0.0025	0.004	0.006
1.000-1.499	0.0002	0.0003	0.0005	0.0008	0.0012	0.002	0.003	0.005	0.008
1.500-2.799	0.00025	0.0004	0.0006	0.001	0.0015	0.0025	0.004	0.006	0.010
2.800-4.499	0.0003	0.0005	0.0008	0.0012	0.002	0.003	0.005	0.008	0.012
4.500-7.799	0.0004	0.0006	0.001	0.0015	0.0025	0.004	0.006	0.010	0.015
7.800-13.599	0.0005	0.0008	0.0012	0.002	0.003	0.005	0.008	0.012	0.025

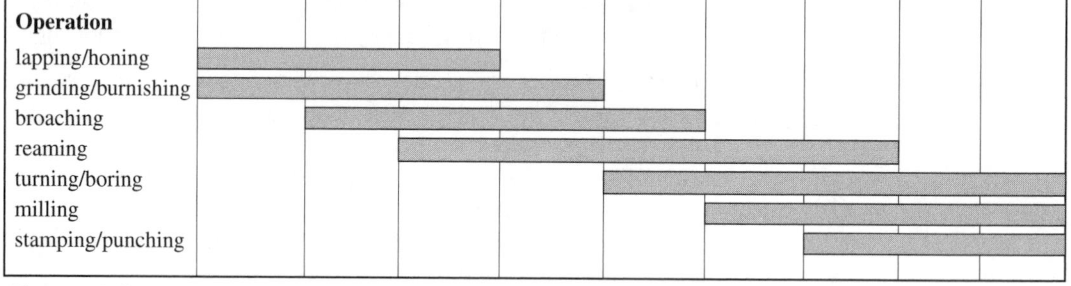

Operation

lapping/honing
grinding/burnishing
broaching
reaming
turning/boring
milling
stamping/punching

Figure 6.3.

Typical tolerances on drills depend on the drill size. Standard drill sizes are fractional in increments of 1/64-inch from 1/16-inch to 4-inch and according to an alphanumeric code. The coded drill sizes range from 80 (.0135 inch) to 1 (.2280 inch) and from A (.234 inch) to Z (.413 inch). The dimensions for the coded drill sizes are widely available in engineering and machinist handbooks. In addition, the proper drill sizes for drilling holes that will be tapped are listed in these handbooks. The standard tolerance for drilled holes is given in Table 6.1.

TABLE 6-1 Standard Tolerance For Drilled Holes

DRILL SIZE (IN.)	TOLERANCE (IN.)	
	Plus	Minus
0.0135 (80)–0.185 (13)	0.003	0.002
0.1875–0.246 (D)	0.004	0.002
0.250–0.750	0.005	0.002
0.7656–1.000	0.007	0.003
1.0156–2.000	0.010	0.004
2.0312–3.500	0.015	0.005

6.4 SURFACE FINISH

All surfaces are rough and irregular on a microscopic scale. The roughness can be described in terms of asperities (peaks or ridges) and valleys. The irregularities of a surface are classified into *roughness* and *waviness*. Roughness describes the small scale, somewhat random irregularity of a surface, while waviness describes a more regular variation in the surface that typically has a wavelength of 0.8 mm or more. The surface can be thought of as a roughness superimposed on waviness. The roughness and waviness can be measured in several ways, but the most common is a profilometer, which drags a fine-pointed stylus over the surface and records the height of the stylus. The roughness is measured in terms of the roughness average (R_a). The roughness average is defined as the average of the absolute values of the deviation of the local surface height from the average height of the surface. This is equivalent to half the average of the peak to valley height. In addition, the *lay*, or predominant direction of the marks left by the machine tools, may be important to describing the surface.

The surface finish resulting from several machining and forming processes are shown in Figure 6.4. This figure shows the range of possible surface roughness averages (R_a) in both micrometers (1μm = 10^{-6} m) and microinches (1μin = 10^{-6} in). For instance, surfaces formed by drilling are likely to have a roughness from 12.5 down to 0.8 μm (500 down to 32 μin). Typically, the roughness is in the middle of the specified range, about 6.3 down to 1.6 μm for the case of drilling. In addition to the machining processes described in Section 6.3, the following processes are also included in Figure 6.4:

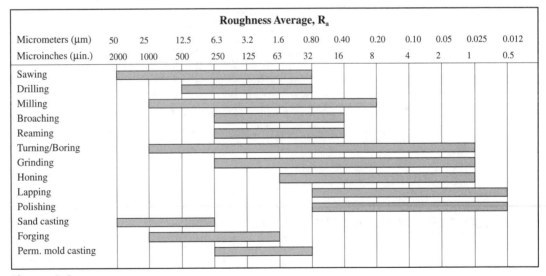

Figure 6.4.

Sawing: Cutting material by moving a toothed blade through the material.

Polishing: Removal of scratches and tool marks on a surface using a belt or rotating wheel of soft material such as cloth or leather, often with a fine abrasive.

Sand Casting: Forming a part by pouring molten metal into a mold made of sand.

Forging: Shaping of metal to a desired form by pressing or hammering, usually with the metal hot.

Permanent Mold Casting: Forming a part by pouring molten metal into a permanent mold.

To put the roughness averages in perspective, consider that a 0.10 μm roughness is a mirrorlike surface, free from visible marks of any kind. A 1.6 μm roughness is a high-quality, smooth machined finish. A 6.3 μm roughness is the ordinary finish from typical machining operations.

The surface finish may be specified on a drawing using the special symbols touching the surface or with a leader line to the surface as shown in Figure 6.5. For the top surface, the roughness is specified as 1.2 μm, corresponding to a high quality, smooth machine finish. The surface finish symbol on the right side of the object includes a horizontal bar that indicates that material removal by machining is required for this surface. The surface finish symbol on the left side of the object indicates that material removal from this side is prohibited. This surface must be that resulting from the original process used to produce the surface such as casting, forging, or injection molding.

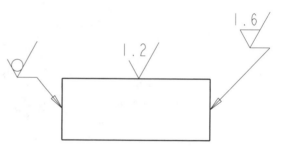

Figure 6.5.

Other notations can be added to the surface roughness symbol. A number to the left of the surface finish mark describes the material removal allowance indicating the amount of stock material to be removed by machining. A symbol to the right of the surface roughness mark indicates the lay, or predominant direction of machining marks: perpendicular, parallel, circular, or radial. Other notations can be used to specify the waviness. Details of surface finish notation are available in engineering and machinist handbooks.

6.5   GEOMETRIC DIMENSIONING AND TOLERANCING

Ideally, engineering drawings should be unambiguous in their interpretation. In many cases, stating dimensions and tolerances provides adequate information so that the part can be manufactured to ensure interchangeability of parts and optimal performance. But sometimes, the traditional dimensioning using the plus and minus scheme does not adequately describe the geometry of the part. For instance, consider the part shown in Figure 6.6. The dimension shown in the drawing could have several possible interpretations. For instance, the dimension at the top edge could be 14.9 mm while the dimension at the bottom edge could be 15.1 mm, resulting in a trapezoidal part instead of a rectangular part. Or the right edge of the part could be bowed so that the part is 15.1 mm wide at the top and bottom, but 14.9 mm wide at the middle. As a result, the part would not fit flush against another flat surface even though the part is 15 ± .1 mm wide at any particular location. In both of these cases, the geometry of the part is not described fully by the plus and minus tolerances on the dimension.

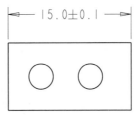

Figure 6.6.

A system known as *geometric dimensioning and tolerancing* is used to prevent such ambiguities in the design to present the design intent more clearly. Geometric dimensioning and tolerancing supplements the traditional dimensioning system with specifications that describe the geometry of the part to enhance the interpretation of the drawing. It is used to indicate dimensions critical to a part's function and ensure part interchangeability. Items related to geometric dimensioning and tolerancing are indicated on a drawing by a feature symbol consisting of a frame or box around information describing the geometry. A complete discussion of geometric dimensioning and tolerancing is beyond the scope of this book—there are entire books on the subject. Nevertheless, several of the key aspects and applications of geometric dimensioning and tolerancing are presented here to familiarize the reader with the basic terminology and symbols that are used.

The various types of tolerances and the characteristics that they describe are indicated in Figure 6.7. Each has its own symbol that is used on a drawing. Perhaps the easiest

	TYPE OF TOLERANCE	CHARACTERISTIC	SYMBOL
FOR INDIVIDUAL FEATURES	FORM	STRAIGHTNESS	—
		FLATNESS	▱
		CIRCULARITY (ROUNDNESS)	○
		CYLINDRICITY	⌭
FOR INDIVIDUAL OR RELATED FEATURES	PROFILE	PROFILE OF A LINE	⌒
		PROFILE OF A SURFACE	⌓
FOR RELATED FEATURES	ORIENTATION	ANGULARITY	∠
		PERPENDICULARITY	⊥
		PARALLELISM	//
	LOCATION	POSITION	⊕
		CONCENTRICITY	◎
		SYMMETRY	=
	RUNOUT	CIRCULAR RUNOUT	↗
		TOTAL RUNOUT	↗↗

Figure 6.7.

type of geometric tolerances to understand are the *form tolerances*, which describe the shape of a single feature. For instance, straightness indicates the limits on how much a surface or axis can bow with respect to a straight line. Figure 6.8 shows the *straightness* specification for a surface. A feature control box with the straightness symbol (a horizontal bar)

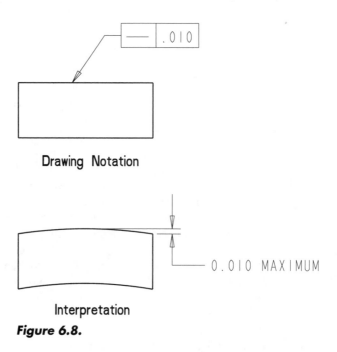

Drawing Notation

Interpretation

Figure 6.8.

and a numerical dimension are connected by a leader line to the surface. The interpretation is that the upper surface must be straight enough so that all points on the surface are within the tolerance zone of 0.010 mm. An example of a *flatness* specification is shown in Figure 6.9. The parallelogram symbol with a numerical dimension in a feature control box

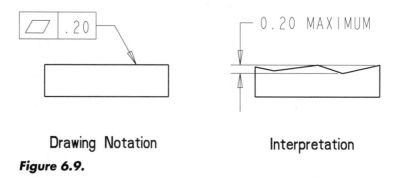

Drawing Notation   **Interpretation**

Figure 6.9.

indicates that the planar surface must lie between two parallel planes 0.20 mm apart. Other single feature specifications include *circularity* or *roundness* (for circular features to be within a tolerance zone defined by two concentric circles), and *cylindricity* (for cylindrical features to be within a tolerance zone defined by two concentric cylinders). Closely related to form tolerances are *profile tolerances*, which define the acceptable deviation of the outline of an object (profile) from that specified in the drawing. These tolerances define a zone on either side of the true profile shown on the drawing within which the line or surface should remain. Profile tolerances can be applied to either a line or a surface.

Orientation tolerances prescribe the relation between features. *Parallelism* controls the degree to which a surface is parallel to a reference plane, or datum plane. In Figure 6.10, the horizontal datum plane that coincides with the bottom edge of the part is identified with a box around B attached to the bottom edge. The parallelism fea-

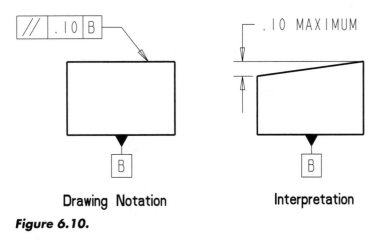

Drawing Notation   **Interpretation**

Figure 6.10.

ture symbol (parallel lines), the numerical tolerance, and the reference datum plane are included in a feature control box with a leader line to the surface to which the tolerance applies. In this case, the upper surface must be within .10 mm of parallel to datum plane B. *Perpendicularity* with respect to a datum plane is indicated in a similar way, as shown in Figure 6.11. Here the vertical plane must be perpendicular to datum plane A to

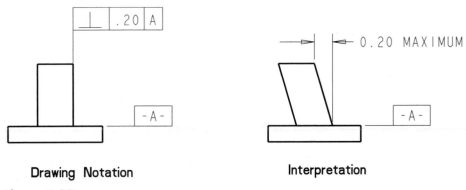

Drawing Notation   **Interpretation**

Figure 6.11.

within .20 mm. In this example, an alternative notation for specifying datum plane A is used. The datum plane symbol used in Figure 6.11 is common, but the datum plane symbol used in Figure 6.10 and Figure 6.12 is preferred. The datum plane symbol can be applied in several different ways as shown in Figure 6.10 and Figure 6.12. Several other relations between features can be specified, including the tolerance zone for *angularity* from a datum plane or axis, the tolerance zone for *concentricity* of a surface of revolution with respect to an axis, the tolerance zone for *symmetry* with respect to a datum plane, and the tolerance zone for *runout*, which describes the circularity with respect to an axis of revolution.

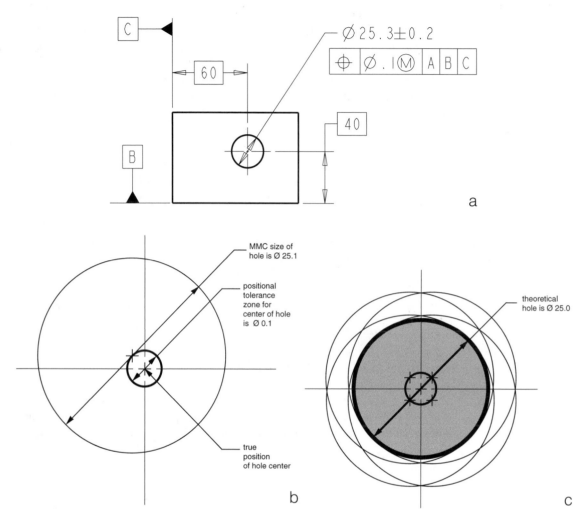

Figure 6.12.

The most difficult concept in geometric dimensioning and tolerancing is the concept of *positional tolerances*. It is demonstrated most easily in indicating the position of a hole, as shown in Figure 6.12a. In this case, the ultimate goal is to have a circular open area (hole) that is at least 25.0 mm in diameter with its center exactly at the position indicated in the drawing. Note that even though we want a 25.0 mm hole, the hole is dimensioned as 25.3 mm in the drawing. The reason for this will shortly become evident.

Rather than describing the position of the hole with a plus-or-minus tolerance, the ideal position of the hole is prescribed. The boxed dimensions indicate that they are basic *true-position dimensions*, which describe the perfect position of the center of the hole. Then the feature control box below the dimension of the hole shows how close the center of the hole should be to the true position. In this case, the hole should be within a circular tolerance zone with a diameter of .1 mm of the true position (indicated by the plus in the circle within the feature control box followed by ⌀ .1). The reference datum planes are also included in the feature control box. Datum plane A is the surface of the part in the plane of the page. Datum planes B and C are references for the true-position dimensions of 40 and 60 mm. These three mutually perpendicular datum planes provide a reference point for the positional tolerance of the hole.

The positional tolerance zone for the center of the hole is shown in Figure 6.12b. The "true position of hole center" is based on the 40 and 60 mm dimensions. Around this center is a circle with a diameter of .1 mm (not drawn to scale in Figure 6.12b) that defines the "positional tolerance zone." The center of the actual hole must be within this circle. For instance, an acceptable hole would be a 25.1 mm diameter hole with its center on the edge of this circular tolerance zone, as shown in the Figure 6.12b.

The M in a circle in the feature control box in Figure 6.12a indicates that the .1 mm circular positional tolerance zone is applied at the *maximum material condition* (MMC). For a hole, the maximum material condition is the smallest acceptable dimension of the hole, because this is the situation in which the most material would be present. For the part in Figure 6.12a, the diameter of the hole for the maximum material condition is 25.1 mm, given a dimension of 25.3 ± .2 for the diameter of the hole. Thus, the circle representing a hole with its center on the edge of the positional tolerance zone has a diameter of 25.1 mm, as shown in Figure 6.12b. Of course, the 25.1 mm diameter hole could be anywhere within the positional tolerance zone or on its edge. Three more 25.1 mm diameter circles are drawn in Figure 6.12c in addition to the original 25.1 mm circle. The centers of all four circles are on the edge of the positional tolerance zone. Note that there is a circle that lies inside all of the 25.1 mm diameter circles, which we call the "theoretical hole." It is relatively straightforward to find the diameter of the theoretical hole, based on the positional tolerance zone for the center of the hole and the MMC size of the hole. The radius of the theoretical hole is the distance from the true position of the hole center to the nearest portion of any one of the MMC circles. Here the theoretical hole has a diameter of 25.0 mm. In fact the theoretical hole always has a diameter equal to the diameter for the maximum material condition minus the diameter of the positional tolerance (in this case, 25.1 mm − .1 mm = 25.0 mm).

The key result is that if the hole diameter is within the specified tolerance (25.3 ± .2 mm) and the center of the hole is within the positional tolerance zone (.1 mm), there will always be a circular opening in the part with a diameter of at least 25.0 mm. Now assume that the hole must mate with a circular pin that is positioned at the true center of the hole and is exactly 25.0 mm in diameter. Given the dimensioning scheme in Figure 6.12a, the pin will always align with the theoretical hole and fit through the theoretical hole, even if the actual hole is not positioned so its center is exactly at the true position of the hole center. Of course, the theoretical hole is based on the maximum material condition (smallest hole allowed). If the hole is at the large end of the acceptable tolerance, 25.5 mm in diameter, circles drawn in Figure 6.12c will be larger. But the theoretical hole will still be open for the pin. Likewise, if the circles drawn in Figure 6.12c are not on the edge of the positional tolerance zone, but inside of the zone, the entire theoretical hole will still be open for the pin. Thus, defining the position and diameter of the hole as in Figure 6.12a forces the existence of an open area (theoretical hole) that is at least 25.0 mm in diameter and centered at the true position of the hole center.

The maximum material condition reflects the practical aspect of assembly. Consider two parts that are bolted together with several bolts. If the bolt holes are not accurately positioned, not all of the bolts can be inserted. Either drilling out the holes to make them larger or using smaller diameter bolts fixes the problem. The idea of the maximum material condition is to capture these trade-offs. The maximum material condition indicates the inner boundary (the theoretical hole) for the actual hole. The boundary of the actual hole must always be outside of this inner boundary. In this way, a bolt or pin that is positioned at the true position of the hole will always fit through the actual hole. Likewise, the least material condition (LMC), or largest hole size, can be used to define a theoretical circle within which the actual hole will be. The boundary for the actual hole must lie inside of the theoretical circle defined by the LMC. Further information regarding geometric dimensioning and tolerancing is provided in handbooks and graphics textbooks.

KEY TERMS

Actual size	Limit dimensions	Positional tolerances
Basic size	Maximum material condition	Roughness
Form tolerances	Nominal size	Target size
General tolerances	Orientation tolerances	Tolerance stackup
Geometric dimensioning and tolerancing	Plus and minus dimensions	True-position dimensions

Problems

1. The part shown in Figure 6.13 is made using a very accurate milling machine by a skilled machinist. The hole is reamed. Specify plus and minus tolerances for each dimension assuming that it is critical to hold all dimensions as close as possible to those specified. Use four digits past the decimal point to specify the tolerances, even though typical practice would be to specify only three digits past the decimal point. Dimensions are in inches.

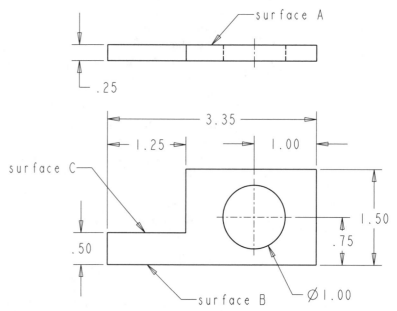

Figure 6.13.

2. The part shown in Figure 6.13 is made by an unskilled student using an old milling machine in a university student shop. The hole is drilled. Specify plus and minus tolerances for each dimension that are reasonable for these conditions. Use four digits past the decimal point to specify the tolerances, even though typical practice would be to specify only three digits past the decimal point. Assume dimensions are in inches.

3. Sketch a view of the object shown in Figure 6.14. Specify the horizontal dimension of the steps using chain dimensioning from the left end. The length of each horizontal section from left to right is .50, .75, 1.25, and .25 inches. Base the plus and minus dimensions on the worst expected tolerances for milling. What are the maximum and minimum dimensions for the overall horizontal length of the object? Use four digits past the decimal point to specify the tolerances, even though typical practice would be to specify only three digits past the decimal point.

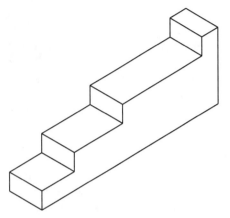

Figure 6.14.

4. Sketch a view of the object shown in Figure 6.14. Specify the horizontal dimension of the steps using datum dimensioning from the left end. The length of each horizontal section from left to right is .50, .75, 1.25, and .25 inches. Base the plus and minus dimensions on the best expected tolerances for milling. What are the maximum and minimum dimensions for the overall horizontal length of the object? Use four digits past the decimal point to specify the tolerances, even though typical practice would be to specify only three digits past the decimal point.

5. Sketch a side view of the shaft shown in Figure 6.15. Specify the horizontal dimension of each section of the shaft using chain dimensioning from the left end. The length of each horizontal section from left to right is .75, 2.00, .50, 1.25, and 3.00 inches. Base the plus and minus dimensions on the best expected tolerances for turning. What are the maximum and minimum dimensions for the overall horizontal length of the object? Use four digits past the decimal point to specify the tolerances, even though typical practice would be to specify only three digits past the decimal point.

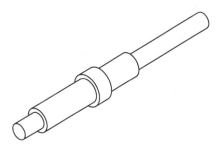

Figure 6.15.

6. Sketch a side view of the shaft shown in Figure 6.15. Specify the horizontal dimension of each section of the shaft using datum dimensioning from the left end. The length of each horizontal section from left to right is .75, 2.00, .50, 1.25, and 3.00 inches. Base the plus and minus dimensions on the worst expected tolerances for turning. What are the maximum and minimum dimensions for the length from the left end to the left edge of the largest diameter section? Use four digits past the decimal point to specify the tolerances, even though typical practice would be to specify only three digits past the decimal point.

7. Draw the appropriate surface finish symbol for:

   a. surface roughness typical for drilling.
   b. surface roughness typical for grinding.
   c. the best possible surface roughness for milling with material removal required.
   d. surface finish of 12.5 microns with material removal prohibited.

8. Sketch the appropriate Geometric Dimensioning and Tolerancing form tolerance for:

   a. an edge straight so that all points on the surface are within a tolerance zone of 0.020 mm.
   b. a surface that is flat to within 0.015 mm.
   c. a surface that is parallel to datum plane C to within 0.20 mm.
   d. a surface that is perpendicular to datum plane B to within 0.10 mm.
   e. a hole that is perpendicular to datum plane B to within 0.12 mm.

9. The part shown in Figure 6.16 is dimensioned in millimeters using the traditional coordinate method. Sketch the same views of the part and dimension using Geometric Dimensioning and Tolerancing procedures so the following functional requirements are met:

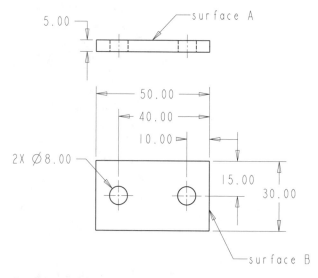

Figure 6.16.

- Set surfaces A and B as datum planes.

- Surface A is flat to within 0.15 mm.

- The upper edge in the front view from which the holes are located vertically is perpendicular to surface B to within 0.20 mm. Set this edge as datum plane C.

- The edge-forming surface A in the top view is straight to within 0.05 mm.

- The 10, 15, and 40 mm dimensions are true-position dimensions.

- The 5, 30, and 50 mm dimensions must be held to the tightest possible tolerance that can be achieved using milling. (Convert the dimensions to inches to determine the tolerances to two places after the decimal (round as necessary). Specify the tolerances as plus and minus dimensions in millimeters.)

- The holes have a tolerance of ±0.05mm. The theoretical hole size is 8.00mm.

- The holes are located within 0.15 mm of the true position at the Maximum Material Condition.

10. The part shown in Figure 6.13 is dimensioned in inches using the traditional coordinate method. Sketch the same views of the part and dimension using Geometric Dimensioning and Tolerancing procedures so the following functional requirements are met:

- Set surfaces A and B as datum planes. Set the right edge as datum plane D.

- Surface A is flat to within .005 inches.

- The hole is perpendicular to surface A to within .010 inches. (Place this tolerance just below the dimension.)

- Surface C is parallel to surface B to within .012 inches.

- The .75 and 1.00 dimensions for the location of the hole are true-position dimensions.

- The 1.50 and 3.35 dimensions must be held to the tightest possible tolerance that can be achieved using milling (use three digits past the decimal point for the tolerances).

- The hole has a tolerance of ±.002. The theoretical hole size is 1.000.

- The hole is located within .004 inches of the true position at the Maximum Material Condition.

11. The part shown in Figure 6.17 is dimensioned in millimeters using the traditional coordinate method. Sketch the same views of the part and dimension using Geometric Dimensioning and Tolerancing procedures so the following functional requirements are met:

- Set surface A as a datum plane.

- Surface B is flat to within 0.10 mm.

- Surface B is parallel to surface A to within 0.05 mm.

- The 40 and 100 dimensions need only be held to the loosest possible tolerance that can be achieved using milling. (Convert the dimensions to inches to determine the tolerances. Specify the tolerances as plus and minus dimensions in millimeters.)

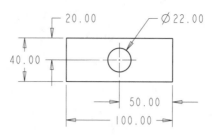

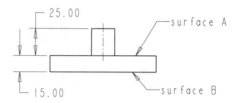

Figure 6.17.

References

ASME Y14.5M-1994, Dimensioning and Tolerancing. New York, NY: American Society of Mechanical Engineers, 1995.

G. R. Bertoline, *Introduction to Graphics Communications for Engineers*. New York, NY: McGraw-Hill, 1999.

P. J. Booker, *A History of Engineering Drawing*. London, England: Northgate Publishing Co. Ltd., 1979.

S. H. Chasen, Historical highlights of interactive computer graphics. *Mechanical Engineering*, November 1981, 32–41.

G. E. Dieter, *Engineering Design: A Materials and Processing Approach*. New York, NY: McGraw-Hill, 1991.

A. R. Eide, R. D. Jenison, L. H. Mashaw, L. L. Northup, and C. G. Sanders, *Engineering Graphics Fundamentals*. New York, NY: McGraw-Hill, 1985.

J. Encarnacao and E. G. Schlechtendahl, *Computer Aided Design*. Berlin, Germany: Springer-Verlag, 1983.

E. S. Ferguson, *Engineering and the Mind's Eye*. Cambridge MA: The MIT Press, 1992.

E. S. Ferguson, The mind's eye: Nonverbal thought in technology. *Science* 197:827–836, 1977.

F. E. Giesecke, A. Mitchell, H. C. Spencer, I. L. Hill, R. O. Loving, J. T. Dygdon, J. E. Novak, and S. Lockhart, *Engineering Graphics*. Upper Saddle River, NJ: Prentice Hall, 1998.

K. Hanks, *Rapid Viz: A New Method for the Rapid Visualization of Ideas*, Menlo Park, CA: Crisp Publications, 1990.

C. M. Hoffman, *Geometric and Solid Modeling*, San Mateo, CA: Morgan Kaufmann Publishers, Inc., 1989.

S. Pugh, *Total Design*, Reading, MA: Addison Wesley, 1990.

D. G. Ullman, *The Mechanical Design Process*, 2nd Edition. New York, NY: McGraw-Hill, 1997.

D. G. Ullman, S. Wood, and D. Craig, The importance of drawing in the mechanical design process. *Computers and graphics*, 14:263–274, 1990.

W. R. D. Wilson, Course Notes for ME B40: Introduction to Mechanical Design and Manufacturing. Northwestern University, March 1998.

7

Getting Started
in Pro/ENGINEER®

OVERVIEW

In this chapter, you begin the modeling of a pizza cutter. First, you set up the Pro/ENGINEER® environment. Then you model the guard of the pizza cutter, which prevents the user's hand from slipping onto the blade. You begin with setting up datum planes. Then you create a two-dimensional (2D) sketch and extrude it to form the guard. Finally, detail features such as a hole and rounded corners are added to the guard.

7.1 THE PIZZA CUTTER

You are about to model an object that you have probably seen numerous times ... a pizza cutter, shown in Figure 7.1. The pizza cutter consists of six different parts. You will model each of these parts, learning various commands along the way. Each concept that you learn will be applied again as you model subsequent parts and work on practice exercises. Once all the individual parts are modeled in Chapters 7, 8, and 9, you will assemble those individual parts to create the pizza cutter model in Chapter 10. In Chapter 11, you will create two-dimensional (2D) engineering drawings of one of the parts and the pizza cutter assembly.

SECTIONS

OBJECTIVES

When you have completed this tutorial chapter, you should be able to:

- Start Pro/ENGINEER
- Create datum planes
- Set up the Pro/ENGINEER environment
- Set up a 2-D sketch plane
- Sketch a 2-D shape
- Constrain a sketch using alignment and dimensions
- Extrude a 2-D shape
- Create rounds
- View the part as wireframe, without hidden lines, or shaded
- Spin the part
- Cut holes

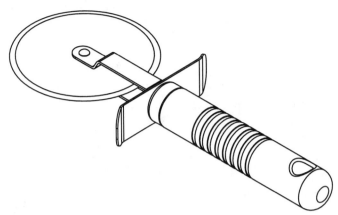

Figure 7.1.

7.2   PRO/ENGINEER BACKGROUND

Pro/ENGINEER® , or Pro/E, is a three-dimensional (3D), feature-based, solids modeling system. It was developed by Parametric Technologies Corporation (PTC) in the late 1980s. Solids modeling represents objects on the computer as volumes, rather than just a collection of edges and surfaces. Features are three-dimensional geometries that have direct analogies to shapes that can be machined or manufactured, such as holes or rounds. Feature-based solids modeling creates and modifies geometric shapes that make up an object in a way that readily represents common manufacturing processes. This makes Pro/ENGINEER a very powerful and effective tool for engineering design.

Originally Pro/ENGINEER was run on computers that use UNIX operating systems to control and operate the basic functions of the computer. These computers are commonly known as workstation computers. Recent versions of Pro/ENGINEER also run on personal computers using the Windows operating system. The latest releases of Pro/ENGINEER perform equally well on both UNIX and Windows computers, and the user interface is identical in both cases.

This tutorial is designed to get you up and running on Pro/ENGINEER quickly. Our goal is to teach you the commands you will encounter most often and to provide you with the foundation to become a more advanced user. You will only learn a very small part of Pro/ENGINEER's capabilities in this tutorial. But with the commands that you learn you should be able to model many types of complicated objects.

As with other computer programs, Pro/ENGINEER organizes and stores data in files. Each file has a name followed by a period (dot) and an extension. The extension is three letters, denoting the type of file. For instance, a "part" file related to a handle could be named "handle.prt". The first portion of the file name (handle) describes the contents of the file and the extension (.prt) indicates the type of file. There are several file types that are used by Pro/ENGINEER. The most common files types and their extensions are:

> *Part files*: .prt
> *Assembly files*: .asm
> *Drawing files*: .drw
> *Table files*: .tbl

Part files are the individual parts that are created or modeled. Part files contain all the pertinent information about the part. Because Pro/ENGINEER is a solids modeling program, the virtual part on the screen will look very similar to the actual part when it is manufactured. *Assembly files* are created from several individual parts that are assembled virtually (on the computer) to create a model of the assembled product. *Drawing files* are the two-dimensional engineering drawing representation of the part and assembly files. The drawings should contain all the necessary information for the manufacture of the part including dimensions, part tolerances, material, packaging information, colors, and so forth. *Table files* are used to store tables of data or information.

The part file is the *driving* file for all other file types. The modeling procedure begins with part files, and subsequent assemblies and drawings are based on the original part files. One advantage of Pro/ENGINEER files is that they are linked dynamically. Any change to a part file will automatically update any corresponding assembly or drawing files. Therefore, drawing and assembly files need to access their corresponding part files in order for them to be opened. Pro/ENGINEER uses text information embedded within the file and the filename to maintain these links automatically.

7.3   STARTING PRO/ENGINEER

Starting Pro/ENGINEER depends on the computer system that is used and how the software is installed. Below are the most common commands to start Pro/ENGINEER for UNIX and Windows operating systems:

UNIX Operating System: Open a shell window; at the prompt type "pro2000i".

Windows Operating System: Using the left mouse button, click "Start" (lower left corner of the screen), click "Programs" , click "ProENGINEER" , click "proe2000i" .

Or

Double-click on the Pro /ENGINEER icon with the left mouse button.

If the method listed here does not work on your system, contact your system administrator for system-specific instructions.

The Main window that appears on the computer screen looks similar to a Microsoft ® Windows interface, as shown in Figure 7.2. The top line of the window is the Menu bar from which menus of various operations can be opened. The next line containing the icon-labeled buttons is the Tool bar, which provides a variety of commonly used operations with a single click of the mouse on the Tool bar. Note in Figure 7.2 the message "Datum planes on/off" just below the Tool bar icon of a parallelogram with a "D." A similar description of the Tool bar button appears whenever the arrow-shaped cursor is moved over one of the buttons. These descriptions are quite helpful as you initially learn the Tool bar buttons. Just below the Tool bar is the Message area where information about the current operation is displayed. This area provides information about whether the last operation was executed properly or what operation is necessary to proceed. The main part of the window is the Graphics window where the model is displayed. At the bottom of the screen is the online Help area. This area provides information and help that is sensitive to the operation being performed. The Message area, Graphics window, and online help area on your screen should be blank at this point.

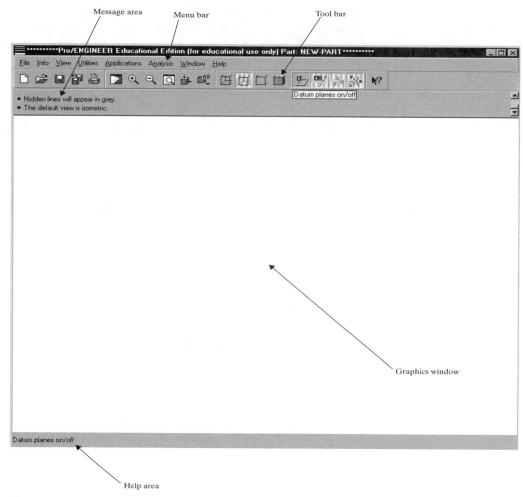

Figure 7.2.

7.4 TUTORIAL CONVENTIONS

This book will follow some basic conventions when presenting information and commands. Below is a list of the conventions that will be used.

All commands will be in **bold** in this text. The following notation is used:

⇒	(arrow) implies moves between menus or menu windows.
|	(pipe) is used to separate the commands within the same menu window.
<select ...>	requires the left mouse button to be clicked on the specified entity in the graphics window.
<enter ...>	requests information that is specified, often followed by **Enter** on the keyboard.
<click ...>	requires a mouse click on a command in a menu or on the screen.

Commands can appear in the Menu bar at the top of the window, in the Tool bar at the top of the window, or in the Pro/ENGINEER Menu Manager to the right of the main window (the Menu Manager is not visible at this point). Commands in each window will be differentiated by the text style:

Plain   commands in the Pro/ENGINEER Menu Manager and in pop-up menus

Underlined   commands or buttons in the Tool bar

Italics   commands in the Menu bar

To be sure that your screens match the ones in this book, use ***Customize Screen*** in the ***Utilities*** menu. To do this, move the arrow-shaped cursor over ***Utilities*** in the Menu Bar using the mouse button. Then move the cursor over ***Customize Screen*** and click the left mouse button. Using the notation in this book these commands are:

Utilities ⇒ ***Customize Screen***

The window shown in Figure 7.3 opens. You will set each item to its default settings. To do this:

<click Toolbars> ⇒ <click Default>

Repeat this command for **Commands**, **Menus**, and **Options**. (**Options** is labeled **Windows** in Pro/ENGINEER, Revision 20.)

Now set up the **Options** (**Windows** in Revision 20) tab so that it is most convenient to use. How this is set up depends on which version of Pro/ENGINEER that you are using.

If you are using Pro/ENGINEER 2000i:

Find the line that says **Left Overlapping Graphics** under **Default Tree settings**.

<click on Left Overlapping Graphics to open the menu> ⇒ <click on Upper right> ⇒ <enter 10 in the Width box>

(To change the **Width** to 10, move the cursor to the right end of the number shown and click. Then use Backspace key on the keyboard to delete the number. Type in 10.)

If you are using Pro/ENGINEER, Revision 20:

<click Above graphics window button>

To apply the settings:

<click OK>

Now the Menu bar and Tool bar should appear as shown in Figure 7.2.

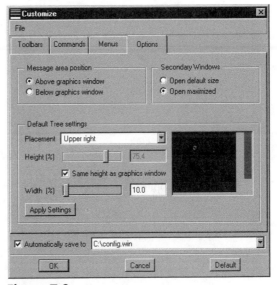

Figure 7.3.

7.5   CREATING A GENERIC PART IN PRO/ENGINEER

7.5.1   Creating a Generic Part

A part is a combination of *features* that model a 3D geometry. Features may be the initial work block for the part, details of the part such as holes or cuts, or items used in the construction of features such as axes. Simple parts can have three or four features, whereas extremely complicated parts might have several hundred features. Any one of these features can be modified at any time.

Keep in mind that most features add or subtract solid geometry to the model. Other features create entities that are necessary for construction of the solid geometry such as datum planes, axes, curves, and so forth. Most of the parts in the pizza cutter are quite simple, so you will not need to create many features for each part.

The part file is the most basic element in the Pro/ENGINEER family of files. To allow for some consistency and prevent replication of similar, necessary steps in the modeling of parts, you will begin by creating a generic part. You will add features to this generic part that are common to all parts. Then you will use this generic part as the starting point for all other parts.

To begin creating the generic part, open a ***New File***. To do this, click with the left mouse button on the word ***File*** in the Menu bar at the top-left of the Pro/ENGINEER window. The menu shown in Figure 7.4 will open. Click on ***New*** to open a new file. The notation used in this book to accomplish the previous two steps is:

> ***File ⇒ New***

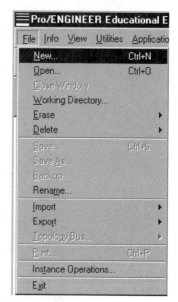

Figure 7.4.

A popup window shown in Figure 7.5 will appear on the screen. Most likely **Part** is activated in the type section and **Solid** is activated in the Sub-type section as indicated by the dot in the circles next to each item shown in Figure 7.5. This opens a part file to create a solid model. If these two items are not selected already, click on them using the left mouse button. To name the generic part "new-part":

> **<enter new-part>** for the name of the generic part file.
> **<click OK>**

Figure 7.5.

Figure 7.6 shows the Menu Manager and Model Tree windows, which have now popped up on the right side of the screen. The Menu Manager contains all of the commands specific to the mode you are currently using (part, assembly, drawing, etc.). Pop-up menus will also appear within the Menu Manager when needed. Available commands are visible, and commands that are not currently available are grayed out (shown as shadows). The Model Tree window (with the truncated title "Mo...") appears to the right of the Menu Manager. It lists every feature of the model that has been created so far. Because no features have been created yet, it currently shows only the part name, NEW-PART. The Model Tree can be minimized or closed using the buttons at the top right of the window, depending on your preference. Leave it open for now.

Figure 7.6.

7.5.2 Environment

To ensure that your screens will match the figures in this tutorial, set the **Environment** variables. Do this by selecting:

Utilities ⇒ Environment (see Figure 7.7)

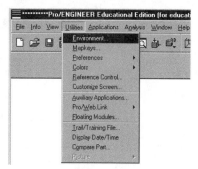

Figure 7.7.

The Environment window shown in Figure 7.8 will pop up. This window is used to control the display of a variety of features. You can turn an item on or off by clicking the box to the left of the item using the left mouse button. The items with a "check-mark" are items that are currently displayed.

Figure 7.8.

Click the items to match Figure 7.8. At the bottom of the window, select **Hidden Line** from **Display Style**. To do this first click on the inverted triangle to the right, and then click on **Hidden Line** from the menu that opens up. In a similar fashion, select **Isometric** from the **Default Orient** menu. When the window matches Figure 7.8, click on **OK** at the bottom of the window to apply the changes and close the **Environment** window.

7.5.3 Creating Default Datum Planes

As you create the model in three dimensions, Pro/ENGINEER needs a way to locate the features within its environment. This is done by creating three default *datum planes*. These datum planes are three mutually perpendicular planes that are created in space as references for constructing features of the part that you are modeling. You might think of them as the x-y, y-z, and x-z planes in a 3D Cartesian coordinate system. The three planes intersect at the origin. Before modeling any part in Pro/ENGINEER, you should create these datum planes.

To **Create** a **Feature** of a **Datum Plane**, select the following commands in the Menu Manager window (shown in Figure 7.9):

Feature ⇒ Create ⇒ Datum ⇒ Plane

Note that appropriate menus appear as the commands above are selected. Finish creating the datum planes by:

Default

Figure 7.9.

Once you have finished the above selections, the screen should look like Figure 7.10. The message in the Message area indicates that the datum planes were created, and the Model Tree now has three features added to it. They are the datum planes DTM1, DTM2, and DTM3. The datum planes are labeled on the screen. There are two sides of a datum plane, a yellow side and a red side. Yellow represents the front side of the datum plane. Red represents the back side. The screen should show the yellow sides of all datum planes, indicating that you are viewing the front of each plane. This is important when orienting a part into different views and also will be used when assembling components.

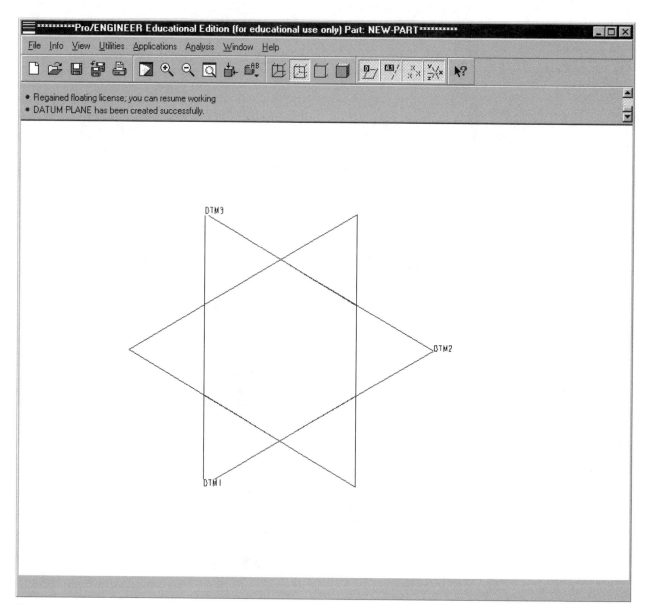

Figure 7.10.

7.5.4 Creating a Default Coordinate System

A coordinate system displays three labeled axes (x, y, z) representing a Cartesian coordinate system in the model space. A coordinate system can be placed anywhere in space and can be rotated to suit your needs. This feature is sometimes useful for dimensioning features, as well as for assembling parts. You will now create a default coordinate system following Figure 7.11. First note that **Feature** is already shown at the top of the Menu Manager window. As a result, only the next steps are needed to create the **Feature**:

Create ⇒ Datum ⇒ Coord Sys ⇒ Default | Done

These steps **Create** a **Datum Coord**inate **Sys**tem at the **Default** location of the intersection of the three datum planes.

Figure 7.11.

A small, yellow coordinate system should be in the center of the window as shown in Figure 7.12. Multiple coordinate systems can be created, but you will create only one. Pro/ENGINEER labels each feature created. Because this is the initial coordinate system created, it has a label of CS0. If another coordinate system was created, it would be labeled CS1.

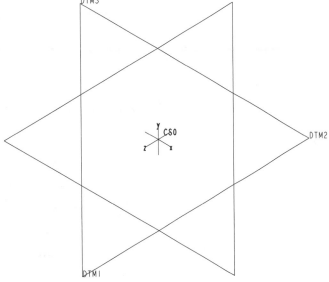

Figure 7.12.

It can be difficult to interpret the datum planes in the isometric view. In the Model Tree window, which is to the right of the main window, click on DTM1. This will highlight the plane that corresponds to DTM1. The datum plane will appear as a parallelogram in this isometric view. This is because DTM1 is at an angle with respect to the screen. Note that the lower edge of DTM1 is at 30 degrees above horizontal to the right, as it should be in an isometric view for the right side of a cube. DTM1 corresponds to the y-z plane, based on coordinate system CS0. Click on the remaining two datum planes in the Model Tree window to visualize their relationship. DTM2 is parallel to the base of an isometric cube corresponding to the x-z plane. DTM3 is parallel to the left side of an isometric cube, with its lower edge 30 degrees above horizontal. It corresponds to the x-y plane. The three datum planes are perpendicular to one another. The intersection of any two datum planes is a line, although the line of intersection is not shown on the screen. For instance, DTM1 and DTM3 intersect along a vertical line forming the y-axis. All three datum planes intersect at a point, the origin. Be sure to spend time now orienting yourself to the datum planes. It is critical to understand their orientation when you start modeling parts.

7.5.5   Setting Up Units

Next you define the units that will be used in the drawing. Pro/ENGINEER uses English units of inches, pounds-mass (lbm), and seconds as its default. But other systems of units are available including meters and millimeters. Pro/ENGINEER should already be using inch-lbm-second units, but you can check the **Set Up** for the Principal System of **Units** by using the following operations in the Menu Manager:

Feature $\Rightarrow$ Set Up $\Rightarrow$ Units

The Menu Manager and window that pops up should look like Figure 7.13. Under the **System of Units** tab, be sure that an arrow appears in front of **Inch lbm Second (Pro/E Default)**. If it is not selected , click on it followed by the **Set** button and **OK**. To finish:

<click Close> $\Rightarrow$ Done

The **Done** command in the Menu Manager completes the changes to the setup.

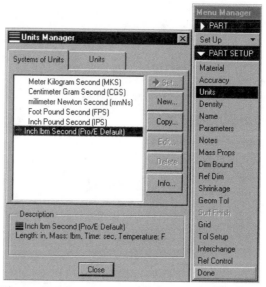

Figure 7.13.

7.5.6   Saving the Generic Part

Congratulations! You have finished creating the generic part which consists only of datum planes and a coordinate system.

Now it is time to save your work. We recommend that you save your work often. Unless you specify otherwise, Pro/ENGINEER will save to the default directory (usually the directory from which Pro/ENGINEER was launched). Your instructor or computer system administrator will provide you with instructions on the proper default directory and device to use. (To create a new folder on the computer hard disk to be your working directory, follow these steps: 1) minimize the Pro/ENGINEER window by clicking the small button with a horizontal bar at the top right corner of the Pro/ENGINEER window; 2) create a new folder using standard Windows commands; 3) maximize the Pro/ENGINEER window by clicking on the Pro/ENGINEER button at the bottom of the screen.) To change the default directory, use:

File ⇒ *Working Directory* ... ⇒ **<navigate to the desired directory or device and click on it so it is highlighted ⇒ OK** (Figure 7.14)

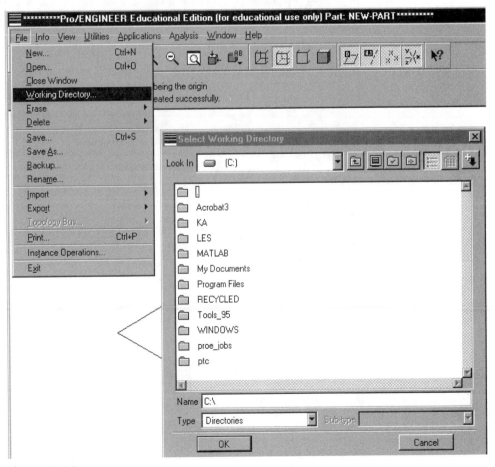

Figure 7.14.

Save the file using:

File ⇒ *Save*

At the top of the main window, you should see the name of the part with its extension ("NEW-PART.PRT"). To complete the **Save** operation:

<Enter> (on the keyboard)

As mentioned at the start of this section, this generic part will be the foundation for each part you model for the pizza cutter. For convenience, you will now save the datum planes that you created to a part file named for each part of the pizza cutter that will be modeled. Use the **Save As** command to create these part files.

File ⇒ **Save As**

Figure 7.15 shows the window that will appear. The Model Name will default to the part that is currently displayed. New Name refers to the file name to which you are copying the part. The first part will be the handle of the pizza cutter:

<enter handle> | **<click OK>**

The .prt extension will be automatically added to the file name that you enter.

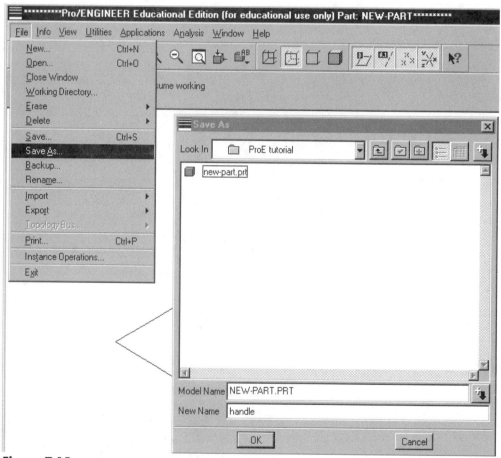

Figure 7.15.

Two parts now exist in your directory, new-part.prt and handle.prt. A number may appear after the .prt extension to indicate the revision number of the part. Each time that you save a part, Pro/ENGINEER will increment the revision number extension by one. Repeat the **Save As** command, and create the following part files: arm, blade, cap, guard, and rivet.

Now your directory will contain all of these parts, each of which is a copy of the new-part.prt file.

7.5.7   Closing a Window

Finally, close the new-part window by using the Menu bar commands:

Window ⇒ Close

7.6   MODELING THE GUARD BASE FEATURE

The first part that you will model is the guard of the pizza cutter shown in Figure 7.16. The guard is between the handle and the cutting blade of the pizza cutter. It is designed to prevent injuries when using the pizza cutter, if the user's hand slips down the handle while slicing a pizza. Because it is a sheet metal part of constant thickness, you will use a **Thin** extrusion. By using a **Thin** feature, you can define the thickness of the part once, and Pro/ENGINEER will calculate the correct thickness across all the bends in the part.

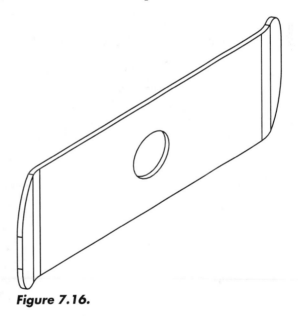

Figure 7.16.

Recall that any part (including the guard) is the combination of a number of features. Each feature defines a portion of the final geometry and the sum of these features models the entire object. Typically the first four features of any part are the three default datum planes and the coordinate system. These features were created in new-part.prt and copied to guard.prt already. The base feature of the guard will be the main shape of the bent rectangle of sheet metal forming the guard. Then the hole will be cut at the center of the guard, and the rounds will be added at the corners of the guard.

7.6.1   Opening a File

First **Open** the guard file:

File ⇒ Open ⇒ <click guard.prt> | <click Open> (Figure 7.17)

Figure 7.17.

The part already has three datum plane features and a coordinate system, which should appear on the screen and in the Model Tree window.

7.6.2   Creating a Protrusion

Begin by creating the base feature of the overall shape of the guard. To **Create** a **Feature** begin by using the menu selections:

Feature ⇒ Create (Figure 7.18)

Figure 7.18.

After selecting **Create**, new menu windows should appear to select the type of **Feature**. In this case, you want model a **Solid** object, the guard. (**Solid** should already be highlighted in the Menu Manager, so it is not necessary to click on it.) The shape of the guard will be created by first drawing the outline of the edge of the guard. Then this outline will be extruded perpendicular to the computer screen to form the flat surfaces of the guard. Because you will create the shape based on the outline of the edge of the guard "protruding" from a datum plane, this feature is called a **Protrusion**. Thus, create a **Solid Protrusion** by selecting the menu items:

Solid ⇒ **Protrusion** (Figure 7.19)

Figure 7.19.

A new menu appears in the Menu Manager with the choice of whether to **Extrude** or **Revolve** a cross-section, along with several other options. In this case, you want to **Extrude** a shape. There is also a choice between a **Solid** feature and a **Thin** feature. A **Solid** feature is used to model parts that are solid, as opposed to hollow or thin-walled. The **Thin** feature is used to model thin-walled parts with a constant wall thickness. The guard is a **Thin** sheet metal part of constant wall thickness:

Extrude | **Thin** | **Done** (Figure 7.20)

The menu shown in Figure 7.20 provides the opportunity to **Quit** working on this feature without affecting the previous features. If you made a mistake in the steps so far, just click on **Quit** instead of **Done** to start over on this feature.

Figure 7.20.

A new window entitled PROTRUSION:Extrude appears (Figure 7.21). This window shows the different elements of the feature that you are creating. We will explain this window in some detail later on. For now, note that this window has a **Cancel** button. If you want to start over on this feature at any time, just click **Cancel**, and repeat the steps to create the feature.

Figure 7.21.

Shortly you will sketch the shape that will be extruded in a "sketching plane." The sketching plane is the plane in which the 2D shape that will be extruded is drawn. Before you can draw the shape, Pro/ENGINEER needs to know whether the sketch will be extruded to only **One Side** of the sketching plane, or if it will be extruded on **Both Sides** of the sketching plane. The guard should be symmetric about the sketching plane. In other words, the sketching plane will bisect the guard. So use **Both Sides**:

Both Sides | Done (Figure 7.22)

Figure 7.22.

From now on we will not show you every menu that will appear on your screen. Instead, we will list the commands. For instance the commands up to this point to create the handle would be given as:

(DO NOT DO THIS) **Feature ⇒ Create ⇒ Solid ⇒ Protrusion ⇒ Extrude | Thin | Done ⇒ Both Sides | Done**

7.6.3 Sketching the Outline of the Guard

It is now necessary to set up a sketching plane. The sketching plane will always be a 2D plane that you will use to draw the cross-section of the geometry that you want to create. The feature you create will "start" at the sketching plane and will be extruded out of this plane to the depth that you specify to create a 3D base feature. For the guard, you will sketch a series of lines that outline the edge of the guard and then specify a depth to extrude the guard on both sides of the sketching plane.

Note that **Setup New**, **Plane**, and **Pick** are highlighted in the Menu Manager, indicating that you are to **Set up** a new **Plane** by **Pick**ing the plane using the mouse. You will use DTM2 (x-z plane) as the sketching plane in this example and extrude the guard to both sides of the sketching plane in the y-direction. We intentionally chose this sketching plane to aid in the orientation of parts with respect to each other when you assemble the pizza cutter in Chapter 10, but any plane could have been chosen. To select DTM2 as the sketching plane, either click on DTM2 in the Model Tree window or click on the *edge* of the datum plane DTM2 in the graphics window. Often the best method is to click on the corner of datum plane DTM2 in the graphics window where the label "DTM2" appears. But it works best to click on the edge of the datum plane itself, not the label "DTM2". If you have not already selected DTM2, the commands are:

Setup New $\Rightarrow$ Plane $\Rightarrow$ Pick $\Rightarrow$ <select DTM2>

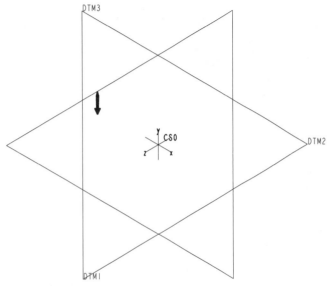

Figure 7.23.

A red arrow should pop up pointing downward from DTM2 as shown in Figure 7.23. The arrow indicates the direction of viewing the sketching plane. Right now the arrow is pointing so that you will be looking toward the yellow side of DTM2. There is no right or wrong way to set up the sketching plane. Most times you select the sketching plane based on personal preference. For the sake of consistency with the figures in this book, set the arrow as shown above. If the arrow is pointing in the other direction, click **Flip** (which is under the DIRECTION menu). Once the arrow is pointing downward:

Okay

The menu shown in Figure 7.24 will appear.

Figure 7.24.

You have already selected the sketching plane (DTM2). Now it is necessary to orient the other datum planes to a particular position. Again, there is no right or wrong orientation, but you should set up the orientation of the datum planes to match the ones shown here for consistency with this tutorial. The four orientations listed in the Menu Manager, **Top**, **Bottom**, **Right**, and **Left**, refer to the side of the screen that the YELLOW side of the selected plane will face. For this example you will "point" the yellow side of the DTM1 toward the **Top** of the screen. Again, when selecting DTM1, the easiest method is to click on the plane near the label "DTM1" in the Graphics window.

Top ⇒ <select DTM1>

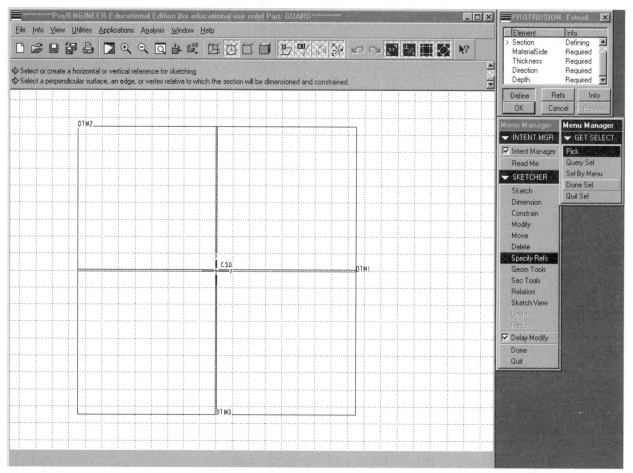

Figure 7.25.

Upon completing this operation, the sketching plane DTM2 will appear in the specified orientation as shown in Figure 7.25. Recall that in Figure 7.23, the arrow indicating the direction of viewing the sketching plane pointed toward the yellow side of DTM2. Thus, the yellow side of DTM2, labeled in the upper left corner of the large square shown in the Graphics window, is parallel to the screen. The yellow side of DTM1, labeled at the right end of the horizontal axis, is facing the top of the screen as specified in Figure 7.24. The red side of DTM1 is facing down. Choosing this orientation for DTM1 automatically forces DTM3 to be vertical with its yellow side to the right. You will be sketching 2D geometry on DTM2; hence it is called the sketching plane. You could have orientated DTM1 and DTM3 in any direction you prefer, but use the orientation in Figure 7.25 for consistency with this tutorial. If the planes are not as shown, click **Cancel** in the PROTRUSION:Extrude window (at the top right of the screen in Figure 7.25) and start over on this feature.

Now that the sketching plane is oriented, you can turn off the coordinate system. To do this:

Utilities ⇒ *Environment* ⇒ **<click off the check box for Coordinate Systems>** ⇒ **<click OK>**

The Sketcher automatically opens with the Intent Manager active as shown in Figure 7.26. The Intent Manager is a powerful tool to assist the designer in sketching the cross-section to be extruded. You will use the Intent Manager later in this tutorial. For now, we prefer to step through the modeling of several parts without using the Intent Manager. This will familiarize you with the fundamentals of Pro/ENGINEER before using the Intent Manager shortcuts. To turn off the Intent Manager:

<click Intent Manager checkbox in the Menu Manager>

All of the commands for sketching the desired geometry originate in the Sketcher menu shown in Figure 7.26. You will draw the 2D geometry on the sketching plane, DTM2, and then fully *constrain* the sketch by adding dimensions, so that the position of every item that you sketched is exactly defined. After you have sketched the 2D profile, you will extrude this cross-section to a specified depth to make a 3D object.

Figure 7.26.

Remember that you are creating the base, or initial, feature of the guard. To start, you will sketch the outline of the edge of the guard. Later the model will be modified by adding other features. Select **Sketch** on the SKETCHER menu (it is probably already selected)

Sketch

The menu shown in Figure 7.27 should also be on the screen. There are several different entities (geometries) that can be drawn. In this case you will use the **Mouse** to **Sketch** the rough outline of the edge of the guard. To do this:

Mouse Sketch (probably already selected)

Figure 7.27.

Begin by sketching the overall shape of the edge of the arm as the three connecting line segments shown in Figure 7.28. The first and third line segments are at angles; the middle line segment connects the angled line segments along the horizontal axis DTM1. Click the left mouse button at the leftmost point and proceed by clicking the left mouse button at each bend. As you move the cursor, the line segments appear. Try to get the horizontal line segment as close as possible to the horizontal axis. Soon you will align this line segment to DTM1, so that they are colinear. This is more easily done when the line segment is close to DTM1. Other than this, you do not have to be exact in

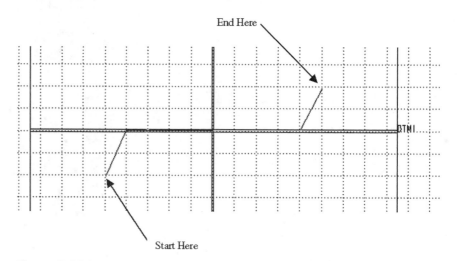

Figure 7.28.

the sketch — just get close. After you click on the rightmost point with the left mouse button, click the middle mouse button to end the **Mouse Sketch**. (If your computer mouse only has two buttons, Shift-left button is equivalent to the middle mouse button.)

If you make a mistake, there are two options. The first option is useful to make minor corrections to a sketch by deleting individual line segments using **Delete** ⇒

<click on each line segment to be deleted>. Once the line segments are deleted, repeat **Sketch ⇒ Mouse Sketch** to sketch the line segments in Figure 7.28. The second option is useful for more major problems. In this case, click **Cancel** in the PRO-TRUSION:Extrude window and start over with Figure 7.18.)

These line segments represent the outline of the edge of the guard. For **Thin** sections like this one, the line segments do not need to connect to form a closed loop. For **Solid** sections, the line segments must form a closed loop. You will see several examples of **Solid** sections later in this tutorial.

Consider the edge of the guard shown in Figure 7.16. Notice that the bends are rounded, not sharp as you have drawn them. To round them, each sharp bend will be changed to a **Fillet**. A **Fillet** is an **Arc** connecting two line segments used to smooth sharp corners. To do this:

Sketch ⇒ Arc ⇒ Fillet ⇒ Pick

Figure 7.29.

The Menu Manager should look like Figure 7.29. To add a **Fillet**, click with the left mouse button on each of the line segments between which an **Arc** should be created. An **Arc** will be created between the two line segments that were selected. Follow Figure 7.30 when selecting the lines. First create Arc 1 between the rightmost Line 1 and the middle Line 2 using the following commands:

<select line 1> <select line 2>

The sharp corner should turn into an **Arc** with the center of the arc marked with a small plus. The radius of the arc will be specified later. Now create Arc 2 between the leftmost Line 3 and the middle Line 2 using the following commands (the commands are already selected):

Sketch ⇒ Arc ⇒ Fillet ⇒ Pick ⇒ <select line 3> <select line 2>

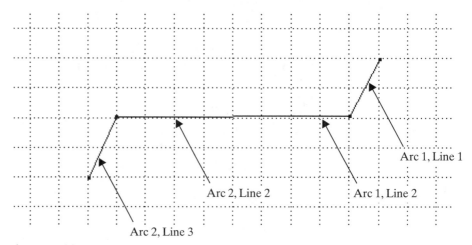

Figure 7.30.

The sketch should now look like Figure 7.31.

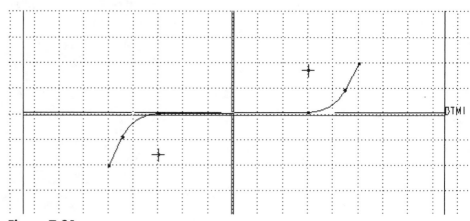

Figure 7.31.

The sketch in Figure 7.31 shows the general shape of the edge of the guard, but it is still necessary to "constrain" the sketch. The sketch is constrained in two ways. First the sketch must be positioned in "space" by locating it with respect to the datum planes. Second, the dimensions of the line segments and angles must be specified. The sketch is constrained using the **Alignment** and **Dimension** commands.

The **Alignment** command tells Pro/ENGINEER to make two entities coincide with one another. In this case, the middle horizontal line segment should coincide with the horizontal axis, DTM1, to fix the vertical position of the line segment. To align a sketched entity (the horizontal line segment) to the existing geometry (DTM1), in the SKETCHER menu in the Menu Manager:

Alignment

The menu on the right in Figure 7.32 will appear.

Figure 7.32.

In the ALIGNMENT menu:

Align (it should already be selected)

Note that **Pick** is highlighted in the GET SELECT menu. This means that you need to **Pick**, or <select>, the two items to be aligned by clicking on them on the sketch. Upon selecting, each item should momentarily turn red to indicate that it was selected. To do this first click on the horizontal line segment, then click on the horizontal axis, DTM1, either to the left or right of the sketched line segment:

<select horizontal line 2 (labeled in Figure 7.30) ⇒ <select DTM1 (to the right or left of line 2)>

If the two entities that were selected have been properly aligned, a message will appear in the Message area to indicate this, as shown in Figure 7.33. It is important to note that in order to align sketched features, the features must be quite close together. In this case, the horizontal line segment must be fairly close to being lined up with DTM1.

Figure 7.33.

It is also possible to verify aligned entities:

Alignment ⇒ Unalign

All of the aligned features will appear in green on the screen. In this case, the horizontal line segment and the DTM1 axis should appear in green. When you are done looking at what segments are aligned:

Quit Sel (on the GET SELECT submenu)

This quits the **Unalign** operation so that the highlighted items remain aligned.

Now continue to "constrain" the sketch by adding dimensions. In this case, eight dimensions must be added to the sketch to indicate fully the length and position of all of the elements of the sketch. In the SKETCHER menu:

Dimension ⇒ Normal

The menu appears as shown in Figure 7.34. In most cases, you can simply use **Normal** dimensioning, which is already highlighted. Once you are a more advanced user, you might use the other dimensioning schemes that are listed in the menu.

Figure 7.34.

Now you can add the dimensions shown in Figure 7.35 starting from left and working to the right. First, the distance of the left end point of the sketched outline from the horizontal axis, DTM1, is dimensioned. This is labeled "sd1" in Figure 7.35. Using the left mouse button, click on the left endpoint and then click on the horizontal axis, DTM1. Using this tutorial's notation these mouse clicks are:

<select left endpoint> ⇒ <select DTM1>

These entities change color when they are selected. Once you have selected both, click the middle mouse button at about the position of sd1 in Figure 7.35 to place the dimension at that location as follows:

<select dimension location with middle mouse button>
(If your computer mouse only has two buttons, Shift-left button is equivalent to the middle mouse button.)

The alphanumeric "sd1" that now appears represents the distance of the left end-point to DTM1. The alphanumeric sd1 is a "parameter" that has yet to be defined as a

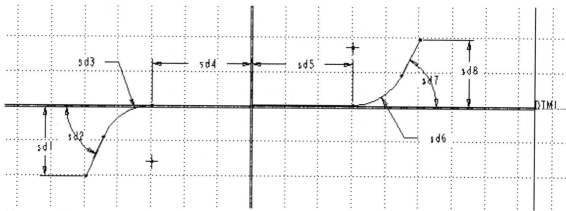

Figure 7.35.

numerical value. This dimension will remain as sd1 until you "regenerate" the sketch. Regeneration is a process where Pro/ENGINEER recalculates the sketch geometry and dimensions to update the model and check for errors. Common regeneration errors include ambiguous geometry and insufficiently dimensioned entities. In either case, the geometry is not fully constrained with adequate alignments and dimensions to define fully the sketched shape. For example, if you tried to regenerate the sketch right now (without fully defining the remaining seven dimensions), Pro/ENGINEER would show an error message because these dimensions are not specified.

If a dimension does not look correct, you can **Delete** it and create it again. To do this, select **Delete** in the SKETCHER menu and **Pick** (<select>) the dimension that you wish to remove. It will immediately disappear when it is selected. Then select **Dimension** in the SKETCHER menu and reapply the dimension. If you do this, the alphanumeric for the new dimension will be incremented by one, so the alphanumeric parameters will not exactly match that in Figure 7.35.

The dimension sd2 is the angle of the left line segment with respect to DTM1. To dimension this:

> **<select leftmost line segment> ⇒ <select DTM1 (near the upper arrow-head for dimension sd2 in Figure 7.35)> ⇒ <select dimension location with middle mouse button>**

The dimension sd2 should appear as shown in Figure 7.35. Note that as dimensions are added, the alphanumeric increases by one. The position of the dimensions on your sketch is not important, so do not worry if your sketch does not look exactly like Figure 7.35.

The dimension sd3 is a radius of the fillet. Radii are dimensioned by clicking once on the arc and then clicking on the position of the dimension with the mouse button:

> **<select left arc> ⇒ <select dimension location with middle mouse button>**

The dimension sd4 indicates the distance of the left endpoint of the horizontal line segment to the vertical axis DTM3. To do this:

> **<select left endpoint of the horizontal line segment> ⇒ <select DTM3> ⇒ <select dimension location with middle mouse button>**

Now add the dimension sd5 in the same way, except select the right endpoint of the horizontal line. Continue by dimensioning the radius of the right arc (a single mouse click on the arc indicates a radius dimension), the angle between DTM1 and the right line segment (click on DTM1 and the right line segment), and the height of the right endpoint above DTM1 (click on the right endpoint and DTM1). Upon completion of these operations, your dimensioned sketch should look similar to Figure 7.35. If a dimension does not work out, you can **Delete** it and create it again. To do this, select **Delete** in the SKETCHER menu and **Pick** (<select>) the dimension that you wish to remove. Then select **Dimension** and reapply the dimension. Try this with one of your dimensions if you like. Recall that the alphanumeric for the new dimension will be incremented by one, so the alphanumeric will not exactly match that in Figure 7.35.

The geometry for the outline of the edge of the guard is now fully defined on the 2D sketching plane. Every point along the outline is exactly defined by the dimensions and alignments that were specified. Now the sketch must be "regenerated" to have Pro/ENGINEER verify that you have created acceptable geometry and have fully constrained the model. In the SKETCHER menu shown in Figure 7.36:

Regenerate

Figure 7.36.

If the model regenerates properly, a statement "Section regenerated successfully" appears in the Message area just above the Graphics window. (The Message area above the Graphics window is often helpful in knowing how to execute various commands. It is worthwhile to monitor it frequently.) In addition, a warning will appear that "Not all open ends have been explicitly aligned." This warning pertains only to **Solid** sections, where the sketched cross-section must be a closed shape. The warning is not pertinent to **Thin** sections like this one. You can ignore the warning.

If you did not properly dimension the sketch, you will get an error message in the Message area when you click **Regenerate**. Pro/E is telling you that you did not exactly define the geometry in the sketch. If this happens, you probably did not include all of the dimensions shown in Figure 7.35 or the horizontal line segment was not properly aligned to DTM1. In this case, click on **Dimension**, add the missing dimension, and **Regenerate** again. If you think that the regeneration problem cannot be addressed in this way, click **Cancel** in the PROTRUSION:Extrude window and repeat all of the steps so far to make the guard.

Upon regeneration, numbers should replace the alphanumeric parameters for the dimensions. Your numbers will probably be different than the numbers in Figure 7.37. You will soon change these numbers to the proper dimensions of the pizza cutter guard.

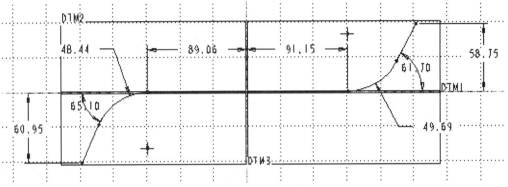

Figure 7.37.

Now that you have successfully regenerated the sketch, you need to **Modify** the dimensions to correct values for the guard. In the SKETCHER menu shown in Figure 7.38:

Modify ⇒ Mod Entity ⇒ Pick (probably already highlighted)

Figure 7.38.

To change the radius of the left arc, select the radius value on the sketch (48.44 in Figure 7.37) by selecting the number with the left mouse button in the Graphics window:

<select left arc radius dimension>

The arc dimension becomes highlighted in red. The new value is typed in at the top of the Graphics window shown in Figure 7.39. Click **<Enter>** the keyboard or click on the green checkmark at the right of the Input window to enter the value:

<enter .25>

Figure 7.39.

Although the numerical value of the dimension changes immediately to .25, the radius of the arc will not change until you regenerate the sketch again. Continuing to use **Modify**, change all of the dimensions to those indicated in Figure 7.40.

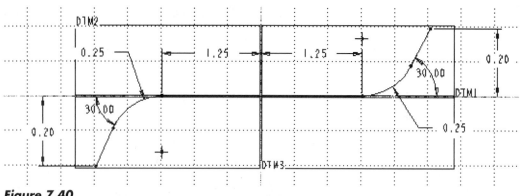

Figure 7.40.

After modifying a dimension, it changes from yellow to white. Once you are done modifying the values, all of the dimensions should be white. The sketch is now ready to be regenerated. In the SKETCHER menu:

Regenerate

Watch the sketch update itself to these new values. Modify the values, if they do not match those in Figure 7.40. (If something goes drastically wrong, click **Cancel** in the PROTRUSION:Extrude window, and repeat the steps to create the base feature of the guard.)

7.6.4 Extruding the Guard

When the values match Figure 7.40 and the sketch has successfully regenerated, finish the sketch by:

Done

The screen should look like Figure 7.41. The arrow shows the direction where the material will be added to the line that you have sketched to give the part a thickness that we will specify. Pro/ENGINEER calls this thickness the "width" of the feature. In this case, the thickness (width) is to be .042. Use **Flip**, if necessary to change the direction of the arrow to that in Figure 7.41. Then:

Okay ⇒ **<enter 0.042>**

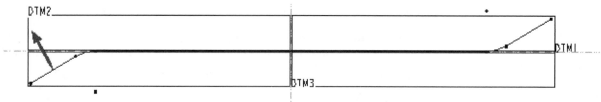

Figure 7.41.

Now that you have specified the 2D cross-section of the guard in the sketching plane, you need to tell Pro/ENGINEER how far to extrude the outline perpendicular to the screen. The depth refers to how far the sketched cross-section is extruded perpendicular to the sketching plane, thus making the section three-dimensional. Specify a **Blind** depth of 1.0:

Blind | Done ⇒ **<enter 1.0>**

This makes the guard a total of 1.0 inches deep. **Blind** indicates that you will specify a numerical value for the depth. Alternatives to using **Blind** will be discussed later. This depth is added on **Both Sides** of the DTM2, which is the plane of the screen, because you initially specified **Both Sides** before sketching the outline of the guard. As a result DTM2 bisects the guard.

On the top right-hand portion of the screen you should see the PROTRUSION:Extrude window shown in Figure 7.42. Expand the size of the box if necessary by moving it (click on the title bar across the top of the box and hold the left mouse button down as you move the mouse) and dragging the lower right corner (click on the lower right corner of the box and hold down the left mouse button as you move the mouse). This box contains all the information necessary to define a solid extrusion as explained below.

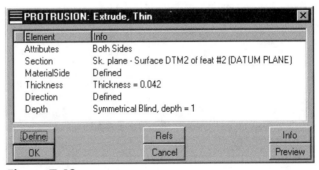

Figure 7.42.

Attributes: The feature being modeled will be extruded on **Both Sides** of the sketching plane. In this way, DTM2 bisects the extrusion. If you had selected **One Side** when creating the extrusion, the solid extrusion would be 1.0 inches deep extending out of only one side of DTM2, making DTM2 on one edge of the extrusion.

Section: The sketching plane is defined as indicated.

MaterialSide: Specifies that the side of the sketched line to which material will be added has been properly defined.

Thickness: Indicates the thickness of the thin section.

Direction: Specifies that the direction of the extrusion has been properly defined.

Depth: Indicates the depth and type of the extrusion.

If you want to modify any one of these elements to match those in Figure 7.42, simply double click on the element title and appropriate menus will appear to modify the information. For example, double click on Depth, and the SPEC TO menu will appear. Click on **Blind | Done** and re-enter 1.0 in the text window above the Graphics Window. (If you had improperly specified the depth, you could correct it this way.)

If the feature is properly specified, the **OK** button will be highlighted in the lower left corner of the PROTRUSION:Extrude dialog box. If the geometry is invalid or missing information, the **OK** button will be grayed out and you will not be able to select it until you have corrected the errors in the feature. To finish the feature:

<click OK>

Now you can view your progress on the guard so far by reverting back to the isometric view. To do this, return to the Default isometric view:

***View* ⇒ *Saved Views* ⇒ <click on Default in the Saved Views window that appears> ⇒ <click Set> ⇒ <click Close>**

The guard should now be shown in an isometric view as in Figure 7.43. Note that DTM2 bisects the guard and that the thickness has been added on the yellow side of DTM1.

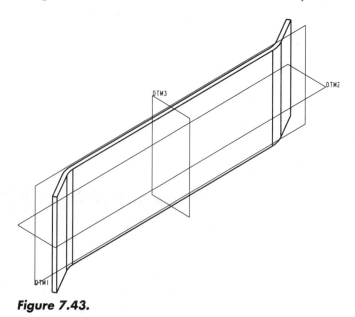

Figure 7.43.

Save your work using **Save** in the **File** menu.

7.7   VIEWING THE PART

Now is a good time to explore some of the buttons on the Tool bar. The eight buttons shown in Figure 7.44 control the way the part appears on the screen.

Figure 7.44.

The four right buttons toggle datum, or reference entities, on and off. From left to right they are **Datum planes on/off**, **Datum axes on/off**, **Datum points on/off**, and **Coordinate systems on/off**. Turn all of these entities off and on by clicking the appropriate button. No datum axes or datum points are visible, because none have been created. Finish by turning all datum entities off.

The left four buttons control the way the object is displayed. The **Wireframe** button displays all solid edges and tangencies as solid lines. This is often a confusing way to display the object. The **Hidden Line** button displays all solid edges and tangencies, but those that are hidden from view are shown in gray. This allows you to view the object as if it were transparent. When hidden lines are printed as hard copy, they are dashed lines. The **No Hidden** button displays the object so that hidden lines do not appear at all. All that is visible are the lines that outline the visible edges and tangencies of the object. This is the way the guard is displayed in Figure 7.43. The **<u>Shading</u>** button shows the object with all surfaces shaded (or rendered), so that it looks as it would in a photograph. This is ideal for seeing the object as it will appear after fabrication. Try all of these buttons.

Pro/ENGINEER allows you to translate, zoom, and rotate the object on the screen with one button. This is done by holding the CTRL key while moving the cursor with one mouse button depressed. The mouse buttons do the following:

Left:	Zoom
Middle:	Rotate/Spin (for a two-button mouse, use CTRL-Shift-left button)
Right:	Translate

Once the mouse button is released, the object will maintain its last position. Try zooming, rotating, and translating the part.

The Tool bar buttons shown in Figure 7.45 are also available to refresh, zoom, and adjust the views. The leftmost button in Figure 7.45 is to **<u>Repaint the screen</u>**. Using this button causes the screen to refresh. This is often helpful when parts are being modeled or when drawings are being created. The next three buttons are used to zoom in and out. To use the **<u>Zoom In</u>** tool (a magnifying glass with a plus sign), click on the **<u>Zoom In</u>** tool, then left click at the position where you want the upper left corner of the new screen to be. Next, click where you want the lower right corner. Pro/ENGINEER then zooms to the region you specified. You can **<u>Zoom Out</u>** (a magnifying glass with a minus) by just clicking that button as many times as necessary. The **<u>Refit the model to the screen</u>** button (a magnifying glass on a screen) adjusts the model so that it fits "full size" on the screen. The fourth button from the left, **<u>Orient the model</u>**, allows the user to orient the model on the screen by specifying the orientation of specific datum planes or axes. We will not use this button. The rightmost button is quite useful. You can always return to the default isometric view using the **<u>Saved view list</u>** Tool bar button and clicking **Default**.

Figure 7.45.

After testing each of these buttons, orient the guard in the default isometric orientation as shown in Figure 7.43. Display it with datum planes visible and no hidden lines

7.8   CUTTING A CIRCULAR HOLE

The next feature to model is the hole at the center of the guard. This is done by extruding a solid cut. Be sure that the guard is shown in **<u>No Hidden</u>** view with the datum planes on and the guard in the default isometric orientation.

Although Pro/ENGINEER has a **Hole** feature, you will use the **Cut** command instead because it is more general and because a hole is simply a circular cut. In this case you want to **Create** a **Feature** that consists of a **Solid Cut** that will be **Extrude**d. To do this:

Create ⇒ Solid ⇒ Cut ⇒ Extrude | Solid | Done ⇒ One Side | Done

Note that you selected **One Side** for the attribute of the cut. This means that the cut will be extruded on only one side of the sketching plane, rather than to both sides of the sketching plane. Look back at Figure 7.16 and 7.43. It is evident that the hole will be perpendicular to DTM1. Because the hole appears as a circle in DTM1, you will set up DTM1 as the sketching plane and sketch a circle:

Setup New ⇒ Plane ⇒ Pick ⇒ <select DTM1>

Note that the message above the Graphics window indicates that in this case the arrow indicates the "direction of feature creation." This is the direction from DTM1 in which material will be removed by the cut. You want to remove material away from the yellow side of DTM1, so that the cut goes through the guard. **Flip** the arrow to indicate the direction shown in Figure 7.46:

Flip | Okay

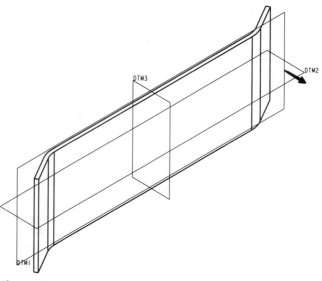

Figure 7.46.

To orient the yellow side of DTM2 toward the **Top** of the screen to result in a sketching plane that looks like Figure 7.47:

Top ⇒ <select DTM2>

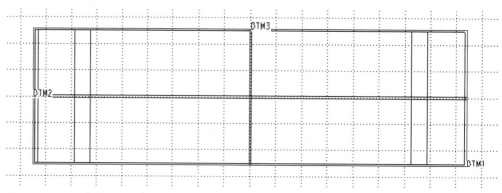

Figure 7.47.

Now you can sketch the circle in the sketching plane:

Sketch ⇒ Circle ⇒ Center/Point

This series of commands creates a circle by specifying the center point of the circle and its radius. Other methods of creating a circle include making a circle **Concentric** to another circle or specifying **3 Point**s on a circle. In the main window draw the circle shown in Figure 7.48 by clicking the left mouse button at the intersection of the two axes to place the center of the circle at the origin. It is important to place the center of the circle as near as possible to the intersection of DTM2 and DTM3, because it will be aligned to the origin shortly. Then move the cursor up and to the right. It does not matter whether you hold down the mouse button or not as you drag the circle to the desired size. Do not worry about making the radius of the circle exactly like the figure, although it should be small enough to fit within the guard. You will specify the radius later. At this point, the size of the circle continues to change with cursor movements. To select the size of the circle, click the left mouse button again. The circle turns blue to indicate that its size is no longer dependent on the mouse position. If something does not look right to you, **Delete** the circle and try again.

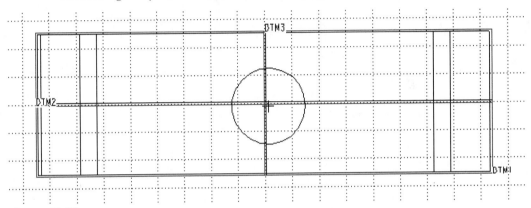

Figure 7.48.

Constrain the location of the center of the circle by aligning it to DTM2 and DTM3. This requires two **Alignment**s, one for each datum plane. In aligning a circle, it is easiest to click on the circle itself (rather than the center of the circle) and then on a datum plane.

Alignment ⇒ Align ⇒ <select circle> ⇒ <select DTM2>

Check in the message area that the entities are ALIGNED. Recall that the sketched features must be quite close together in order to be aligned. In this case, the center of the circle must be fairly close to being lined up with DTM2. (If this is not the case, move the circle by selecting **Geom Tools ⇒ Move Entity** and then selecting the center of the circle. Move the circle center so that it is at the origin. Then left click again to fix its position.) After you have aligned the circle center to DTM2, align the circle with the DTM3 axis.

Alignment ⇒ Align ⇒ <select circle> ⇒ <select the DTM3 axis>

To verify aligned entities, select **Alignment ⇒ Unalign** and all the aligned features will appear in green on the screen. In this case, the center of the circle, the DTM2 axis, and the DTM3 axis should appear in green. When you are done looking at what segments are aligned, select **Quit Sel**. This quits the **Unalign** operation so that the highlighted items remain aligned.

The only other constraint that needs to be added is the diameter of the circle. Recall that a radius was dimensioned by a single mouse click (left button) followed by a click on the middle mouse button to place the dimension. In this case, you need to dimension the diameter of the hole. To dimension a diameter, double-click on the circle followed by a click on the middle button to place the dimension. Thus, the commands to create a diameter dimension are:

Dimension ⇒ <double-click on circle> ⇒ <select dimension location with middle mouse button>

After creating this dimension, the sketch should look like Figure 7.49.

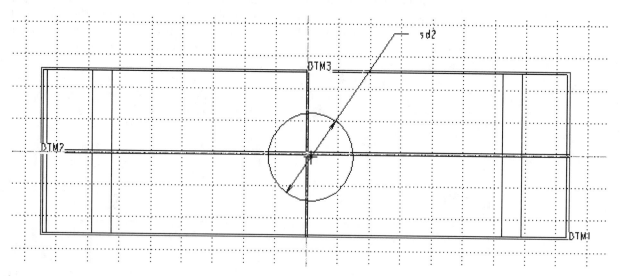

Figure 7.49.

The sketch is now fully constrained and ready to **Regenerate**:

Regenerate

Upon regeneration, the alphanumeric variables are replaced with numeric dimensions. The numeric dimensions may not have three digits after the decimal point. If so, the number of digits can be changed by:

Sec Tools ⇒ Sec Environ ⇒ Num Digits ⇒ <enter 3> (Figure 7.50)

This command sets the number of digits after the decimal point to 3.

⇨ Number of decimal places for dimensions | 3

Figure 7.50.

Now **Modify** the dimension for the diameter to be .404 inches and finish the sketch:

Modify ⇒ <click on the diameter dimension> ⇒ <enter .404> ⇒ Regenerate

After regenerating the sketch should look like Figure 7.51.
Once you have the circle sketched and dimensioned as shown in Figure 7.51, select:

Done

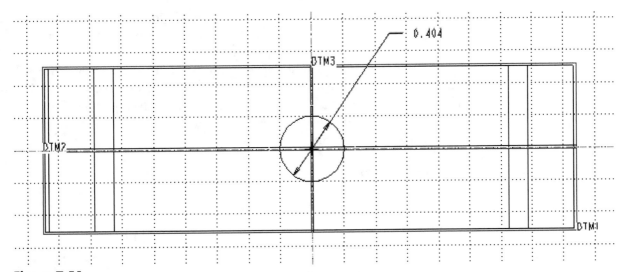

Figure 7.51.

Now a red arrow should appear on the sketch as shown in Figure 7.52. The arrow indicates the direction that material is removed as noted in the Message area. The arrow should point from the circle that you just sketched inward, so that material is removed on the inside of the circle. If necessary, **Flip** the arrow so it points inward. When the sketch looks like Figure 7.52:

Okay

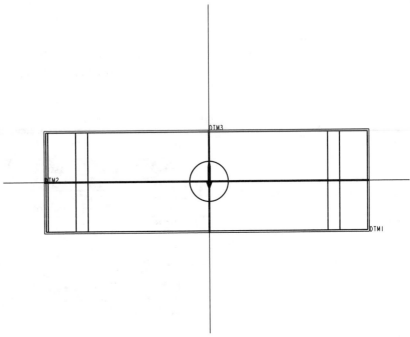

Figure 7.52.

Return to the isometric view using the <u>**Saved view list**</u> Tool bar button and clicking **Default**. The arrow in Figure 7.53 shows the direction that the material will be removed. Now the type and depth of the cut must be specified. The options for feature depth that are used most frequently are **Blind**, **Thru Next**, and **Thru All**. A **Blind** cut will go a specified distance only. The **Thru Next** cut will remove all solid material until it reaches the next part surface. The **Thru All** cut will remove all material through the part. In this case there is only one surface, so **Thru Next** and **Thru All** accomplish the same cut:

Thru All | Done

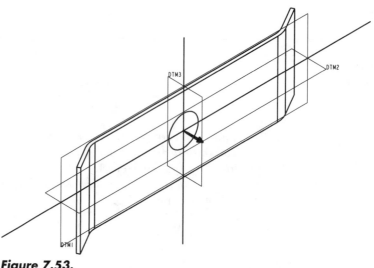

Figure 7.53.

Review the feature elements that you have created as shown in Figure 7.54. This feature should be sketched in Surface DTM1 with a depth of Through All. To complete the cut:

<click OK>

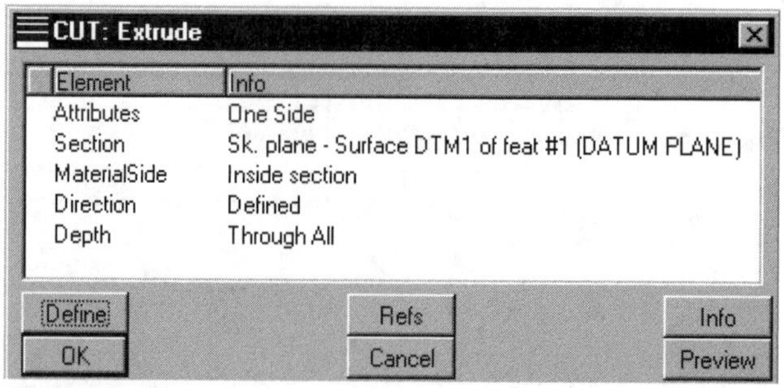

Figure 7.54.

Spin and shade the part to see the hole.

7.9   CREATING A ROUND AT THE CORNERS

Rounds on each corner are the last feature to add to the model of the guard. Use the Tool bar buttons to set the model in **<u>Hidden Line</u>** view with the datum planes on and the guard in the default isometric orientation (using **<u>Saved view list</u>**).

There are four corners that need to be rounded. This can be done one corner at a time or as a group. If it is done one corner at a time, each round is a separate feature. If the rounds are done as a group, they are a single feature. In this case the rounds will be created as a group, so that the radius of all four rounds can be later modified as a group, rather than individually. To do this, you will **Create** a **Solid Feature** called a **Round**:

Create $\Rightarrow$ Solid $\Rightarrow$ Round $\Rightarrow$ Simple | Done $\Rightarrow$ Constant | Edge Chain | Done $\Rightarrow$ One By One

This is a single (**Simple**) **Round** of **Constant** radius. **Edge Chain** indicates that you will select a sharp edge to be rounded. An alternative is to select two surfaces between which there is a round (**Surf-Surf**). You want to select the four edges at each corner of the guard, shown in Figure 7.55. This is done by selecting each edge **One By One** in the graphics window. It is a little tricky to select the correct edge, especially for edges that are behind surfaces. The most certain way to do this is to **Query Select**. To do this, use **Query Sel** in the GET SELECT menu. This command allows you to choose among several nearby features. Upon selecting a feature in the Graphics window using a mouse click, you can either **Accept** that selection or move to the next nearby

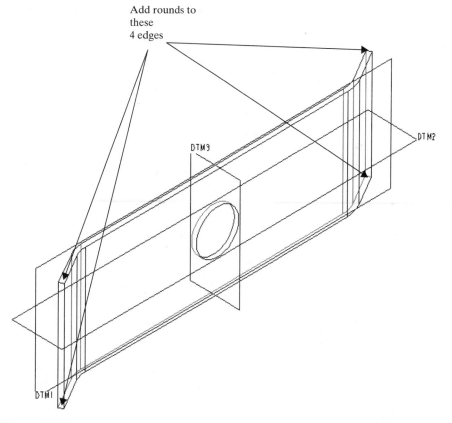

Figure 7.55.

feature. The **Query Sel** command provides a list of possible selections in a window called the **Query Bin**. Clicking on any item in the list highlights the item in the Graphics window. When the desired item is chosen, clicking on **Accept** will select that item. This is particularly useful if lines or curves are close together or behind other surfaces, making it difficult to **Pick** in the usual way. To select the upper right corner of the guard:

Query Sel ⇒ **<select the edge at the top right corner of the guard>**

When you select an item, it will change color. If the proper edge is highlighted, click **Accept**. If not, click on the next item in the **Query Bin** until the correct edge is highlighted. Then click **Accept**. Now continue to select the other three edges using **Query Sel**ect:

Query Sel ⇒ **<select the remaining three edges one at a time>**

It may help to spin the guard to get better access to make the initial selection. When you have finished selecting all four edges for the round (all four are highlighted), complete the operation with:

Done

Enter a radius of .35 for the round in the dialog box that appears in the Message area above the Graphics window.

<enter .35>

The ROUND:General window, shown in Figure 7.56, shows the information about the round. Note that the elements listed in this dialog box for a round feature are different from the elements that were listed for the extrusion of the guard base feature or the extruded cut of the hole in the guard. Double clicking on any element brings up the appropriate menus to modify any of the elements. You can preview the round by clicking **Preview** in the ROUND: General window. To see the rounded corners more clearly, it may help to turn off the datum planes by toggling the **Datum planes on/off** button in the Tool bar. To finish the feature:

<click OK>

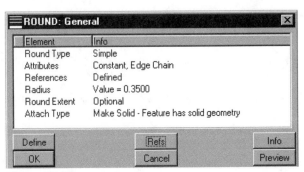

Figure 7.56.

After creating the rounds, the guard should look like Figure 7.57. You can check the dimension of any feature to make sure that it is correct. For instance to check the radius of the rounds:

Feature ⇒ **Modify** ⇒ **<select a round>**

This command will show the radius of the round as shown in Figure 7.57. Then click **Done** and **Repaint the screen** to end the **Modify** command and remove the dimension.

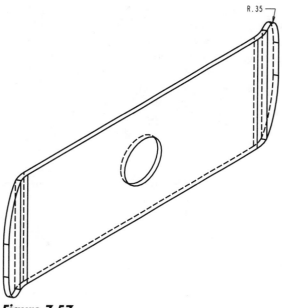

R.35

Figure 7.57.

Congratulations! You have finished the first of six individual parts that make up the pizza cutter. Finish up by saving the guard.prt file. Previously you used *Save* in the *File* menu to save a part. But there is a quicker alternative. Find the **Save** button in the Tool bar (an icon of a floppy disk near the left end of the Tool bar). Move the mouse cursor over the icon to be sure that it indicates Save. Then click on the button. Hit Enter on the keyboard or click on the green checkmark in the Message area to complete the save operation.

It is also possible to **Print** the image of the guard that is in the Graphics window. To do this find the **Print** button in the Tool bar (an icon of a printer near the left end of the Tool bar). Move the mouse cursor over the icon to be sure that it indicates Print. Then click on the button. Depending on how your computer is configured with the printer, a window will appear to lead you through the printing process. Printing can also be done from the menu system as *File* ⇒ *Print*. (Because printing is somewhat computer/printer system specific, you may need to get more detailed instructions about printing from your computer system administrator if the above commands do not work.)

Shade and rotate the finished guard to see what it looks like. Close the guard window using:

Window ⇒ *Close*

If you want to quit, either click the X button at the top right corner of the Pro/ENGINEER window or use:

File ⇒ *Exit*

Pick and Place Features

"Pick and place" commands create standard features that occur frequently as parts are designed. The features are quite easy to create because Pro/ENGINEER makes assumptions about certain aspects of the geometry. A **Round** is an example of a pick and place command. One pick and place command that is not used in this tutorial is the **Hole** command. A hole can be created using a circular **Cut**, or the **Hole** pick and place command can be used. When the **Hole** command is used, it is not necessary to sketch the circular cross-section of the hole, just indicate the hole's location and diameter. Nevertheless, anything that can be done with the **Hole** command can also be done using a circular **Cut**.

KEY TERMS

Align	Extrude	Regenerate
Base feature	Feature-based modeling	Round
Blind	Fillet	Sketching plane
Constrain	Protrusion	Solids-based modeling
Cut	Query select	Thin feature
Datum planes		

Problems

1. Model the guard, except make both ends of the guard bend 30 degrees in the same direction rather than opposite directions.

2. Model the guard so that the plane of the hole is parallel to DTM2 instead of DTM1. Make the angle of the bends 20 degrees rather than 30 degrees. (Hint: Begin by determining the proper sketching plane.)

3. Model the guard so that it is extruded to one side of the sketch plane, DTM2. (Note: One edge of the guard will be coincident with DTM2 when finished.) In addition, make the radius of the bend .15 rather than .25.

8

Modeling the Handle

OVERVIEW

In this chapter, you continue by modeling the handle of the pizza cutter. You begin by creating a 2D sketch of a circle and extruding it to form the cylindrical base feature for the handle. Then several detail features are added to the handle including a round, a rectangular slot, a circular hole, and grooves.

8.1 MODELING THE HANDLE BASE FEATURE

Now that you have some experience in modeling using Pro/ ENGINEER, you will tackle a much more complicated part, the handle of the pizza cutter shown in Figure 8.1. The handle is generally cylindrical in shape with a circular hole at one end to hang the pizza cutter on a hook, and a rectangular hole at the other end to accept the arms that hold the cutting blade. Grooves on the handle provide a better grip for the user.

Recall that any part is the combination of a number of features. Each feature defines a portion of the final geometry and the sum of these features models the entire object. Typically the first features of any part are the default datum planes and the coordinate system. These features were created in new-part.prt and copied to handle.prt already. The base feature of the handle will be the main solid cylinder of the handle. You will model this solid geometry as the extrusion of a circle to form a cylinder. Then you will modify the cylinder by removing material as features are added to obtain the desired handle geometry.

OBJECTIVES

When you have completed this tutorial chapter, you should be able to:

- Set up a 2D sketch plane
- Sketch a 2D shape
- Constrain a sketch using alignment and dimensions
- Extrude a 2D shape
- Create rounds
- Revolve a cut
- Cut slots and holes
- Create a patterned feature

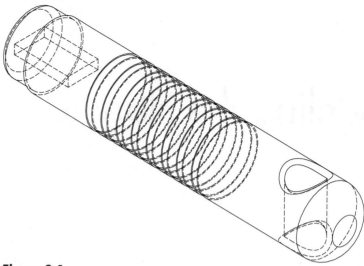

Figure 8.1.

If Pro/ENGINEER is not open, start it using the appropriate commands for your computer. Be sure that the *Environment* (in the *Utilities* menu) is set to **Spin Center** off, **No Hidden**, and **Isometric**. Also set up the **Default Tree settings** (in the *Utilities ⇒ Customize Screen ⇒ Options* menu) as in Figure 7.3. Finally, set up the proper *Working Directory* (in the *File* menu).

Open the handle file:

File ⇒ Open ⇒ < click handle.prt > | < click Open >

The part already has three datum plane features and a coordinate system, which should appear on the screen. (If they do not appear, be sure that the <u>**Datum planes on/off**</u> and <u>**Coordinate systems on/off**</u> buttons are on.) You will begin by **Creat**ing a base **Feature** of the overall cylindrical shape of the handle. The handle will be modeled as a **Solid Protrusion**. You want the circular cross-section of the handle to "protrude" from datum plane DTM1, forming a cylinder. Thus:

Feature ⇒ Create ⇒ Solid ⇒ Protrusion

A new menu appears in the Menu Manager with the choice of a **Solid** feature or a **Thin** feature. The **Thin** feature is used to model parts with a constant wall thickness, like the guard. Here you need to **Extrude** a part that is a **Solid** cylinder:

Extrude | Solid | Done

A new menu appears along with a window entitled PROTRUSION:Extrude, which shows the different elements of the feature that you are creating. Recall that this window has a **Cancel** button, if you want to start over on this feature at any time.

You want to extrude the part to one side of the sketching plane that you will soon specify, so:

One Side | Done

Pro/E now asks you to set up a sketching plane. Recall that the sketching plane is the plane that you will use to draw the cross-section of the geometry that you want to create. The feature you create will "start" at the sketching plane and will be extruded out of this plane to the depth that you specify to create a 3D base feature. For the handle, you will sketch a circle and then specify a depth to extrude the cylindrical handle.

Setup New, **Plane**, and **Pick** are already highlighted in the Menu Manager to indicate that you are to **Set up** a **New Plane** by **Pick**ing the plane using the mouse. You will use DTM1 (y-z plane) as the sketching plane in this example and extrude the handle in the x-direction. We intentionally chose this sketching plane to aid in the orientation of parts with respect to each other when you assemble the pizza cutter in Chapter 10, but any plane could have been chosen.

< **select DTM1** >

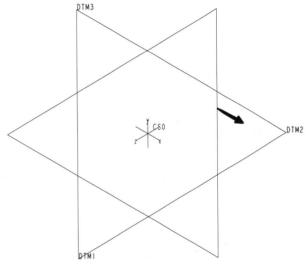

Figure 8.2.

A red arrow should pop up pointing to the right from DTM1 as shown in Figure 8.2. The arrow indicates the direction that the feature will be extruded from the sketching plane. Right now the arrow is pointing away from the yellow side of DTM1 in the positive x-direction. Remember that there is no right or wrong way to extrude the feature. Set the arrow as shown in Figure 8.2 for consistency with this tutorial using **Flip** if necessary. When the arrow matches Figure 8.2

Okay

Now it is necessary to orient the other datum planes. Again, there is no right or wrong orientation, but you should set up the orientation of the datum planes to match the ones shown here for consistency later on in this tutorial. In this case, you will "point" yellow side of DTM2 toward the **Top** of the screen:

Top ⇒ < **select DTM2** >

The screen shown in Figure 8.3 will appear. If the Intent Manager is checked, click on the checkbox to turn it off.

The yellow side of DTM1 is the sketching plane, which is parallel to the screen. In Figure 8.2 the arrow indicating the direction of the extrusion came out of the yellow side of DTM1, so the solid will be extruded out of the screen toward the viewer. Now that the sketching plane is oriented, you can turn off the coordinate system using the **Coordinate systems on/off** Tool bar button.

The cross-section of the handle is circular, so:

Sketch ⇒ **Circle**

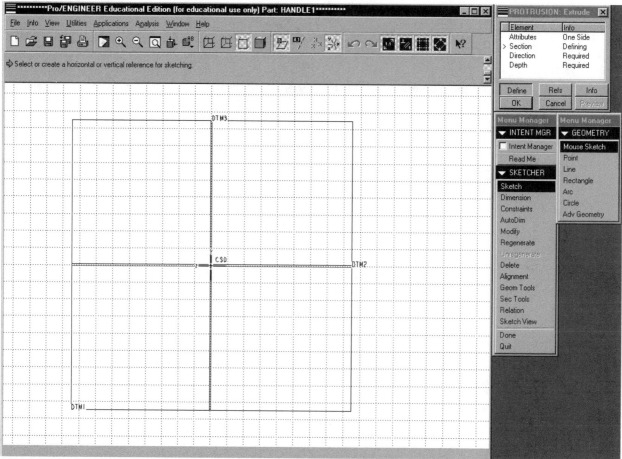

Figure 8.3.

A new menu appears with **Geometry** and **Center/Point** already highlighted, so that you can create a circle by specifying the center point of the circle and its radius. (Other methods of creating a circle include making a circle **Concentric** to another circle or specifying **3 Points** on a circle.) In the main window draw the circle shown in Figure 8.4 by clicking the left mouse button at the center of the circle and moving the cursor up and to the right. It does not matter whether you hold down the mouse button or not as you drag the circle to the desired size. Do not worry about positioning the center of the circle exactly where it is shown or making the radius of the circle exactly like the figure. You will specify these items later. To select the size of the circle, click the left mouse button again. The circle turns blue to indicate that its size is no longer dependent on the mouse position.

Now you need to define the exact location of this circle relative to the datum planes by dimensioning. In the SKETCHER menu:

Dimension

To fully constrain a circle, you need to define the location of its center and specify its diameter as shown in Figure 8.5. First:

< **select the center of the circle** > ⇒ < **select DTM3** > ⇒ < **select dimension location with middle mouse button** >

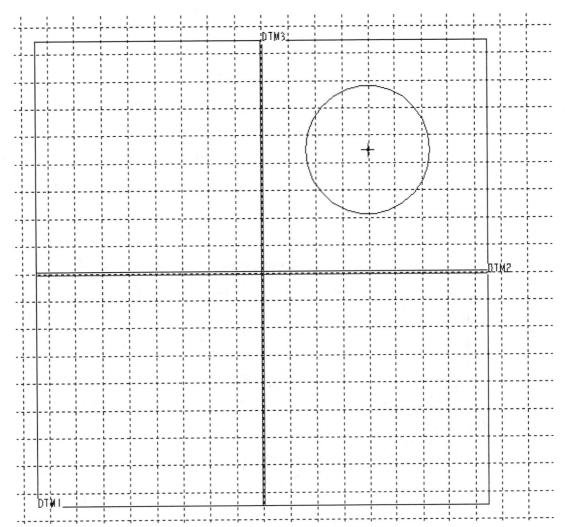

Figure 8.4.

Place the dimension of the circle center to DTM2 the same way as the first dimension by clicking on the center of the circle, then DTM2, and then placing the dimension with the middle mouse button. To specify the diameter of the circle, double click on the circle and then click the middle mouse button to place the dimension as shown in Figure 8.5. If you clicked on the circle only once while dimensioning, the radius would have been specified. Either dimensioning works, but we prefer to click on the circle twice to use a diameter dimension.

The geometry for this circle is now fully defined on the 2D sketching plane. Every point along the circle is exactly defined by the coordinates of the circle center and the diameter of the circle.

Regenerate

Check that the statement "Section regenerated successfully" appears in the Message area above the Graphics window. The sketch should look like Figure 8.6, except for different numerical values.

Now **Modify** the dimensions to the right size for the pizza cutter.

Modify ⇒ < **select diameter dimension** > ⇒ < **enter 1.0** >

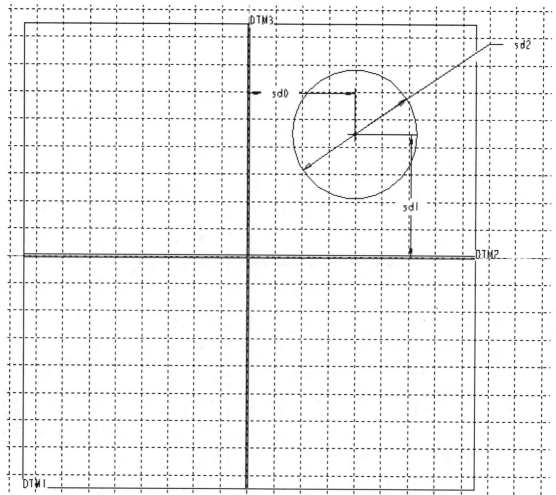

Figure 8.5.

<blockquote>
< select dimension to DTM2 > ⇒ < enter 0 >

< select dimension to DTM3 > ⇒ < enter 0 >
</blockquote>

Even though the circle was originally sketched in the upper right quadrant of the sketching plane, these commands have constrained it to have its center at the origin. To have the circle update to the new values:

Regenerate

This demonstrates the power of Pro/ENGINEER as a constraint-based modeler. Even though the circle was not originally sketched with its center near the origin, it was constrained to be located at the origin by the dimensions. It would have worked just as well to sketch the circle with its center near the origin and then align the center to the origin. In fact, this is often the preferred method to locate a feature. To finish the sketch:

Done

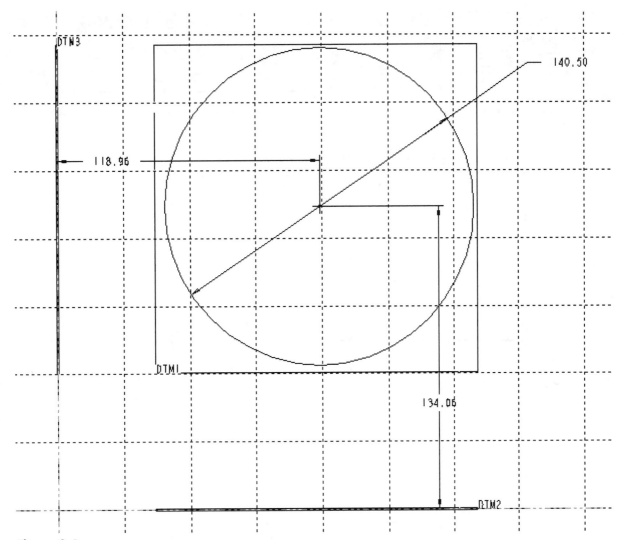

Figure 8.6.

Now that the 2D cross-section of the handle shaft is specified in the sketching plane, you need to tell Pro/ENGINEER how far to extrude the circular shape perpendicular to the screen. The screen should look similar to Figure 8.7. Note the small concentric red circles at the center of circle in the figure. These circles (representing the point of an arrow) indicate that the depth of the feature will be extruded out of the screen toward you. If you see a red X (indicating the tail of an arrow), the feature will be extruded into the screen, away from you. Continue with:

Blind | Done

The command **Blind** indicates that you want to control the depth of the feature by specifying a dimension for the depth. To extrude the handle to 5.25 inches long:

< enter 5.25 >

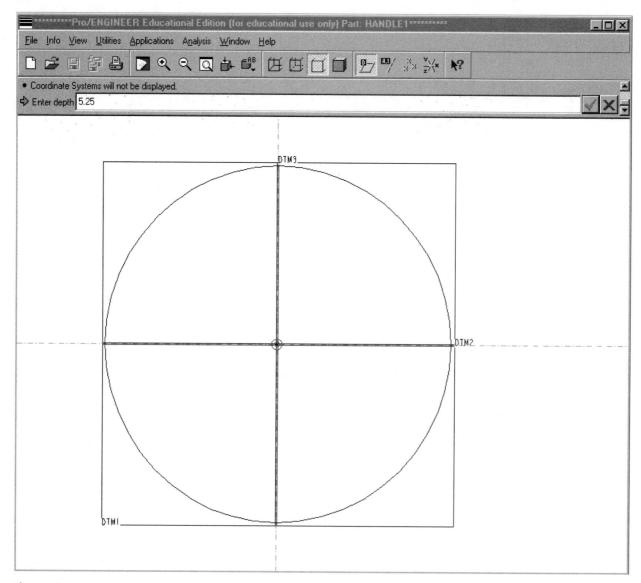

Figure 8.7.

Examine the PROTRUSION:Extrude window at the top right-hand portion of the screen. To finish the feature:

< click OK >

To see the feature, return to the isometric default view by clicking on the **Saved view list** button in the Tool bar and clicking **Default**. If you have created the handle properly, you should see the shape shown in Figure 8.8 with the datum planes as shown. The handle has been extruded from the yellow side of DTM1 as you originally specified. The axis "A _ 1" appears along the axis of the handle. If the axis is not shown, toggle the Tool bar button **Datum axes on/off** to display it. Before continuing toggle the axis off.

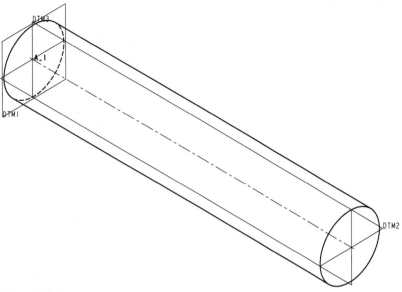

Figure 8.8.

To verify that we have created this shaft with the correct dimensions:

Feature ⇒ **Modify** ⇒ < **select handle** > (by clicking on the right end of the handle)

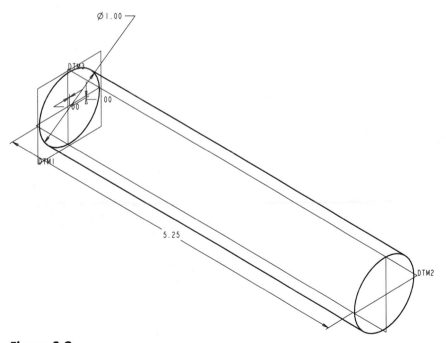

Figure 8.9.

The dimensions that you specified are shown as in Figure 8.9. The handle diameter is 1.0 inch, the circle center is at (0,0), and the handle length is 5.25 inches. Click the **Repaint the screen** Tool bar button to remove the dimensions.

8.2 CREATING A ROUND

The finished geometry for the handle is shown in Figure 8.10. The handle has a rounded right end, a smaller diameter and rectangular slot at the left end, grooves around it in the middle, and a hole near the right end. You have created the base feature of the handle as a solid cylinder. Now you need to add additional detail features. The next feature you will model is the round on the right end of the handle. Often rounds are the last features added in a Pro/ENGINEER model, because they depend on other features. This is known as a parent-child relationship. A new feature, the child, depends on its parents to exist. In this case, the round at the right end of the handle could not exist without the base feature of the extruded cylinder shown in Figure 8.9. All features except the default datum planes have parents. Not all features have children. Because the round at the right end of the handle depends only on the handle base feature to exist, the round can be created now. To model the round:

Feature ⇒ Create ⇒ Solid ⇒ Round ⇒ Simple | Done ⇒ Constant | Edge Chain | Done ⇒ Tangnt Chain ⇒ Pick ⇒ <select the circle forming the right end of the handle (as displayed in Figure 8.9)> ⇒ Done

Here you are **Creat**ing a single (**Simple**) **Solid Feature** of **Constant** radius to **Round** the edge that you selected. **Edge Chain** indicates that you select an edge to be rounded rather than selecting two surfaces between which there is a round (**Surf-Surf**). You want to select the edge that is the circle forming the right end of the handle. This circle is actually made up of two semicircular edges. Using **Tangnt Chain** selects edges that form a continuous tangent chain of edges, so if one semicircular edge is selected the other one will also be selected automatically. When you select the circle forming the right end of the handle, it will change color. Once you have selected the circular edge, **Done** completes the operation.

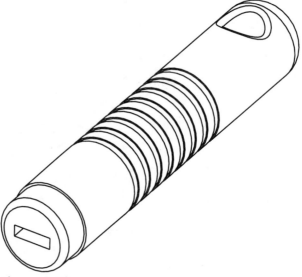

Figure 8.10.

Enter the radius for the round in the dialog box that appears in the Message area.

< enter .30 >

Preview the round by clicking **Preview** in the ROUND:General window. If you are satisfied, click **OK**. The handle will now appear as shown in Figure 8.11 after turning off the datum planes using the **<u>Datum planes on/off</u>** Tool bar button.

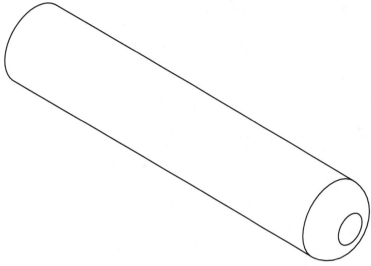

Figure 8.11.

To verify the dimension of the radius for the round, click on **Feature** ⇒ **Modify** and then select the round at the right end of the handle. The dimension of the round should appear on the screen. **<u>Repaint the screen</u>** to remove the dimension.

The handle now has six features listed in the Model Tree window. (The Model Tree window may be minimized at the bottom of the screen. Click on it once to open it up.)

1. DTM1 — Datum 1
2. DTM2 — Datum 2
3. DTM3 — Datum 3
4. CS0 — Coordinate system 0
5. Protrusion — Solid extrusion to form a cylinder for the handle shaft
6. Round — Round at right end of the handle

Now would be a good time to save your work using *Save* in the *File* menu or the **<u>Save</u>** Tool bar button.

8.3   CREATING A CUT

The next feature to model is the reduced diameter at the left end of the handle, as shown in Figure 8.10. The diameter is reduced so that a mating part, the cap, can fit over this end of the handle. At this point it is helpful to be sure that the environment is set up so that hidden lines are not shown. Use the **<u>No Hidden</u>** Tool bar button or use the *Environment* dialog box in the *Utilities* menu to change the **Display Style** to **No Hidden**. Also turn on the datum planes, and turn off the datum axes, datum points, and coordinate systems, if they are on.

To reduce the diameter of the left end, you will **Extrude** a **Solid Cut** along the axis of the handle to cut away a ring of material on **One Side** of a datum plane (DTM1):

Feature ⇒ Create ⇒ Solid ⇒ Cut ⇒ Extrude | Solid | Done ⇒ One Side | Done

Now you need to select a sketching plane on which you can sketch the cut. The solid cut will be extruded along the axis of the handle perpendicular to DTM1. Thus, use DTM1 as the sketch plane:

Setup New ⇒ Plane ⇒ Pick ⇒ < select DTM1 >

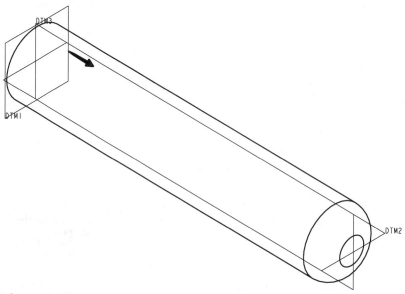

Figure 8.12.

It is helpful to check the Message area above the Graphics window frequently. At this point the message should be "Arrow shows direction of feature creation. Pick FLIP or OKAY." Be sure the arrow is pointing in the direction shown in Figure 8.12 so that the material will be removed in the direction shown by the arrow. If the arrow is not pointed in the right direction:

Flip | Okay

Next, you need to select a datum plane to orient the sketching plane. Orient the front (yellow) side of DTM2 toward the top of the screen as shown in Figure 8.13:

Top ⇒ < select DTM2 >

The red side of DTM1 is the sketching plane. Since the arrow shown in Figure 8.12 points outward from the yellow side of DTM1, the cut will be extruded into the screen from the sketching plane.

Rather than sketching a circle using the **Center/Point** method as was done with previous features, you will create a circle that is **Concentric** to the circle already shown:

Sketch ⇒ Circle ⇒ Geometry | Concentric ⇒ < select the circle >

Clicking on the existing circle defines the circle to which the new circle will be concentric.

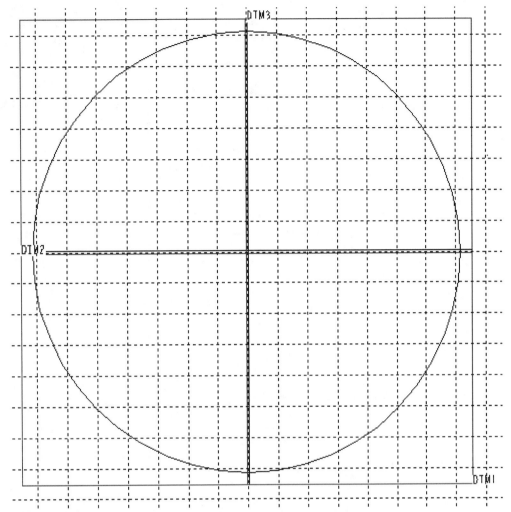

Figure 8.13.

       < select a point inside of the existing circle > ⇒ < select a point on the new circle just inside of the existing circle >

The new circle will appear. The second click fixes the diameter of the new circle slightly smaller than the circle already on the sketch, as shown in Figure 8.14.

When you sketched the circle that was extruded to form the handle, the diameter of the circle was dimensioned. Although this method would work here, you will dimension the distance from the inner circle to the outer circle instead.

       Dimension ⇒ < select the right side of the inner circle just above the horizontal axis > ⇒ < select the right side of the outer circle just above the horizontal axis > ⇒ < place the dimension with the middle mouse button just to the right of the two circles >

The dimension does not appear right away, because Pro/ENGINEER does not know whether you want to dimension the distance between the outside edges of the circles or the distance between the centers of the circles. A new menu, shown in Figure 8.15, appears in the Menu Manager that prompts you to specify **Center**

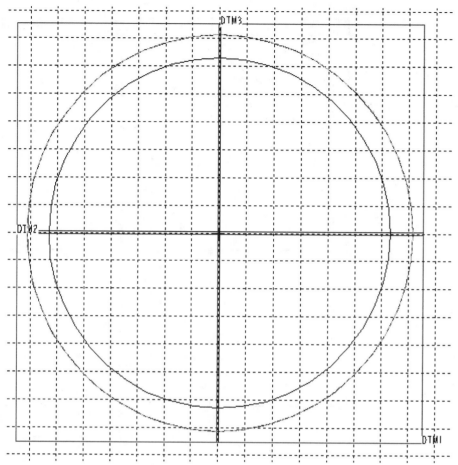

Figure 8.14.

(distance between centers of the circles) or **Tangent** (distance between tangents to the circles). Use:

> **Tangent**

Figure 8.15.

Another new menu, shown in Figure 8.16, appears before the dimension can be placed. Pro/ENGINEER now asks if the dimension should be the **Vert**ical distance between the edges of the circles or the **Horiz**ontal distance. You want the horizontal dimension shown in Figure 8.17:

> **Horiz**

Figure 8.16.

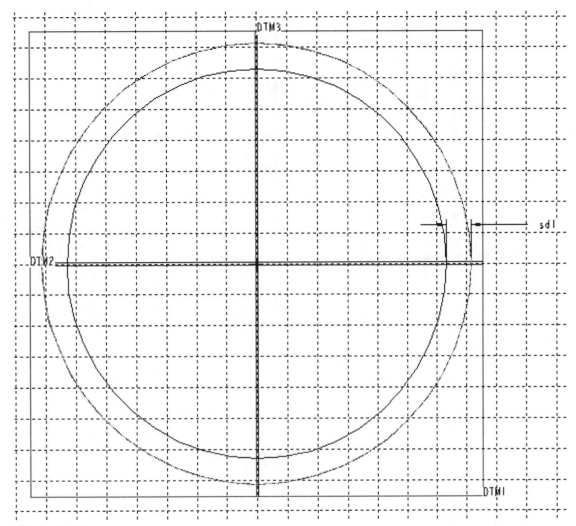

Figure 8.17.

The inner circle shown in Figure 8.17 is now fully constrained. This may be surprising, because no dimensions have been applied to locate the center of the new circle, nor has the center of the new circle been aligned to DTM2 and DTM3. But recall that this circle was constructed to be concentric to the original circle. Thus, the position of the center of the new circle is automatically constrained to be identical to the position of the center of the original circle. This is another example of a parent-child relationship. The new circle (child) is constrained to move with the original circle (parent) if the location of the center of the original circle is changed. To continue:

Regenerate

The result should look similar to Figure 8.18, although the dimension will probably be different.

Modify the dimension between the circles to be .030 inches using **Modify**.

Modify ⇒ < select the dimension between circles > ⇒ < enter .030 > ⇒ Regenerate

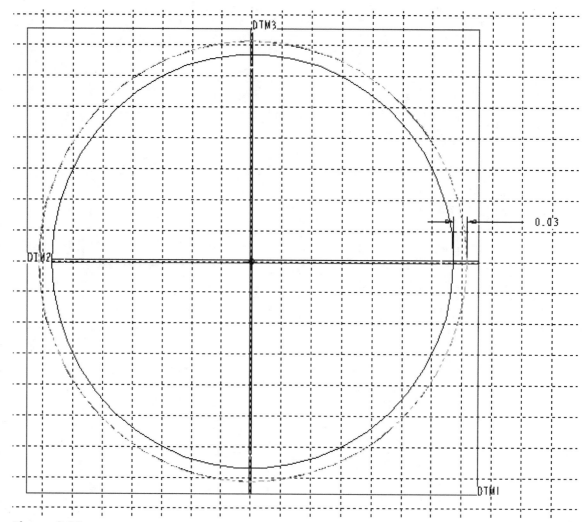

Figure 8.18.

The model should look like Figure 8.18. If the sketch looks like this:

Done

A red arrow appears as shown in Figure 8.19. Pro/E provides help about what the arrow means in the Message area above the Graphics window, shown in Figure 8.20. The text indicates that the arrow points toward the solid geometry that will be removed with the cut. Remember that you are reducing the diameter of the handle at one end so the arrow should be pointing in the direction shown in Figure 8.20 to remove material outside the smaller circle.

Flip (if necessary) | Okay

Now Pro/ENGINEER prompts for the depth of the cut into the plane of the sketch. Change the view to the isometric view shown in Figure 8.21 by clicking the **Saved view list** button and **Default**. The arrow shows the direction that the cut will be extruded.

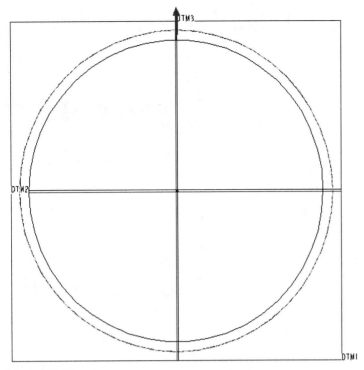

Figure 8.19.

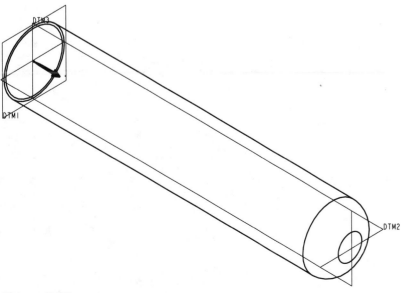

Figure 8.20.

Figure 8.21.

Now that you are sure what direction the cut will be extruded, create a blind cut of a specified depth of .4:

Blind | Done ⇒ **< enter .4 >**

Element	Info
CUT: Extrude	✕
Element	Info
Attributes	One Side
Section	Sk. plane - Surface DTM1 of feat #1 (DATUM PLANE)
MaterialSide	Outside of section
Direction	Defined
Depth	Blind, depth = 0.4

Define　　　　Refs　　　　Info
OK　　　　　Cancel　　　　Preview

Figure 8.22.

Double check the feature properties shown in Figure 8.22. Click **Preview** to see what the cut will look like. If there is a problem with the cut, click **Cancel** or double-click on one of the elements in the CUT:Extrude window to change that element. When satisfied:

OK ⇒ **Save**

Orient the handle as shown in Figure 8.23 using the Control (Crtl) key and the middle mouse button. Then display it with no hidden lines and no datum planes.

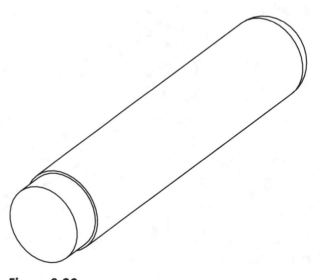

Figure 8.23.

By dimensioning as shown in Figure 8.18, the radius of the circle of the cut will be .030 inches less than the handle radius. If you change the outer diameter of the handle, the radius of the cut will still be .030 inches smaller. If you had instead dimensioned the diameter of the cut circle, changing the diameter of the handle would have no effect on the cut circle diameter. The key point is that you should consider the design intent when dimensioning features. For example, you might have a cap to fit over this end of the handle that is only available in one size. Therefore, you would want to assign a dimension to the diameter of the circle for the cut. Thus, any changes to the handle diameter would not have an effect on the diameter that the cap must fit over. In the case you specified in Figure 8.18, you assume that you will to use a cap that is .030 inches thick and is flush with the handle diameter.

8.4 CUTTING A RECTANGULAR SLOT

Next you will model the rectangular slot at the left end of the part shown in Figure 8.10. The arms that hold the cutting blade of the pizza cutter are inserted in this slot. The cross section of the finished handle is shown in Figure 8.24. The slot extends into the handle only to a specified depth, so it is a blind cut.

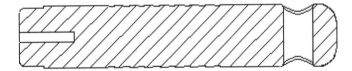

Figure 8.24.

We begin a slightly different approach to describing the commands that you will be implementing now. Up to this point, we have usually specified commands as lines of bold text separated from the description of the operations. But now that you have experience implementing several different commands, you do not need to be told every single command. From now on we will just tell you *what to do* for operations and commands that you have done before, rather than giving you step-by-step details of the commands. For instance, we may tell you to "draw a circle" instead of giving you the specific set of commands to draw the circle. This may seem a little more difficult at first. However, it helps you to learn Pro/ENGINEER more quickly. It also encourages you to understand the effect of the commands that you are implementing, rather than following "cookbook" instructions. For new or difficult commands we will still provide a separate line of text in bold that gives the exact commands to use.

Begin by turning on the datum planes and returning to the default isometric orientation. To model the rectangular hole at the left end of the handle, **Create** a **Solid Cut** feature that is **Extruded** on **One-Side** of the sketching plane. Select the same surfaces for the sketching plane and the orientation reference as were selected for the previous blind cut that reduced the diameter of the handle. In other words, use the datum plane on the left end of the handle (DTM1) in Figure 8.21 as the sketching plane. Be sure that the arrow shows the proper direction for the cut at the left end of the handle. Use **Flip**, if necessary. Then orient the yellow side of DTM2 to face the **Top** of the screen. The sketching plane should look like Figure 8.25 with the red side of DTM1

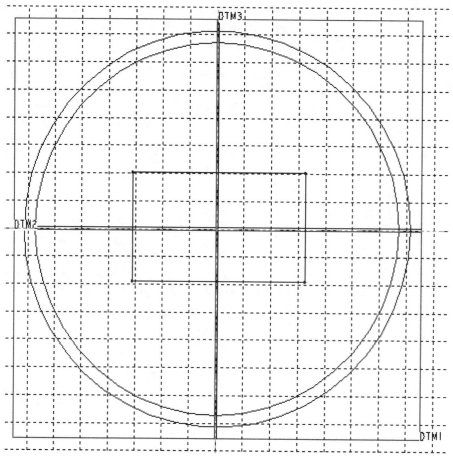

Figure 8.25.

being the sketching plane and the yellow side of DTM2 facing the **Top** of the screen. (If the sketching plane is not as shown in Figure 8.25, click **Cancel** in the Cut: Extrude window and start over.)

When **Sketch**ing the cut, instead of selecting **Circle** on the sketch menu, use the **Rectangle** option. Sketch the rectangle shown in Figure 8.25 by clicking on the sketch at one corner of the rectangle and then clicking at the diagonal corner.

Several schemes can be used to dimension the rectangular cut. One possibility is shown in Figure 8.26. Use **Dimension** to create the dimensions in Figure 8.26. To do this, select the top side of the rectangle and then select the horizontal axis. Middle-click to place the dimension, sd0. Repeat for the other dimensions.

After you set up this dimensioning scheme, **Delete** all of the dimensions, so that you can try another method. Another possibility for dimensioning is shown in Figure 8.27. Again, try creating this dimensioning scheme. Be sure to click on **Dimension** before beginning to add dimensions so that you do not delete the rectangle.

Clearly there are many other ways to dimension the slot cut. One of the quickest is the **Autodim** command. This is a quick way to dimension a sketch automatically by specifying datum planes to which the dimensions should be referenced. Before continuing, **Delete** the current dimensions. In the SKETCHER menu, select **Autodim**.

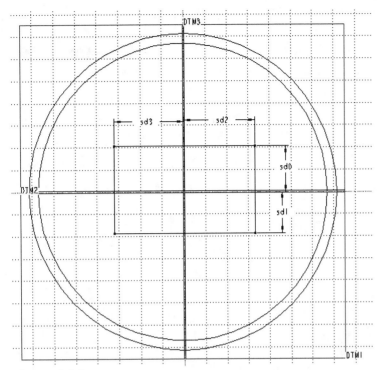

Figure 8.26.

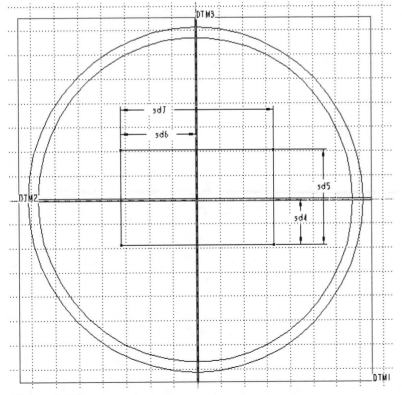

Figure 8.27.

Now you are prompted in the Message area as in Figure 8.28.

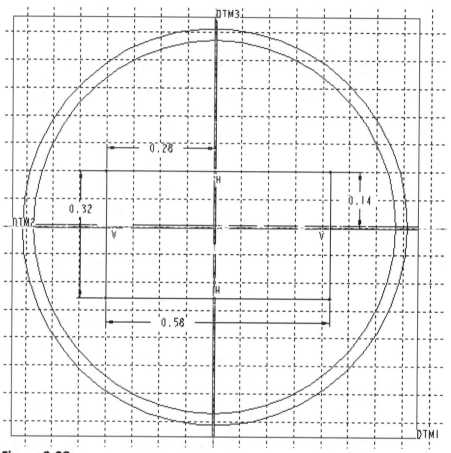

⇨ Select references to be used for locating the section.

Figure 8.28.

Select DTM2 and DTM3 as the references to which dimensions that are automatically generated will be related. Finish with **Done Sel** to indicate that you are done with the selections of references.

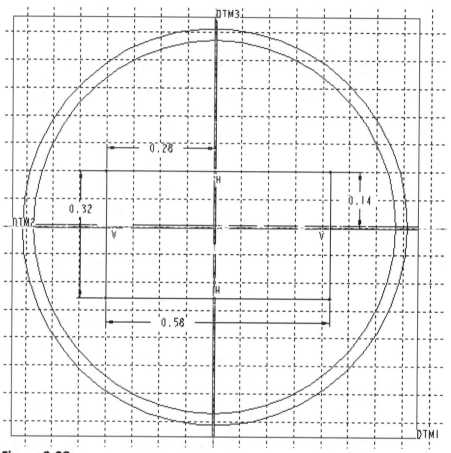

Figure 8.29.

Pro/ENGINEER automatically assigns dimensions necessary to create the sketch relative to the reference features that you specified (in this case, DTM2 and DTM3), as shown in Figure 8.29. The numbers and dimension locations in your sketch will probably be different.

The rectangle should be centered about the origin. This can be done using a **Relation**. To use a **Relation** in this case, it is best if the dimensions for the rectangle use the scheme shown in Figure 8.27 rather than that shown in Figure 8.26. If **Auto-dim** created any dimensions in the format shown in Figure 8.26, **Delete** those dimensions and use **Dimension** to match the format in Figure 8.27. Now **Relation** can be used to center the rectangle about the origin:

Relation ⇒ **Add**

Upon this operation, all of the numeric values for the dimensions change to alphanumeric parameters, similar to those shown in Figure 8.27, although the numerical part of the alphanumeric will probably be different. In addition, a text box appears in the Message area in which you can enter a relation. In this case, with reference to Figure 8.27, you want sd5 to be twice sd4. The equation is entered in the text box using the parameters on your screen, not sd4 and sd5:

> **< enter sd5=2 * sd4 (or equivalent using the parameters on your screen) >**
> ⇒ **< Enter (2 times) >**

This sets up a relation that sd5 is two times sd4. The first Enter (or click on the green checkmark) finishes the text line. The second Enter finishes the input operation. **Add** a second relation between the horizontal dimensions that appear on your screen corresponding to sd6 and sd7 in Figure 8.27.

Regenerate and **Modify** the dimensions of the part to those shown in Figure 8.30. Note that you can only change the dimensions that are the parent dimensions (.25 and .075). The other dimensions (.5 and .15) are dependent upon the parent dimensions and cannot be modified. If you try to modify a child dimension, a warning appears in the Message area above the Graphics window. If three digits past the decimal place are not shown, use **Sec Tools** ⇒ **Sec Environ** ⇒ **Num Digits** to change the number of digits.

Regenerate to have the sketch update to the latest values. You might want to move the dimensions using **Geom Tools** ⇒ **Move Entity** to make it look like Figure 8.30. Note the V next to the vertical lines and the H next to the horizontal lines. These letters indicate that Pro/ENGINEER has assumed that your design intent is to make the sides of the rectangle horizontal and vertical.

The most important factor to consider when dimensioning a sketch is the "design intent." For example, this rectangular slot is being created for another part to fit into. Therefore, you should dimension it independent of other features in the handle. You would not want to dimension the slot relative to the handle diameter because if the handle diameter changes, the geometry of the slot will change. Because the mating part will not change, the parts will not fit together properly. It is sometimes difficult to know the best dimensioning scheme when you first model a feature. However, remember that you can go back and modify the dimensions or dimensioning scheme of any feature later on.

When your sketch is dimensioned and regenerates properly, click **Done**. Be sure that the arrow points inward from the edge of the rectangle to indicate that the rectangle represents the material to be removed. Click **Flip** to change if necessary, then **Okay**. Change to the default isometric view to see which direction from the sketching plane that material will be removed. Make the **Blind** cut have a blind depth of .90 " (" is the same as inches). **Preview** and click **OK**. The cut will disappear at this point because the view is shown using no hidden lines.

The final step remaining to finish the left end of the handle is to create the small round visible in the view of the handle shown in Figure 8.31. Rotate the handle to the orientation shown in Figure 8.31 and turn off the datum planes. **Create** a **Simple Round** of **Constant** radius on the left end using the same steps as used to create the round on the right end in Section 8.2. Use **Edge Chain** to indicate that the round is along a series of edges. The radius of the round is .075 inches. Check to be sure that the round looks right using the **<u>Shading</u>** button to view the handle. Click **Ok** to finish.

If you make a mistake and the round does not look right, it can be deleted. Return to the **No Hidden** view, then

> **Delete** ⇒ **Normal** | **Select** | **Pick** ⇒ **< select the round >** ⇒ **Done**

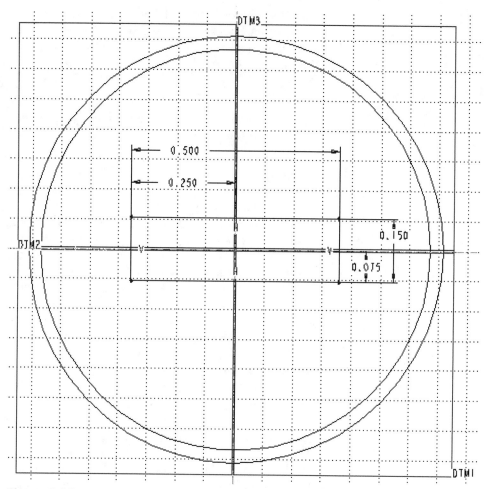

Figure 8.30.

Try this procedure to **Delete** the round that you just created. Then **Create** the **Round** again. The handle should now look like Figure 8.31. Rotate the part and use the different ways of viewing (hidden line or shading) to be sure that the rectangular slot and round look correct.

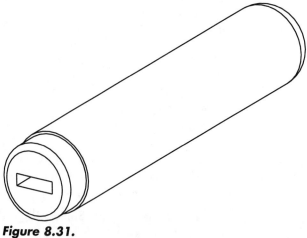

Figure 8.31.

8.5   CUTTING A CIRCULAR HOLE

The next feature to model is the hole at the right end of the handle. This is done by extruding a solid circular cut. Return to <u>**No Hidden**</u> view with the datum planes on and the handle in the default isometric orientation. To **Create** a **Solid Cut Feature** for the hole:

Create ⇒ Solid ⇒ Cut ⇒ Extrude | Solid | Done ⇒ Both Sides | Done

Note that you selected **Both Sides** for the attribute of the cut. This means that the cut will be extruded on both sides of the sketching plane. In this case the hole will be perpendicular to DTM2, so DTM2 will be the sketching plane. Because DTM2 is in the middle of the handle, the hole must be cut on **Both Sides** of it.

Select DTM2 for the sketching plane, because the hole is perpendicular to this plane. The message above the Graphics window indicates that in this case the arrow indicates the "direction of viewing the sketching plane," not the direction of feature creation. Because you are creating a cut on both sides of the sketching plane, there is no direction of feature creation to specify. When the arrow is as shown in Figure 8.32, the yellow side of DTM2 is the sketching plane. If necessary, **Flip** the arrow to the direction shown in Figure 8.32, then **Okay**.

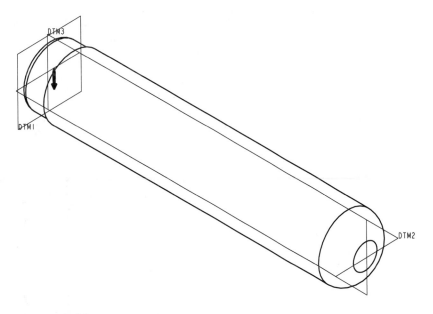

Figure 8.32.

Click **Top** and DTM1 to orient the yellow side of DTM1 toward the top of the screen to result in a sketching plane that looks like Figure 8.33.

Now you will sketch the circular hole. Instead of clicking on **Circle** in the GEOMETRY menu, you will use a mouse shortcut.

Be sure **Sketch** is selected on the SKETCHER menu and **Mouse Sketch** is selected in the GEOMETRY menu (as shown in Figure 8.34). In this mode, the middle mouse button or shift-left button on a two button mouse can be used to create circles using the **Center/Point** method. Position the cursor near the top of the handle where the center of the hole is to be. Click the middle mouse button and drag the cursor to create a circle that is changing size with the cursor movement. Move the size of the circle until it looks like Figure 8.35. Click the middle mouse button again to fix the size of the circle. Try to sketch the circle so that its center is close to DTM3, so that you can align the center of the circle to the axis of DTM3. If you do not like the circle you created, **Delete** it and sketch a new one.

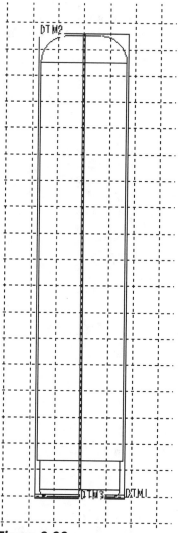

Figure 8.33.

Figure 8.34.

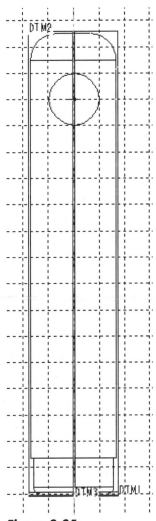

Figure 8.35.

Constrain the center of the circle by aligning it to DTM3 using **Alignment** and selecting the circle and the axis of DTM3. You will not notice any change, but when the sketch is regenerated the circle will be constrained so its center is on the vertical axis. Place the dimensions shown in Figure 8.36. Remember to click twice on the circle for a diameter dimension.

Regenerate the sketch. **Modify** the dimensions to the values in Figure 8.37 (0.5 and 4.6) and **Regenerate** again. Once the circle is sketched, dimensioned, and regenerated as shown in Figure 8.37, select **Done**.

If necessary, **Flip** the arrow that appears, so that material is removed on the inside of the circle. When the arrow points from the edge of the circle inward, click **Okay**. Change the view to the default isometric view.

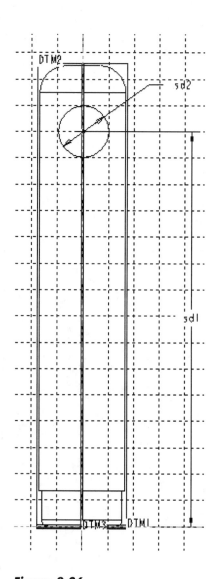

Figure 8.36.

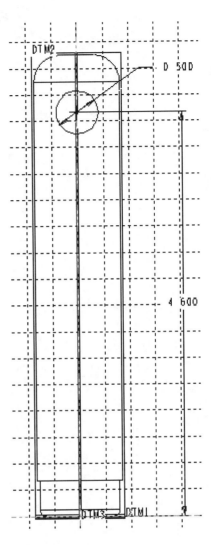

Figure 8.37.

Now specify the depth of the cut. The other features that you created were **One Side**, so you only needed to specify one depth for the cut. However, this feature has depth on **Both Sides** of the sketching plane, DTM2. The cut on two different sides of the sketching planes can have two different depths. For example, you can specify that one side of the cut should be .2 " deep, while the other side of the cut should be .4 " deep. Pro/ENGINEER will prompt you for the depths on each side and indicate the direction in which material is removed with the red arrow (as in Figure 8.38). For this hole feature, you want the cut to remove all the material on both sides of the sketching plane. Click **Thru Next | Done** so that material will be removed from above DTM2 in the direction of the arrow through to the next part surface

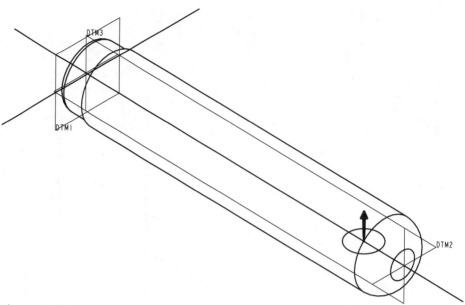

Figure 8.38.

Now the arrow flips as shown in Figure 8.39, indicating that material will be removed from the other side of DTM2. Click **Thru Next** | **Done** again for the depth in the direction below DTM2.

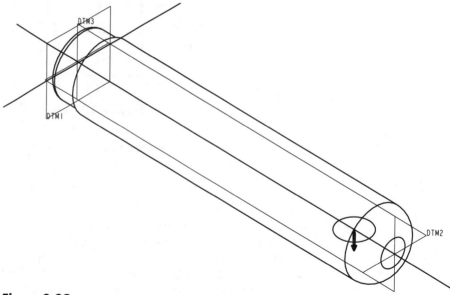

Figure 8.39.

Review the feature elements that you have created as shown in Figure 8.40. Note that there are two depths specified in the Depth element, because the cut is made on two sides of DTM2. Click **OK** when satisfied.

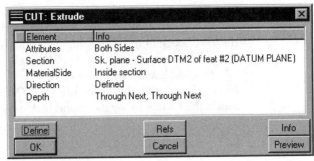

Figure 8.40.

The resulting cut should look like Figure 8.41. It is fun to shade the handle and spin it (CTRL and middle mouse button) to look through the hole that you just modeled.

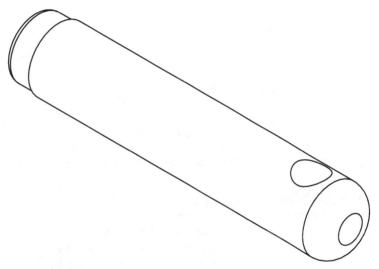

Figure 8.41.

Change the view to the default isometric and **Hidden Line** so that you can see both the top and bottom edge of the hole. Now **Create** a **Round Feature** using **Edge Chain** and **Tangent Chain**. You should round both the top and bottom edge of the hole at the same time. To do this, use **Query Sel** in the GET SELECT menu. This command allows you to select from a list of nearby features in the **Query Bin** and then **Accept** the desired feature. This is particularly useful if lines or curves are close together and difficult to **Pick** in the usual way. To select the upper edge of the hole:

Query Sel ⇒ < **select the top edge of the hole** >

Probably half of this edge will be highlighted. Because you used **Edge Chain**, the other half of the hole will also be selected. If an edge on the top of the hole is highlighted, click **Accept**. If not, click on the next item in the **Query Bin** list until the upper edge of the hole is highlighted. Then click **Accept**. The power of **Query Sel** is more evident when selecting the bottom edge of the hole:

Query Sel ⇒ < **select the bottom edge of the hole** >

When selecting the bottom edge it is easy to mistakenly select the round on the end of the handle or some other edge. In this case click items in the **Query Bin** until the lower edge of the hole is highlighted. Then click **Accept**. Now both the upper edge of the hole and the lower edge of the hole should be highlighted. Click **Done** to indicate that you have finished selecting edges for the round. Then type in the radius of .050 inches. Finish the round feature with **OK**. The handle should look like Figure 8.42. Shade the handle to see the round that you just created more easily.

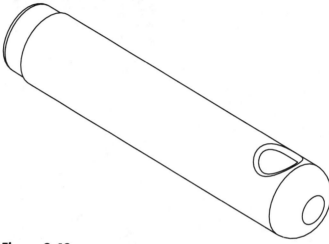

Figure 8.42.

It is wise to <u>**Save**</u> the part before continuing.

8.6 CREATING PATTERNED FEATURES

The last features of the handle to be modeled are the grooves shown in Figure 8.43. Although the grooves look like a lot of work, they can be created easily using a **Pattern** feature. To do this, you will create one feature that has the desired shape for one groove and then **Pattern** that feature seven more times to create the other grooves.

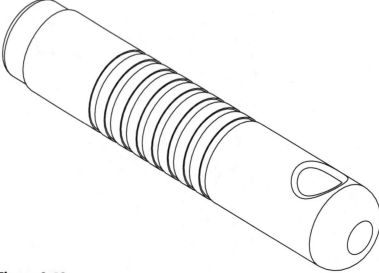

Figure 8.43.

All of the features that you have created so far have been Extruded features. This means that a sketched cross-section is extruded perpendicular to a plane for a specified depth. However, some types of geometry like these grooves are difficult to model as extruded features. Fortunately, there are other feature types available for you to use including:

Revolve
Sweep
Blend
Use Quilt
Advanced

You probably will not need **Blend**, **Use Quilt**, or **Advanced** until you are a more advanced Pro/ENGINEER user. Most basic solid geometries can be created with a combination of **Extrude**, **Revolve**, and **Sweep** features. (The **Sweep** feature is not covered in this tutorial. It permits the extrusion of a section along a user-defined trajectory rather than along a straight line as occurs with **Extrude**.)

The groove feature will be created using **Revolve**. A **Revolve** feature is similar to an **Extrude** feature in that a sketching plane is defined and a cross-section is sketched. However, in a **Revolve** feature the cross-section is revolved about an axis of revolution rather than extruded linearly.

To begin the groove feature, switch to <u>**No Hidden**</u> line and default view. Then turn on the axes and datum planes. You should see an axis that represents the intersection of DTM3 and DTM2 as shown in Figure 8.44. This axis and the one through the center of the hole were created automatically when you sketched a circle to model the cylindrical handle and the hole. The axis down the center of the handle will be used as the axis of revolution for the groove feature. This axis is labeled as A_2 in Figure 8.44. It may have a different number in your case.

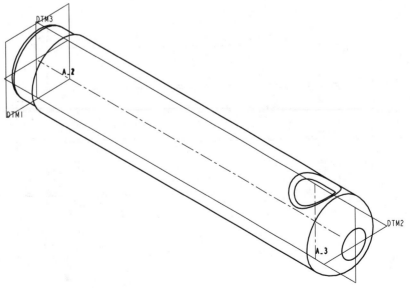

Figure 8.44.

To **Create** a **Revolved Solid Cut** extending on **Both Sides** of the sketch plane:

Create ⇒ **Solid** ⇒ **Cut** ⇒ **Revolve** | **Solid** | **Done** ⇒ **Both Sides** | **Done**

Note that the commands are very similar to those used to **Extrude** a cut feature, except that **Revolve** is substituted for **Extrude**.

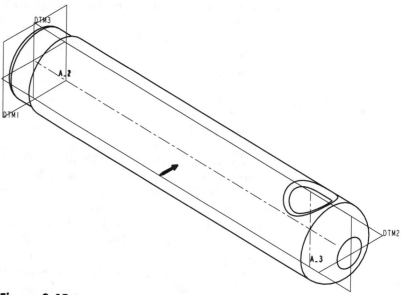

Figure 8.45.

The sketching plane must be a plane in which the cross-section of the cut can be drawn. In this case either DTM2 or DTM3 could be used as the sketch plane. Select DTM3 as the sketching plane with the arrow as shown in Figure 8.45. In this way you view the yellow side of DTM3, as noted in the Message area above the Graphics window. Orient the yellow side of DTM2 so it faces the **Top** of the Graphics window to result in the sketching plane in Figure 8.46.

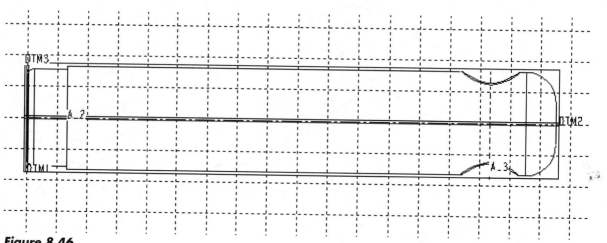

Figure 8.46.

In a **Revolve** feature, a cross-section is sketched and revolved about an axis of revolution to create the feature. Therefore, in the sketch you need to model a cross-section of one groove and define an axis about which to revolve the cross-section.

Zoom in to the left end of the handle using the **Zoom In** Tool bar button to obtain a close up of the sketch plane as shown in Figure 8.47. Click the middle mouse button to end the zoom.

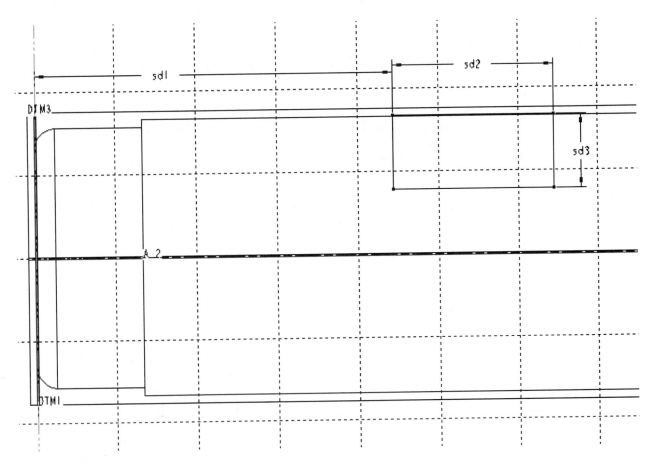

Figure 8.47.

Sketch the rectangular cross-section of the groove using **Sketch ⇒ Rectangle**. Try to have the top edge of the rectangle coincide with the top edge of the handle as shown in Figure 8.47. The groove can be sketched much larger than its actual size, because adding dimensions will constrain it to the proper size. Use **Alignment** to align the top edge of the rectangle to the surface of the handle. Be sure that "-ALIGNED-" appears in the Message area above the Graphics window. **Dimension** the groove as shown in Figure 8.47. The long dimension is from the left end of the handle to the left side of the rectangle.

Now you need to specify an axis of revolution for the groove. In this case, you will **Sketch** a **Horizontal Centerline** to be used as the axis of revolution:

> **Sketch ⇒ Line ⇒ Centerline | Horizontal ⇒ < select a point on the axis down the centerline of the handle >**

When you select **Horizontal** you only have to click once to place a line, because you already defined the line as horizontal. Selecting a single point on the axis down the centerline of the handle places the horizontal axis of revolution as close as possible to the axis of the handle. You may need to **Refit the model to the screen** to see this centerline extending past the ends of the handle. This centerline is the axis of revolution for the sketched rectangle.

After you have placed the horizontal centerline, align it to DTM2 using **Alignment**. Using **Alignment** can be quite tricky. The entities to be aligned must be close enough together so that Pro/ENGINEER accepts them to be aligned. Two methods may work to align the new centerline with DTM2. In the first method, <u>**Zoom In**</u> and use **Query Sel** ⇒ < **select line** > ⇒ **Accept** to be sure that you select the right lines and datum planes. Check the Message area above the Graphics window to be sure that the entities are aligned. If a message "Entities cannot be aligned" appears, use **Geom Tools** ⇒ **Move Entity** to move the new centerline closer to DTM2. Then align using **Query Sel** again. Check the message area for the "-ALIGNED-" response to indicate that the entities have been properly aligned. A second method to align the new centerline to DTM2 is to <u>**Refit the model to the screen**</u>. Now select the centerline on the screen where the centerline is easily visible extending past the ends of the handle. Next < **select DTM2** > either on the screen or (more easily) in the Model Tree window. Again it may be necessary to use **Geom Tools** ⇒ **Move Entity** to move the new centerline closer to DTM2, if they are not close enough initially.

Regenerate the sketch and **Modify** the dimensions to match Figure 8.48. The 1.450 inch dimension is from the left end of the handle. The rectangle is 0.1" by 0.015". **Regenerate** and click **Done**.

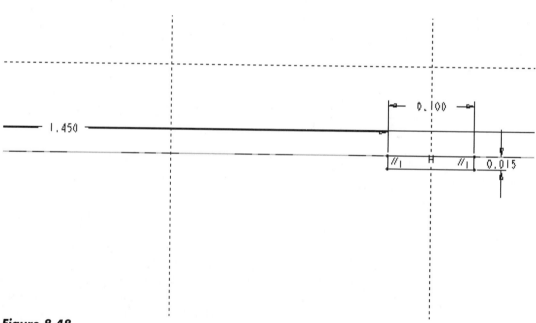

Figure 8.48.

Use <u>**Zoom In**</u> to see the sketched cross-section of the groove to be sure that the arrow properly reflects the material to be removed. **Flip**, if necessary, and click **Okay**. Define the revolve angle to **360** degrees to remove material all around the circumference of the handle. Click **Done**. Return to the default isometric view and click **Preview** in the CUT: Revolve dialog box. If the cut looks correct, click **OK**. The result should look like Figure 8.49.

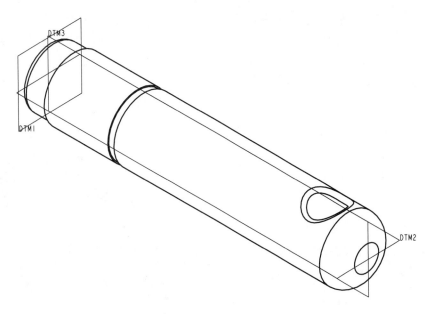

Figure 8.49.

You have created a single groove feature in the handle. To model the rest of the grooves, you will **Pattern** this feature. A **Pattern** is used to create multiple copies of a single feature. There are eight grooves in the handle, so you will need to **Pattern** this feature seven more times. To **Pattern** this feature:

Pattern ⇒ Select ⇒ Query Sel

Return to the default view, **<u>No Hidden</u>** line, and turn off the datum planes and axes. Use **Query Sel** to be sure to select the groove and not some other feature of the handle. Select the groove by clicking on it. If it is highlighted, click **Accept ⇒ General | Done**.

The dimensions that you used to create the first groove will appear as shown in Figure 8.50. In the Message area above the Graphics window, Pro/ENGINEER asks you to select pattern dimensions in the first direction. In other words, specify which dimension will be changed to create the desired pattern. In this case, you want a series of grooves spaced along the axis of the handle. The next groove will be further from the left end than the groove that is shown, so the 1.450 inch dimension will be changed to create the remaining grooves. Thus, select the 1.450 dimension in the Graphics window. Now Pro/ENGINEER asks you to specify a dimension increment, as shown in Figure 8.51. In other words, how much should this 1.450 dimension be changed to create the desired pattern. In this example, the dimension increment is the distance from groove to groove. Enter .25 for this value.

Now Pro/ENGINEER asks you to select another dimension for First direction or select **Done**. Select **Done**. If you had wanted to vary the pattern with more than one variable, you would select another dimension. For example, you could have a groove with equal spacing of .25 inches apart, but with the depth of the groove changing by a value of .010 with each groove.

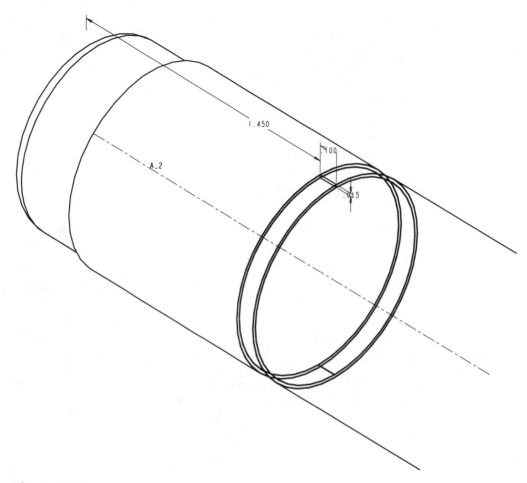

Figure 8.50.

Figure 8.51.

Finally, Pro/ENGINEER prompts you to enter the total number of instances of the feature in this direction. The handle should have eight grooves in all, so enter "8" in the text window shown in Figure 8.52.

Figure 8.52.

To complete the creation of the pattern, click **Done**. The handle now has eight identical groove features as shown in Figure 8.53.

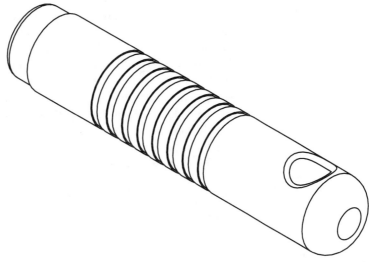

Figure 8.53.

Congratulations! You have completed modeling a very complicated part and learned some of the most important steps for creating features in Pro/ENGINEER. **Save** the part file now. Shade and rotate the part to see what it looks like. Close the handle window using the ***Close*** command in the ***Window*** menu at the top of the screen.

KEY TERMS

Constraint-based modeling
Design intent
Detail feature

Model Tree
Parent-child relation
Pattern

Relation
Revolve
Solid feature

Problems

1. Model a 12-inch long, 1-inch diameter broomstick as an extruded circle. Make one end flat and the other end with a 0.25 inch radius round.

2. Make a copy of the handle modeled in this chapter and save it as "handle2." Open "handle2" and delete the grooves by selecting Delete in the Menu Manager and clicking on the grooves. Recreate the groove feature but add .015-inch rounds on the inside corners of the grooves. Repeat the pattern to create 10 grooves with the same spacing as in the original handle.

3. Make a copy of the handle modeled in this chapter and save it as "handle3." For this copy, delete the rectangular hole by selecting Delete in the Menu Manager and clicking on the hole. Then create a solid circular cut with a diameter of .75 inches and a depth of 5.125 inches to hollow out the handle. Add a round at the end of the cut to make the wall thickness at the rounded end constant.

9

Creating More Parts

OVERVIEW

Pro/ENGINEER allows the modeling of parts in several different ways. In this chapter you will model the sheet metal parts of the pizza cutter, such as the arm and cap, as Thin sections, both Extruded and Revolved. The Revolve capability will be used to create axisymmetric parts including the cap, rivet, and blade, both Solid and Thin. The Mirror feature will be used to reflect a symmetric section about the axis of symmetry. The Intent Manager will be introduced to enhance sketching capabilities in the sketcher mode.

9.1   THIN EXTRUDE FEATURES—THE ARM

Six individual parts are needed for the pizza cutter. The guard and handle were completed in the last two chapters. You will now model the other parts of the pizza cutter beginning with the arm shown in Figure 9.1. The arm connects the handle to the blade of the pizza cutter. Because this sheet metal part has a constant thickness, it is modeled using a **Thin** extrusion. Although the basic Pro/ENGI-NEER system works quite well to model simple sheet metal parts, Pro/ENGINEER also has a sheet metal module that is specifically designed to model sheet metal parts. Discussion of this module (and the many other modules that are available) is beyond the scope of this book.

SECTIONS

OBJECTIVES

After working through this tutorial chapter, you should be able to:

- Extrude thin sections
- Revolve thin sections
- Add cuts to thin parts
- Add rounds and fillets to thin parts
- Sketch arcs
- Revolve solid sections
- Mirror sketch entities about an axis of symmetry
- Trim lines in sketches
- Use the Intent Manager

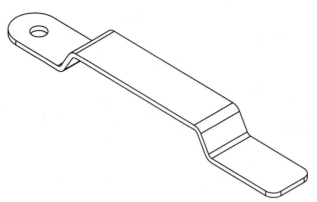

Figure 9.1.

To begin, start Pro/ENGINEER and open the arm part file. (Be sure that *File* ⇒ *Working Directory* is properly set to the working directory that you are using; *Utilities* ⇒ *Environment* is set to **Spin Center** off, **No Hidden**, and **Isometric**; and *Utilities* ⇒ *Customize Screen* ⇒ **Options** ⇒ **Default Tree settings** is properly set.) To open the arm file, use the **Open** button (an open folder) near the left end of the Tool bar.

Open ⇒ < select arm.prt > ⇒ < click on Open >

Be sure that the datum planes are turned on. The arm consists of only the three datum plane features and a coordinate system at this point. To begin, **Create** a **Thin**, **Solid Protrusion**.

Feature ⇒ **Create** ⇒ **Solid** ⇒ **Protrusion** ⇒ **Extrude | Thin | Done** ⇒ **Both Sides | Done** ⇒ < select DTM3 > ⇒ **Okay** ⇒ **Top | < select DTM2 >**

A **Thin**, **Extrude** is being used because the part has a constant thickness. The **Thin** option allows you to specify the thickness once. **Both Sides** indicates that the part will be extruded from both sides of the sketching plane so that it is symmetric about the sketching plane. The choice of the yellow side of DTM3 as the sketch plane is somewhat arbitrary. Use DTM3 in this case so that when the arm is assembled into the rectangular slot at the end of the handle, DTM3 of the handle and DTM3 of the arm are coplanar. This choice is not necessary, but it will make the assembly of the parts easier later on.

Ensure that the screen matches Figure 9.2. DTM3 will be parallel to the screen with its yellow side toward you. The yellow side of DTM2 will be facing upward. If this is not the case, click **Cancel** in the PROTRUSION: Extrude window and start over.

Turn off the axes, datum points (not datum planes), and coordinate system display because they are not needed for this part. Also turn off the Intent Manager, if it is on.

Begin by sketching the overall shape of the edge of the arm, including the two bends.

Sketch ⇒ **Mouse Sketch**

Sketch the five line segments in Figure 9.3. Click the left mouse button at the leftmost point and proceed by clicking the left mouse button at each bend. Note that the line segments at either end of the part coincide with DTM2. Try to get these line segments close to DTM2, so that you can align them to DTM2 later on. Otherwise, you do not have to be exact in the sketch, just get close. After you click on the rightmost point, click the middle mouse button to end the sketch.

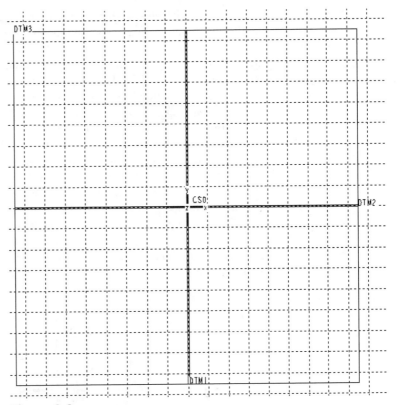

Figure 9.2.

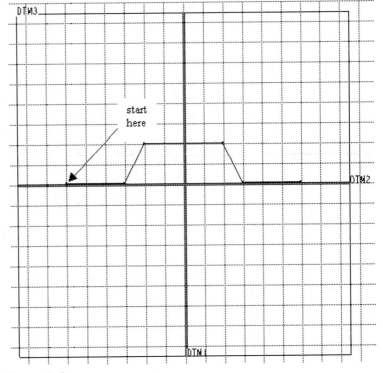

Figure 9.3.

Unlike solid features, thin features do not require closed loop sections. Recall from the handle model that every solid section that was created required that the sketch be "closed," meaning that there were no endpoints. For example, you created a complete circle in the sketch for the handle shaft and a closed rectangle for the groove. With a thin feature, Pro/ENGINEER adds a thickness to the lines that outline the edge of the part. A closed section is not required.

Now using the same techniques you learned with the guard and handle, dimension and align the part per Figure 9.4 using the **Dimension** and **Alignment** commands. Either **Dimension**ing or **Alignment** can be done first. The numeric portion of the alphanumeric parameters may be different from Figure 9.4 depending on what order you dimension and align items. Dimensions sd0, sd2, and sd4 can be added in two ways. Either click on each end of the line segment and place the dimension, or click on the middle of line segment and place the dimension. Try it both ways. The angles sd1 and sd3 are dimensioned by clicking on both line segments that form the angle and then placing the angle dimension. An explicit dimension to locate the section vertically with respect to DTM2 is not needed. Instead, align the two lower horizontal legs to DTM2. This tells Pro/ENGINEER exactly where the part is located vertically. The dimension sd6 in Figure 9.4 locates the section the horizontally.

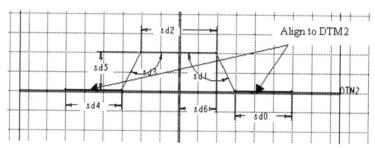

Figure 9.4.

Regenerate the sketch and check the Message area above the Graphics window to see that the regeneration was successful. Ignore the warning that open ends are not aligned. (If this were a **Solid** extrusion, the ends of the lines would need to meet to form a closed section. But this is not necessary for a **Thin** extrusion.) **Modify** the dimensions per Figure 9.5. After a dimension is modified, it will change color. This helps ensure that you **Modify** all dimensions before regenerating. As you can see, we are ensuring that DTM1 remains in the center of the section by making that dimension half of the length of the top line. **Regenerate** the sketch after changing all of the dimensions.

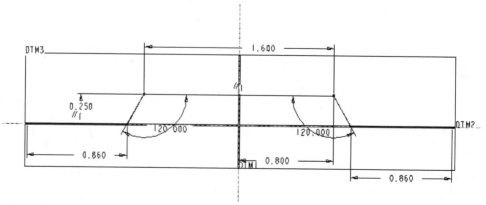

Figure 9.5.

You may want to move the dimensions so they show up more clearly. This is done by **Geom Tools** ⇒ **Move Entity**. Click **Done** to finish the sketch. The red arrow indicates the side of the line segments that you sketched to which the thickness will be added. Be sure the arrow is pointing up as in Figure 9.6, so that the material is added to the top of the lines that you sketched. If arrow is pointing up, click **Okay**; otherwise, **Flip** | **Okay**.

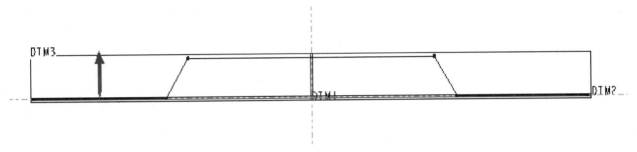

Figure 9.6.

< **Enter .05** > for the width of the thin feature to make the arm .050 inches thick, a standard thickness for stainless steel sheet metal.

Now you will be prompted for a depth of the arm. The depth refers to the amount of material added into the plane of the screen, thus making the section three dimensional. Specify a blind depth of .5" :

Blind | **Done** ⇒ < enter .5 >

Now, click **OK** in the PROTRUSION: Extrude dialog box to complete the feature. Figure 9.7 shows the result. Use **Saved view list** ⇒ **Default** to see the isometric view of the arm. Notice that DTM3 bisects the part. This is a result of selecting the **Both Sides** option in the initial **Protrusion** command.

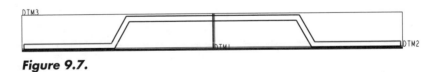

Figure 9.7.

You will now create the circular cut (hole) that the rivet goes through to hold the blade. This hole will be made on the upper surface shown in Figure 9.8. This is a **Solid Cut** that is **Extrude**d from **One Side** of the sketching plane.

Create ⇒ **Solid** ⇒ **Cut** ⇒ **Extrude** | **Solid** | **Done** ⇒ **One Side** | **Done**

Use **Query Sel** to select the upper surface indicated in Figure 9.8 as the sketch plane. Be sure that DTM3 or the lower surface are not selected. You need to remove material from the top surface into the part, so be sure that the arrow for direction of feature creation points downward toward the part before clicking **Okay**. In this case the yellow side of DTM1 should face the **Bottom** of the screen, so

Bottom | < select DTM1 >

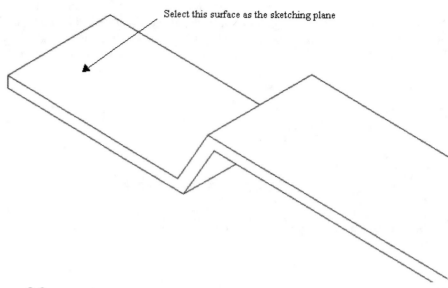

Select this surface as the sketching plane

Figure 9.8.

The sketcher view should look like Figure 9.9.

Figure 9.9.

To create a hole, sketch a circle near the top of the arm so that its center is near the DTM3 axis as shown in Figure 9.10.

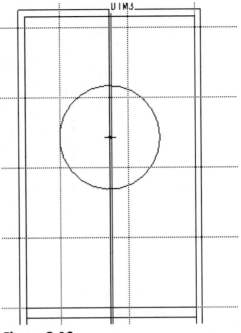

Figure 9.10.

Dimension the circle per Figure 9.11. Use the **Alignment** command to align the center of the circle to DTM3. If you are having trouble using the Alignment command, it is probably because the features are not close enough for Pro/ENGINEER to align them. You can use the **Geom Tools** ⇒ **Move Entity** command to move the center of the circle closer to DTM3.

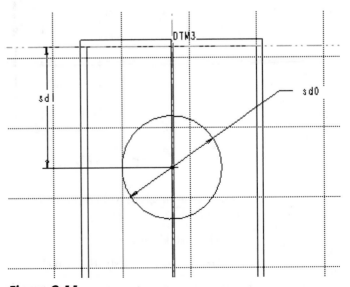

Figure 9.11.

Regenerate and then **Modify** the dimensions to match Figure 9.12. Note that .17 is the diameter of the circle. If you only clicked once on the circle when dimensioning, you dimensioned the radius of the circle. This is okay; just use .085 for the radius.

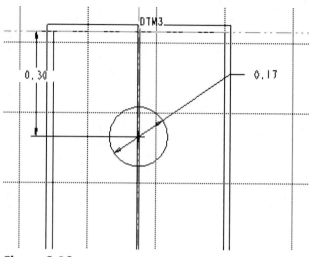

Figure 9.12.

Regenerate | Done

Click **Okay** if the arrow is pointing from the edge of the circle toward the center of the circle as in Figure 9.13, in order to remove material inside the circle.

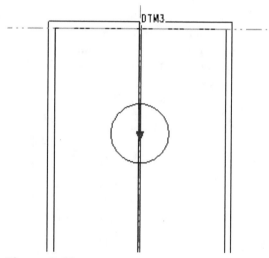

Figure 9.13.

Because this hole will go through the entire thickness of the arm, use the **Thru All** for the depth.

Thru All | Done

OK (in the CUT: Extrude dialog box)

The isometric view of the arm should look like Figure 9.14.

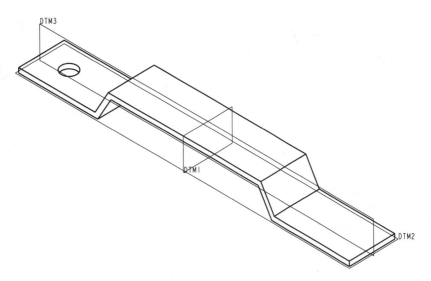

Figure 9.14.

You will now create the rounds of the arm. It has four sets of rounds (see Figure 9.1). The first round is a full round at the end of the part with the hole. The next two sets of rounds curve the bends in the metal, so the part will appear more like a real part fabricated from sheet metal. Recall that for the guard the rounded bends were modeled using a **Fillet** in the sketch before the part was extruded. In this case, you will **Round** each bend after the part is extruded. In most cases the **Fillet** method used for the guard is faster and more representative of how a real sheet metal part is bent. But you will use rounds as an alternative here. The final set of rounds are two small rounds on the corners at the end of the arm opposite the hole.

Begin with the full round near the end with a hole. Turn off the datum planes, turn on **<u>Hidden Line</u>**, spin the part, and **<u>Zoom In</u>** to help you select the correct surfaces shown in Figure 9.15. Remember to click the middle mouse button to end the zoom.

> **Create** ⇒ **Solid** ⇒ **Round** ⇒ **Simple | Done** ⇒ **Full Round | Surf-Surf | Done**

A **Full Round** creates a round that completely removes a part surface, in this case the end of the arm. The **Surf-Surf** option indicates that the round is created between two selected surfaces. The bounding surfaces are the side edges of the arm. The surface to remove is the end edge of the arm. It is quite helpful to read the information in the Message area above the Graphics window as you choose each surface. Initially, the Message area indicates "Select first surface reference for round/fillet." **Query Sel**ect the first bounding surface indicated in Figure 9.15. Next, the Message area indicates "Select second surface reference for round/fillet." **Query Sel**ect the Second bounding surface shown in Figure 9.15. Finally, the Message area indicates "Select a surface to be replaced by a round." **Query Sel**ect the surface to remove indicated in Figure 9.15. This surface is completely replaced by the round.

Click **OK** from the ROUND dialog box to finish the round, as shown in Figure 9.16. Because the round is bounded by two surfaces, it is not necessary to define a radius for the round.

Now create the second set of rounds for the bends in the arm. Return to the default isometric view, be sure that **<u>Hidden Line</u>**s are visible, and use **<u>Refit the model</u>**

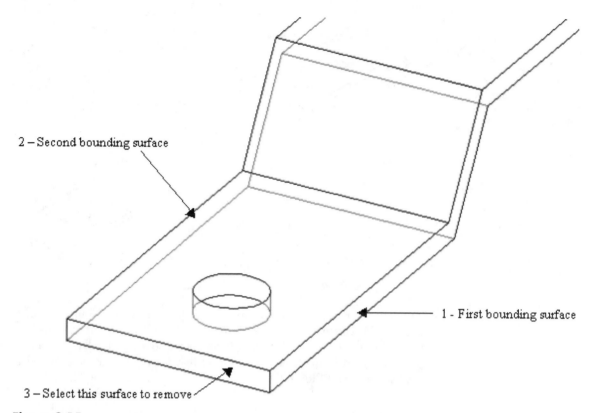

2 – Second bounding surface

1 - First bounding surface

3 – Select this surface to remove

Figure 9.15.

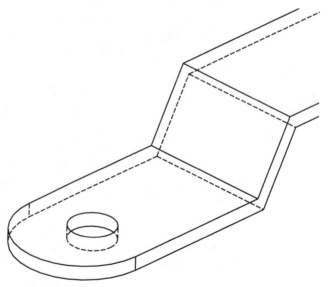

Figure 9.16.

to the screen followed by **Zoom In** to have the model appear as in Figure 9.17. To create **Simple Rounds** for the edges that are selected **One By One**:

> **Create** $\Rightarrow$ **Solid** $\Rightarrow$ **Round** $\Rightarrow$ **Simple | Done** $\Rightarrow$ **Constant | Edge Chain |**
> **Done** $\Rightarrow$ **One By One** $\Rightarrow$ < **Query Sel the four lines indicated in**
> **Figure 9.17; these lines are the " outside " edges of the four bends** >

If you accidentally select the wrong line, use the **Unselect** option to correct the error.

Done ⇒ < **enter .1 for the radius of all four rounds** > ⇒ **OK** (in the ROUND dialog box)

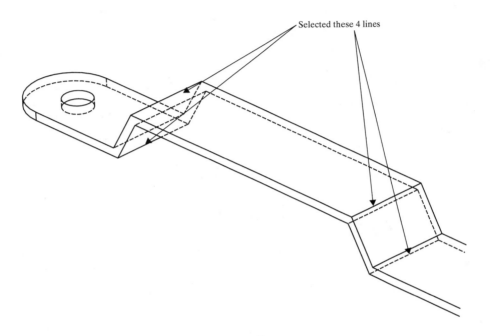

Selected these 4 lines

Figure 9.17.

The result should match Figure 9.18.

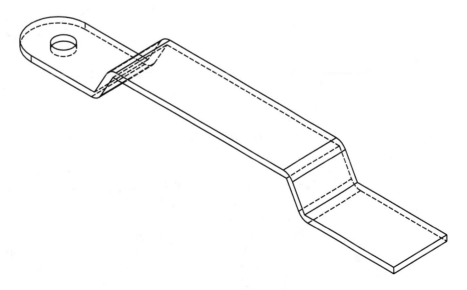

Figure 9.18.

Now add the corresponding rounds to the "inside" edges of the four bends, opposite the edges just rounded. Repeat the steps to create rounds, except select the inside edges shown in Figure 9.19. < **Enter .05** > for the radius.

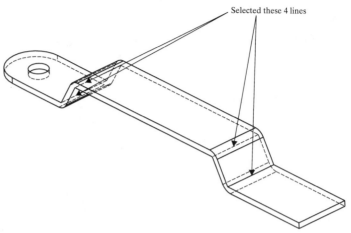

Selected these 4 lines

Figure 9.19.

Upon clicking **OK**, the arm should look identical to Figure 9.20. It helps to shade the part and spin it to be sure that you have rounded both sides of all four bends. Return to the default isometric, hidden line view.

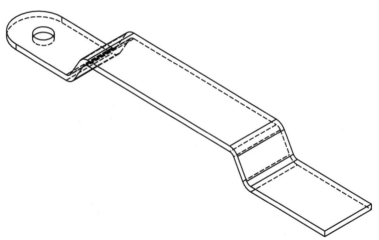

Figure 9.20.

Finally, repeat the commands to create rounds at the corners on the end of the arm opposite the hole. This time use **Edge Chain** and **One By One** to round the selected edges indicated in Figure 9.21. Use a radius of .1 to round these corners. The result should look like Figure 9.22.

It would have been possible to combine the rounds for the outside edges of the bends and for the right end of the arm, because they all have the same radius of .1" . However, you created these rounds separately, so that they could later be modified separately, if necessary.

Congratulations! You have finished the third part of the pizza cutter. **<u>Save</u>** the arm, and ***Close*** the arm.prt ***Window***.

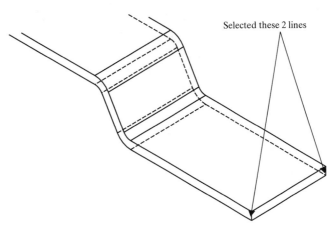

Figure 9.21.

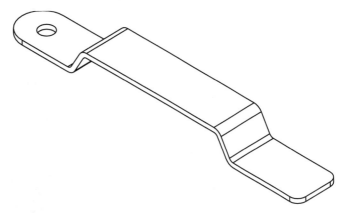

Figure 9.22.

9.2 SOLID REVOLVE FEATURES WITH ARCS—THE RIVET

The first three parts have demonstrated the use of the **Extrude** (**Thin** and **Solid**) option of the **Protrusion** command as well as numerous **Cut**s and **Round**s. The next three parts will all take advantage of the **Revolve** option of the **Protrusion** command. The first part that you will model using the **Revolve** option is the rivet shown in Figure 9.23. The rivet will be modeled to look like it would after it has been deformed to fasten the cutting blade to the arms.

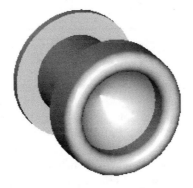

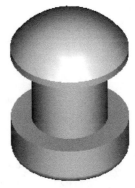

Figure 9.23.

The rivet looks complicated in the 3D views. By viewing its cross-section in Figure 9.24, its shape is much more obvious. In the planning stages of part design, imagining the cross-section of a part often allows the modeling of a complex part using simple geometries. A simpler cross-section results if you initially ignore the round at the bottom of the rivet as shown in Figure 9.25.

Figure 9.24.

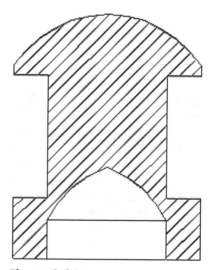

Figure 9.25.

The rivet is symmetric about a vertical axis. Taking advantage of this symmetry makes it much simpler to model the part in Pro/ENGINEER. The section in Figure 9.26 can be revolved about a vertical axis to create the rivet. Adding the round at the bottom of the rivet completes the part using only two features (a **Revolve**d section and a **Round**). You could create the bottom round before the revolve, thereby modeling this part with a single feature; however, the section sketch to be revolved is already quite complex. Therefore, you will add the round after revolving the section.

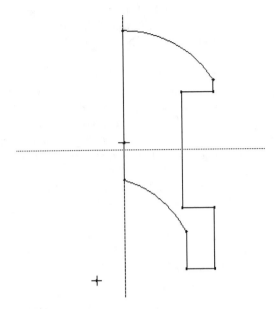

Figure 9.26.

To start, **Open** the rivet part file. Model the rivet as a **Solid Revolve Protrusion** extending from **Both Sides** of the sketch plane. Set up the yellow side of DTM3 as the sketching plane as shown in Figure 9.27 with the yellow side of DTM2 toward the **Top** of the screen. The setup of the sketching plane is arbitrary, but you should set it up as indicated to be consistent with later sections of the tutorial.

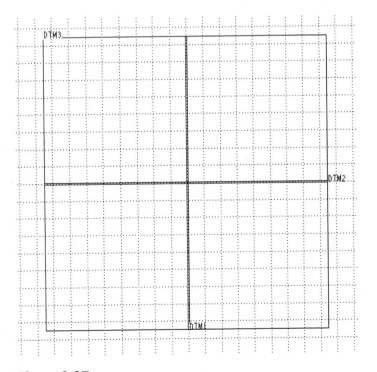

Figure 9.27.

Use the **Line** command to sketch the shape shown in Figure 9.28. This works like the **Mouse Sketch** command except that by setting the line to either **Horizontal** or **Vertical** all of the lines will be parallel to the grid.

Sketch ⇒ **Line** ⇒ **Geometry | Vertical**

Click a **Vertical** line on top of DTM1 starting as shown in Figure 9.28. After the second click with the left mouse button at the top of the line, Pro/ENGINEER automatically toggles to a **Horizontal** line. This **Vertical/Horizontal** toggling continues until you click the middle mouse button to end the **Line** command. After the vertical line along DTM1 add nine more line segments working clockwise around the shape as shown in Figure 9.28. Do not worry if the ending point does not meet exactly with the starting point. Just be sure that the last horizontal line crosses the first vertical line.

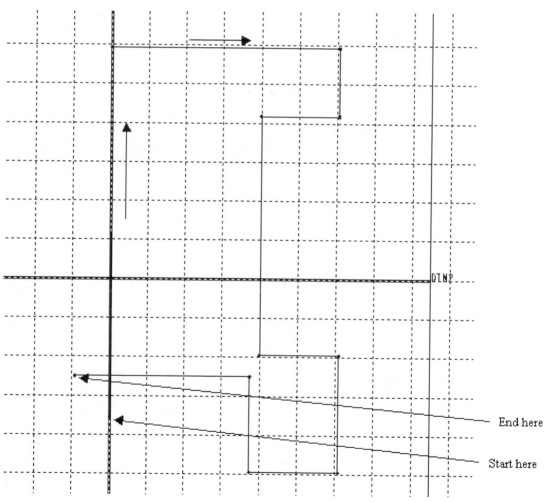

Figure 9.28.

Turn off the datum planes so that the sketch resembles Figure 9.29. You will now **Trim** the line segments so that the starting and ending points join. The **Trim Corner** command will create a clean corner between two intersecting lines.

Geom Tools ⇒ **Trim** ⇒ **Corner** ⇒ < select line 1 > | < select line 2 >

Select the line where the arrows in Figure 9.29 are pointing. Where you click on the line is IMPORTANT. Click on the side of each line that you want to keep.

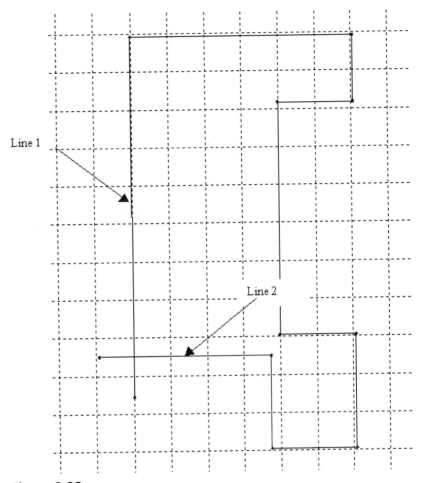

Figure 9.29.

Figure 9.30 shows the result of the **Trim** ⇒ **Corner**.

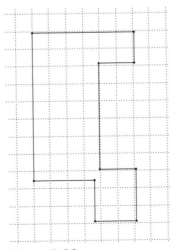

Figure 9.30.

Now you will add the arcs to the sketch to form the curved surfaces of the rivet. You used the **Arc ⇒ Fillet** earlier to create a tangent arc between two lines. This time **Sketch** the **Arc** explicitly by defining **3 Point**s on the arc. Use Figure 9.31 as a guide. Make Point 1 just to the left of the vertical line so that the vertical line and the arc intersect. Likewise make Point 2 just to the right of the vertical line. You will **Trim** the intersection shortly. The crosses that appear on the figure indicate the centers of the arcs. The upper cross corresponds to the upper arc and the lower cross corresponds to the lower arc.

> **Sketch ⇒ Arc ⇒ 3 Point ⇒** < **select Point 1** > (Start point of arc) | < **select Point 2** > (End point of arc) | < **Move the mouse and click a third time when the arc and location of the arc center look similar to Figure 9.31 to define the curvature of the arc** >

Repeat the **3 Point Arc** command but select Points 3 and 4.

Now the sketch needs to be cleaned up by deleting two lines and trimming the arcs. First **Delete** the line segments indicated in Figure 9.32.

Delete ⇒ < **select Line 1** > | < **select Line 2** >

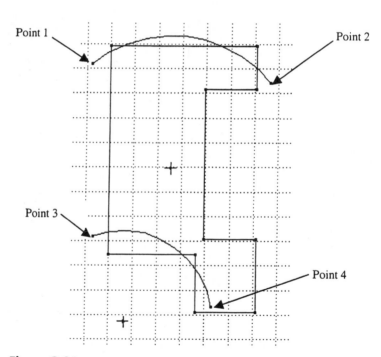

Figure 9.31.

The result should look like Figure 9.33. Now trim the intersections of the arcs and line segments using **Geom Tools ⇒ Trim**. Select Points 1 and 2 to trim the corner between the upper arc and the leftmost vertical line. Then trim at Points 3 and 4, 5 and 6, and 7 and 8. Remember to select the part of the line segment that is to be retained. If you accidentally trim a section that you did not want to trim, use the **Untrim Last** command to undo the selection.

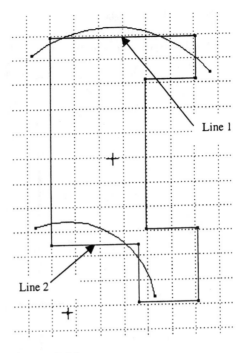

Line 1

Line 2

Figure 9.32.

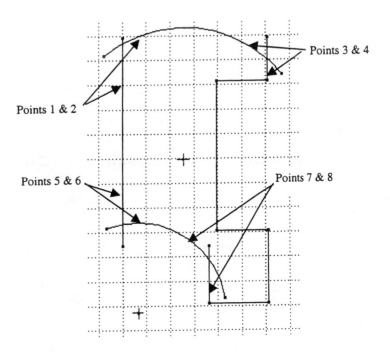

Points 3 & 4

Points 1 & 2

Points 5 & 6

Points 7 & 8

Figure 9.33.

Turn the datum planes on. The resulting section should resemble Figure 9.34. A **Revolve** feature needs an axis of revolution to revolve the section about. Sketch a vertical centerline coinciding with DTM1:

Sketch ⇒ Line ⇒ Centerline | Vertical ⇒ < click on DTM1 >

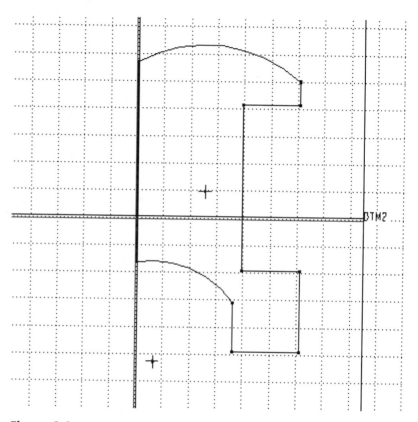

Figure 9.34.

A vertical dashed (or dotted) line will display on top of DTM1. Turn off the datum planes to see the centerline more clearly. It may also help to toggle off the grid using the **Toggle the grid on/off** button at the right end of the Tool bar (blue button showing a grid). Pro/ENGINEER needs to know to where the centerline is located, so use **Alignment** to align the centerline to DTM1 as in Figure 9.35. It is easiest to align the centerline by selecting it first (at either end of it) and then selecting DTM1 in the Model Tree window. (You may need to display the Model Tree window by clicking on the Model Tree button at the bottom of the screen.) Check the Message area above the Graphics window to be sure that the alignment occurred.

Dimension/Align the rest of the sketch per Figure 9.36. Recall that the numeric part of the alphanumeric variables for the dimensions depend on the order in which you dimension and align items, so your variables may be different from Figure 9.36. Dimensions sd8, sd9, sd10, and sd11 dimension the diameter of the revolved section with respect to the axis of revolution, which is the centerline that you just created. A special technique using an extra mouse click is used to dimension diameters of a revolved section. To create this type of diameter dimension, first click on the edge that you wish to dimension (Point 1), then click on the centerline (Point 2 on the centerline, NOT on

DTM1), *then click back on the original entity* (Point 1), and place the dimension with the middle mouse button. When the dimension is created, a vertical line on the left end of the dimension indicates the position of the specified diameter for the revolved section that is not yet shown. Be sure that you include all 13 dimensions. **Align** the left side of the sketched section with DTM1. Here again it is easiest to select the left side of the sketch in the graphics window and then select DTM1 in the Model Tree window.

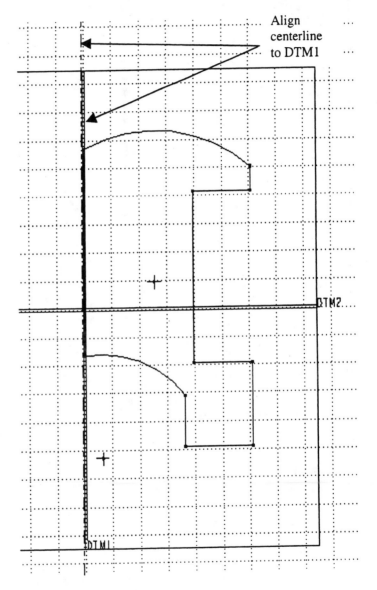

Figure 9.35.

Note that the upper arc was defined by fixing the arc radius (sd7), the location of the left point of the arc (sd1 and on the centerline), and the distance of the center of the arc from the centerline (sd4). The lower arc is defined by the position of both the left end (sd2 and on the centerline) and right end (sd3 and sd10) of the arc along with the arc radius (sd13).

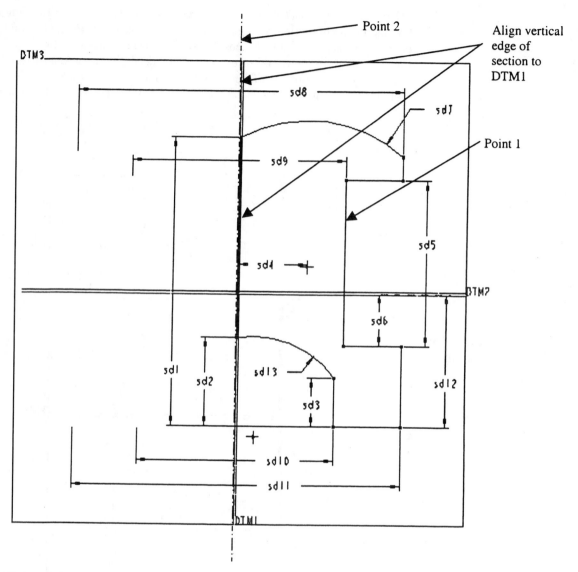

Figure 9.36.

Regenerate | Modify

Change the dimensions to the values specified in Figure 9.37. Note that sd4 is set to 0.0. Be sure to change all of the dimensions to the proper values before regenerating, or else the rivet will be very odd looking upon regeneration. Modified dimensions appear in white instead of yellow. (Turn off the datum planes to see only the sketch and dimensions.) Note that the sketch is a closed section, which is necessary for a **Solid Revolve**. After double-checking that all dimensions have been modified to the correct values, finish the sketch:

Regenerate | Done

(A query box may pop up asking whether you wish to additionally align features after the regeneration. This sometimes happens if Pro/ENGINEER detects two (or more) entities that are sufficiently close to be aligned. In this case, you have already explicitly aligned the entities, so click **Done** in that dialog box.)

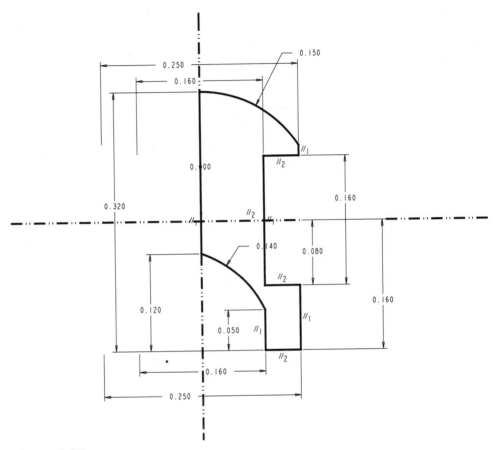

Figure 9.37.

You want a full revolve about the axis of revolution, so:

360 | Done ⇒ OK

The rivet is almost complete. Return to the default isometric view and orient the part per Figure 9.38. Turn on **Hidden Line**, if it is not already on. The last step is to add a **Full Round** on the bottom of the rivet. This time, instead of using bounding surfaces for the **Full Round** (as with the arm), select two edges. The round is created through the **Edge Pair**, with its radius being determined by the distance between the edges.

Create ⇒ Solid ⇒ Round ⇒ Simple | Done ⇒ Full Round | Edge Pair | Done ⇒ < select the two edges in Figure 9.38 >

If you are uncertain whether you selected the correct edges, click **Preview** in the ROUND: General dialog box and use a **Shading** view. If the round looks correct, click **OK**. Otherwise click **Cancel** and repeat the above steps.

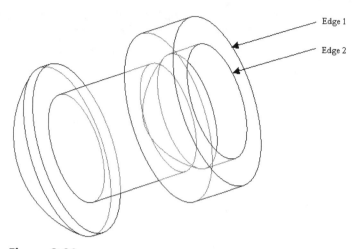

Figure 9.38.

The final rivet looks like Figure 9.39. Shade and spin the rivet. Note that this complex part was created with only two features, a **Revolve** and a **Round**. <u>**Save**</u> the rivet and **_Close_** the window.

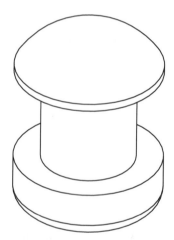

Figure 9.39.

Sweeps and Blends

Solids modeling software eases the creation of smooth, curved features called sweeps and blends. Sweeps are used to create features that have a cross-section defined along a trajectory. An example of a sweep is the handle of a ceramic coffee mug. The cross-section of the handle is usually oval in shape. A mug handle can be created by "sweeping" the oval cross-section through a trajectory shaped like a sideways U. To create a sweep, the **Sweep** option is used instead of **Extrude** or **Revolve** when the feature is created.

First, the trajectory along which the sweep is to occur is sketched. Then the oval cross-section is sketched. Finally, the cross-section is swept along the defined trajectory.

Blends are smooth transitional surfaces between at least two planar sections. For instance, imagine a ventilating duct that transitions from a circular cross-section to a rectangular cross-section. A blend is used to create the transition surface of the duct. A blend feature is created using the **Blend** option for a **Protrusion**.

9.3   THIN REVOLVE FEATURES WITH THE INTENT MANAGER—THE CAP

It should be evident by now that there are several ways to model a part using Pro/ENGI-NEER. The trick is to determine the best possible approach to minimize the number of features and to allow for easy modification should a change be needed.

You have already created a solid extrusion (handle), thin extrusions (arm and guard), and a solid revolve (rivet). The cap shown in Figure 9.40 has a uniform thickness and is axisymmetric. The **Thin Revolve** feature works perfectly to model this part.

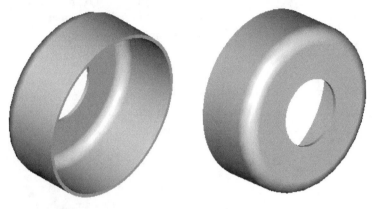

Figure 9.40.

Open the cap part file. This time we will not tell you the exact sequence of commands to use. You should be able to determine the proper commands based on your past experience. **Create** a **Revolve Protrusion** using the **Thin** option. Use **One Side** so the material is added to one side of the sketched curve that will be revolved to create the cap. Set up the sketching plane as shown in Figure 9.41 with the yellow side of DTM2 facing you in the plane of the screen and the red side of DTM1 up. Again the datum planes are oriented in this way so that like datum planes are parallel when you assemble the parts. It is not necessary to do this, but it works nicely for this tutorial.

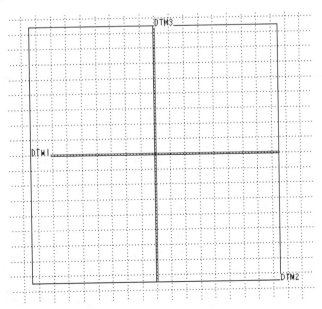

Figure 9.41.

For this sketch, you will use the Intent Manager capability of Pro/ENGINEER. The Intent Manager helps the user by assuming design intent as the cross-section is sketched. This happens in several ways:

- The section is dimensioned and constrained "on the fly" as it is sketched.
- The sketch "snaps" to the grid.
- Alignment occurs automatically.
- There are **<u>Undo</u>** and **<u>Redo</u>** Toolbar buttons to correct mistakes.
- Entities can be dragged to different positions using **Move**, and dimensions and constraints adjust automatically.
- Dimensions can be updated as they are changed, rather than waiting for regeneration.

To start the Intent Manager, click the **Intent Manager** box in the Menu Manager as shown in Figure 9.42. The menus in the Menu Manager change slightly when the Intent Manager is used.

Figure 9.42.

When the Intent Manager is started, **Specify Refs** is highlighted. Because the Intent Manager dimensions, aligns, and constrains as you sketch, it needs to know the references (datum planes, axes, etc.) to which dimensions, alignments, and constraints should be related. In most cases, it is best to dimension, align, and constrain with respect to the datum planes. In this case, reference with respect to DTM1 and DTM3:

Specify Ref ⇒ < **select DTM1** > ⇒ < **select DTM3** >

Note that a brown dashed line appears along DTM1 and DTM3 to indicate that these are references for sketching. Sketching the cross-section using the Intent Manager is done in the same way as without the Intent Manager, except that constraints and dimensions appear as you sketch. If the grid does not appear, begin by toggling on the grid using the **<u>Toggle the grid on/off</u>** button at the right end of the Tool bar (blue button showing a grid). When the grid is displayed, sketch the section shown in Figure 9.43.

Sketch ⇒ Line ⇒ Geometry | 2 Points

Start at the left end of the horizontal line and click at each endpoint of the horizontal line segment. Note that the line "snaps" to horizontal as you draw it (indicated by H next to the line). Continue with the vertical line segment, placing the lower endpoint on DTM1. The line "snaps" to vertical (indicated by V next to the line), and the lower endpoint "snaps" to be aligned on the horizontal axis, DTM1. Click the middle mouse button to finish. Upon clicking the middle mouse button, numerical dimensions automatically appear in gray without regenerating the sketch. The "snapping" to vertical and horizontal, the automatic alignment of the final point to DTM1, and the automatic appearance of dimensions are features of the Intent Manager. The dimensions that appear usually do not look as nice as those in Figure 9.43. We cleaned them up for clarity in the figure.

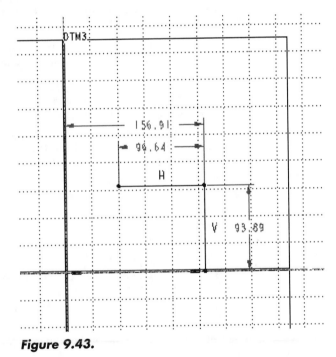

Figure 9.43.

Any of your steps can be undone. Click the **Undo** Toolbar button shown in Figure 9.44 to undo the lines that you just sketched. Then click the **Redo** button to redo the sketch.

Figure 9.44.

Next add the **Fillet** at the corner shown in Figure 9.45. Note that new dimensions appear after the fillet is added.

Sketch ⇒ Arc ⇒ Fillet ⇒ < select the horizontal line segment >
⇒ < select the vertical line segment >

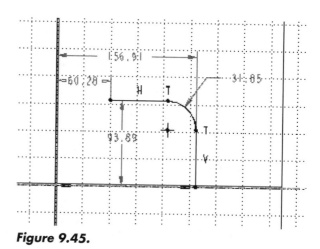

Figure 9.45.

Before correcting the dimensions, a **Centerline** must be added as the axis of revolution. The centerline will be vertical:

Sketch ⇒ **Line** ⇒ **Centerline | 2 Points** ⇒ < **select a point on DTM3 above the horizontal axis** > ⇒ < **select a point on DTM3 below the horizontal axis** >

The centerline is automatically vertical and aligned with DTM3.

Now the desired dimensions can be added to the sketch as shown in Figure 9.46. First, **Dimension** the outer diameter by clicking on the vertical line segment, clicking on the centerline above the top of datum planes, and clicking on the same vertical line segment with the left mouse button. Place the dimension with the middle mouse button. Note that as you do this, one of the dimensions that was generated previously by the Intent Manager disappears, because it is not needed anymore. (Use **Undo** and **Redo** to see this.) Second, **Dimension** the diameter to the left endpoint of the horizontal line by clicking on the left endpoint, the centerline (above the top of the datum plane), and the same left endpoint with the left mouse button. Place the dimension with the middle mouse button. Again one of the dimensions that was originally placed by the Intent Manager disappears.

There should be two gray-colored dimensions that remain from the initial dimensioning by the Intent Manager. These dimensions are called "weak" dimensions, because they are removed automatically when a dimension is added. Two weak dimensions have already been removed by adding the two dimensions above. These new dimensions are yellow. One of the remaining weak dimensions is the radius of the fillet, and the other is the vertical height dimension.

Now the proper dimensions can be specified using **Modify** per Figure 9.47. When the four dimensions are modified, **Regenerate** the sketch.

Although the dimensions shown in Figure 9.47 are correct, we will demonstrate some of the capabilities of the Intent Manager. At this point, the **Delay Modify** box in the SKETCHER menu is not checked. When this box is not checked, modifications to dimensions occur when the dimension is changed even without regeneration. To see this, **Modify** the .38 dimension to .30. The shape of the section changes even though the sketch was not regenerated. **Undo** this to return to the proper dimension. Now check the **Delay Modify** box and make the same change to the .38 dimension. In this case, the dimension does not immediately update. Use **Regenerate** to update the dimension. Click **Undo** two times to return to the .38 dimension.

Another feature of the Intent Manager is that parts of the sketch can be changed dynamically using the **Move** command. To show this:

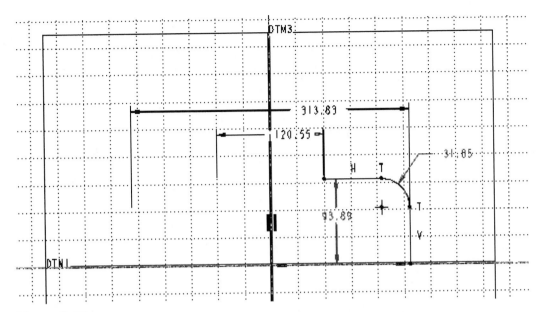

Figure 9.46.

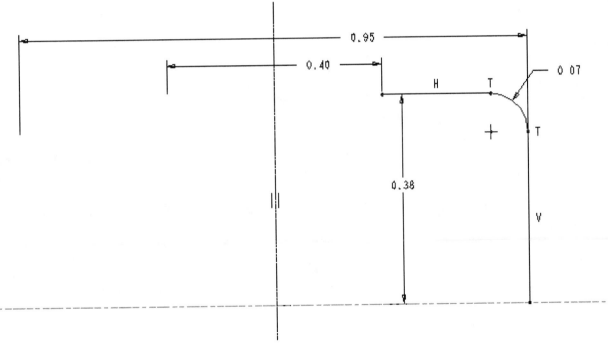

Figure 9.47.

Move

Now click on the horizontal line segment and drag it lower. Note that the vertical dimension to the line segment changes as you move it. Click again and the line segment stays where it was dragged. The new dimension is updated automatically to reflect the position of the line segment. Click **Undo** to return to the proper vertical dimension.

At this point, the sketch is complete, so click **Done**. Remember that this is a thin section, so you can ignore the warning that "Not all open ends have been explicitly aligned."

The arrow should be pointing up or to the right toward the outside of the sketch as in Figure 9.48, to add material on the outside of the sketched lines.

Flip *(if necessary)* | **Okay**

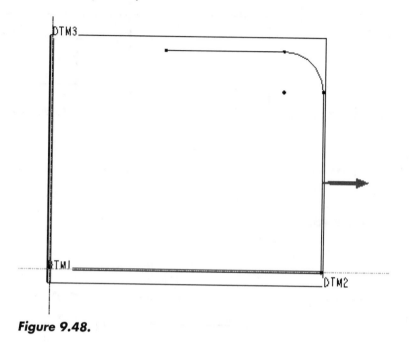

Figure 9.48.

< **enter .020 for the width (thickness) of the thin feature** > ⇒ **360** | **Done** ⇒ **OK**

The result should look like Figure 9.49 with hidden lines displayed. Change to the default isometric view. Shade and spin the part to be sure it looks like Figure 9.40. **Save** the cap and **Close** the window.

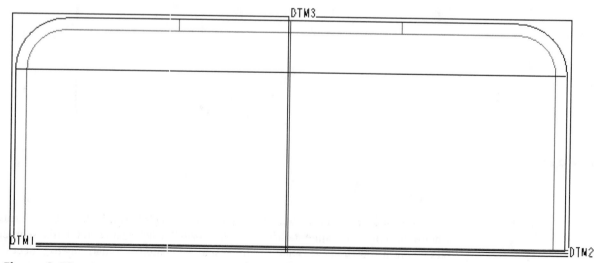

Figure 9.49.

What Is the Best Approach to Model a Part?

Many different approaches to model the same part are possible. Which is the best approach? The answer to this question depends on the skill of the CAD user, the complexity of the part, the potential for redesign of the part, the design intent, and the preferences of the user. Unskilled users may prefer to "carve up" a solid block of material by using rounds, cuts, and chamfers, whereas skilled users may extrude or revolve a cross-section that already includes many of these features. Simple parts can often be modeled with only a few strategic features, but complex parts may require hundreds of features. For a simple part, the order in which features are modeled is unlikely to be critical. For a complex part, it may be necessary to model one feature before another one can be created. If redesign of the part is likely, several features may be added to the model separately so that each could be removed or modified individually. If redesign is unlikely, these features could be combined. Design intent can play a key role in how a feature is created and which features are

modeled first. The parent-child relationships, how features are dimensioned with respect to other features, and what features are likely to be modified all play a role. Finally, some users prefer to model using the fewest features possible by extruding or revolving very detailed sketches. Others prefer to mimic the operations that a machinist might use in making a part. They begin with a stock shape of material (a simple base feature) and add cut features and detail features such as holes and rounds just as a machinist would machine the initial block of material.

The bottom line is that there are always several ways to model a part, and there is rarely one "best" way to model a part. Think ahead about the easiest way to visualize the part, the most efficient method to extrude or revolve the cross-section, the best way to add details, the critical dimensions of the part, what might be redesigned in the part, and how the part fits with other parts. Then proceed with the knowledge that there are many approaches that may work equally well.

9.4   MIRRORING TO MODEL THE BLADE

The final part is the blade of the pizza cutter, shown in Figure 9.50. The blade is a simple **Solid Revolve**, but you will use the **Mirror** command in the sketching section to make this part.

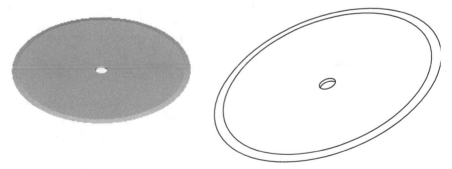

Figure 9.50.

Open the blade part file. Start by creating a **Solid**, **Revolve**d **Protrusion (One Side)**. Sketch the section on the yellow side of DTM3, and orient the yellow side of DTM2 to the **Top** of the window.

Turn on the Intent Manager if it is not already on by checking the box in the Menu Manager. Begin by specifying the references:

Specify Refs $\Rightarrow$ < **select DTM2** > $\Rightarrow$ < **select DTM1** >

Now sketch two centerlines. The first centerline is always assumed to be the axis of revolution for the revolve. In this case, the axis of revolution is along the vertical axis DTM1:

Sketch ⇒ Line ⇒ Centerline | 2 points ⇒ < click on DTM1 at two different points >

Next **Sketch** a horizontal **Centerline** along DTM2 using similar commands. This is the axis about which the sketched geometry will be "mirrored." To sketch the geometry shown in Figure 9.51:

Sketch ⇒ Line ⇒ Geometry | 2 points

Sketch the three line segments (a short vertical line segment on the left side, a long horizontal line segment, and a short angled line segment on the right side) to make the section shown in Figure 9.51. Be sure that the start point on the lower end of the left line segment and the endpoint on the right end of the angled line segment are both on the horizontal centerline.

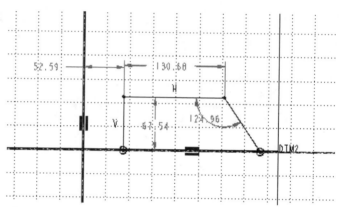

Figure 9.51.

Due to symmetry, this section can be mirrored about the horizontal centerline that is aligned with DTM2. Use the **Mirror** command to complete the section:

Geom Tools ⇒ Mirror ⇒ < select the horizontal centerline > ⇒ All

The horizontal centerline is the line that the geometry is mirrored about. **All** tells Pro/ENGINEER to **Mirror** all the sketch entities. You could alternatively select each line that you wish to mirror individually. The result should look like Figure 9.52.

Add the following dimensions using **Dimension**:

1. diameter to the right endpoint of the horizontal line with reference to the vertical centerline;

2. diameter to the vertical line with reference to the vertical centerline.

Modify all of the dimensions except the angle, per Figure 9.53. (Use **Sec Tools ⇒ Sec Environ ⇒ Num Digits** to change the number of digits, if you need to.) **Regenerate** when done.

Now **Modify** the angle from the horizontal line to the angled line to be 170 degrees. It might help to **<u>Zoom In</u>** to the pointed edge of the blade. The angle should immediately update to the new value, because **Delay Modify** is unchecked after the first regeneration. (Ideally, you should be able to modify all of the dimensions including the angle prior to the first regeneration. But this sometimes results in a "Section regeneration failed" error. To avoid this problem, modify all dimensions except the angle, regenerate, modify the angle, and regenerate again.)

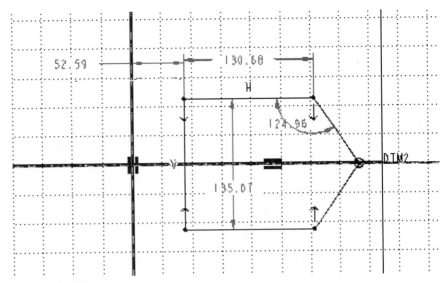

Figure 9.52.

Complete the blade by revolving 360 degrees:

Done ⇒ **360** | **Done**

Click **Preview** and revert to the shaded default view (isometric). If the blade looks correct, click **OK**. Figure 9.54 shows the final result. The blade was modeled using only one feature.

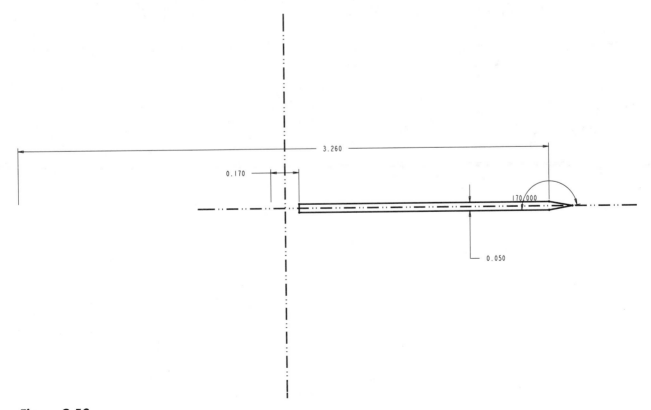

Figure 9.53.

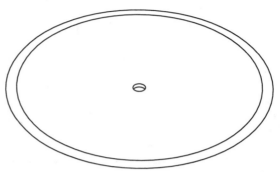

Figure 9.54.

Spin the blade to see the part. <u>**Save**</u> the blade and ***Close*** the window. Congratulations! You have successfully created all six parts of the pizza cutter. The next chapter will step you through the assembly mode of Pro/ENGINEER to assemble these parts into a pizza cutter. The final chapter will describe how to create 2D drawings of the parts and the assembly.

PROFESSIONAL SUCCESS

Screw Threads

Pro/ENGINEER allows the creation of thread features. The individual threads are not drawn (although this could be done using a helical sweep). Instead, the threads are represented schematically on a part. Both internal and external threads can be created, depending upon which surface is selected. If the surface of a hole is selected, then an internal thread is created. If the surface of a cylinder is selected, then an external thread is created. For an internal thread, start by modeling a circular cut with the size of the tap drill diameter. Then use the commands:

Feature ⇒ Create ⇒ Cosmetic ⇒ Thread ⇒ < Query Select the hole surface >

Pro/Engineer will prompt for the surface where the thread starts and an arrow will appear to show the direction of the thread creation. Then Pro/ENGINEER will prompt for the depth, either blind or to a selected surface, and the major diameter. The details of the thread (threads per inch, form, etc.) can be specified in the table that appears upon using the command:

Mod Params

Upon exiting the thread parameters table, click **Done/Return** and **OK**. A schematic representation of the threads will appear.

KEY TERMS   Intent Manager   Mirror   Reference

Problems

1. Model the cap as a thin section without the hole. Add the hole as a circular, extruded cut.

2. Two arms that face one another are needed in the pizza cutter. Design a single thin extrusion that will replace the two arms and still fit in the rectangular hole at the end of the handle.

3. Model the blade as a solid extrusion of a circle (extrude the circle by the thickness of the blade). Use revolve cuts to model the cutting edge of the blade.

4. Model the cap using a solid extrude of a cylinder with a round on one end. Then use a revolved cut to remove material from the inside of the cylinder. Finally, cut the circular hole on the flat end of the cap. (Note: Be sure to keep the wall thickness constant.)

5. Model the arm beginning with a solid, rectangular extrusion of a cross-section that is .30" high and .50" wide. Cut away material to obtain the shape of the arm. Add rounds and the hole.

6. Model the handle using a solid revolve of a section that includes the rounds and reduced diameter. Then add the circular hole, grooves, and rectangular hole.

7. Measure the dimensions of a nail and then model it in three different ways:

    a. Revolve a single cross-section.

    b. Extrude a cylinder the size of the head and then revolve a cut to make the shaft of the nail.

    c. Extrude a cylinder of the shaft diameter to one side of a datum plane, and extrude a cylinder of the head diameter to the other side of the datum plane. Revolve-cut the pointed end of the nail.

10

Modeling an Assembly

OVERVIEW

One of the key features of Pro/ENGINEER is the capability to assemble parts in a virtual environment. This makes it possible to check for fit or interference between parts and to visualize the overall assembly. Assembly involves orienting parts one by one with respect to the datum planes of the assembly and with respect to each other. Once the parts are assembled, the interference between parts can be checked. Then errors in the design of individual parts can be corrected.

10.1 CREATING ASSEMBLY DATUM PLANES

One of the great advantages of Pro/ENGINEER is that an engineer or designer can assemble parts that have been modeled to create a virtual assembly. This allows the designer to work out problems with parts that do not fit together properly early in the design process, before the parts have ever been made. Pro/ENGINEER has features that will check automatically for clearances and interferences between parts in the assembly. The assembly also permits the designer to see what the object looks like before it is fabricated. In this chapter, you will begin by setting up the datum planes for the assembly. Then each part of the pizza cutter will be brought into the assembly and oriented. After assembling the pizza cutter, you will examine the fit between mating parts and modify the parts to eliminate the interferences. The final pizza cutter assembly will look like Figure 10.1.

SECTIONS

- 10.1 Creating Assembly Datum Planes
- 10.2 Bringing the First Part into the Assembly
- 10.3 Adding Other Parts to the Assembly
- 10.4 Checking Interference in the Assembly
- 10.5 Fixing Errors in Parts
- 10.6 Assembly After Correcting Part Errors

OBJECTIVES

After working through this tutorial chapter, you should be able to:

- Open a new assembly
- Bring parts into the assembly
- Orient and constrain parts with respect to datum planes and other parts
- Check for interference in an assembly
- Correct errors in parts while assembling
- Continue assembly after correcting part errors

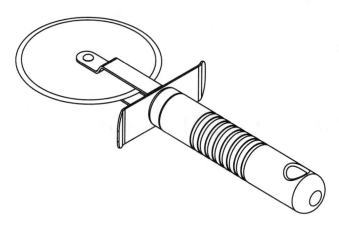

Figure 10.1.

Similar to the generic new-part that you created as a starting point for all parts, it·
is convenient to create a generic assembly to use as the starting point for all assemblies.
(Be sure that *File* ⇒ *Working Directory* is properly set to the working directory that
you are using and that *Utilities* ⇒ *Environment* is set to **Spin Center** off, **Query Bin**
on, **Hidden Line**, and **Isometric**. Also set up the **Options** tab in *Utilities* ⇒ *Customize Screen* as in Section 7.4.) Use the **Create new object** Tool bar button to open a
new file:

> **Create new object** ⇒ < **click Assembly button** > ⇒ < **enter new-assembly** >
> ⇒ < **click OK** >

As with the new-part, it is best to first create default datum planes shown in
Figure 10.2. Use **Feature** ⇒ **Create** to create **Default Datum Planes**. Note that the
datum planes in the assembly are listed as ADTM. The "A" prefix differentiates these
assembly datum planes from the datum planes of individual parts. **Save** the assembly.

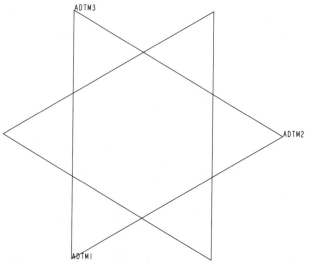

Figure 10.2.

Use the **Save As** Tool bar button to copy the generic assembly datum planes to
the new assembly with the name "pizzacutter." *Close* the new-assembly window.

10.2 BRINGING THE FIRST PART INTO THE ASSEMBLY

<u>**Open**</u> the pizza cutter assembly. Now that the pizza cutter assembly datum planes are specified, the parts (**Component**s) that were created in the previous chapters will be brought into the assembly one by one and aligned with the assembly datum planes or other parts.

Component ⇒ Assemble

The file directory window should appear with all of the parts listed as .prt files as shown in Figure 10.3.

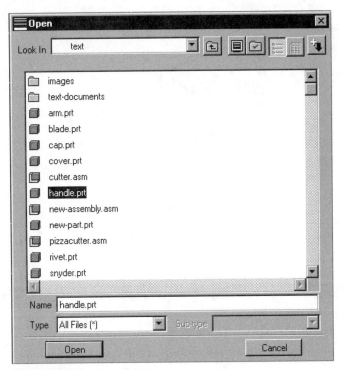

Figure 10.3.

Part files from this directory or from other directories can be added to the assembly by clicking through the file structure. In addition, assemblies can be assembled into a larger assembly. Begin by bringing the handle into the assembly window:

< click handle.prt > ⇒ < click Open >

The screen should look like Figure 10.4 showing the handle in addition to the assembly datum planes ADTM1, ADTM2, and ADTM3. Turn off axes and coordinate systems using the Tool bar buttons so that the screen looks like the figure. Pro/ENGI-NEER has placed the handle into the pizza cutter assembly in a random orientation, although the part datum planes and the assembly datum planes may be aligned. In fact, you may not be able to see the assembly datum planes, because they are underneath the handle's part datum planes. A hint of this is that the datum planes may appear as DTM22, where the second 2 in the expression is actually the 2 from the assembly datum plane ADTM2 that is under DTM2.

The Component Placement window on the right side of the screen is used to specify how parts should be assembled into the pizza cutter assembly. Take a moment to

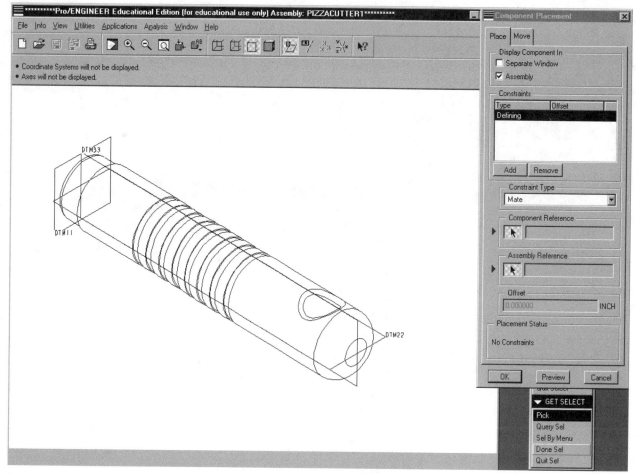

Figure 10.4.

review the Component Placement window. The key areas of this window are the Constraints list, the Constraint Type, the Component and Assembly References, and the Placement Status, each of which is described below.

Constraints—This window lists the assembly constraints as you create them. Right now, there are no constraints, so the window indicates "Defining". After creating a constraint, it can be modified by double clicking on the constraint in the list so its relevant attributes will appear in the Component References.

Constraint Types—Click **Mate** in the drop-down menu as in Figure 10.5 to show the different types of assembly constraints that are available. While all of these can be useful, the most commonly used constraints are **Mate**, **Mate Offset**, **Align**, and **Align Offset**. **Mate** places two planar surfaces so that the outward normal vector from the selected surfaces point in *opposite* directions, and the surfaces become coplanar. In this way the selected surfaces face each other. **Mate Offset** is similar, except that the surfaces are separated by a specified offset, instead of being coplanar. **Mate** and **Mate Offset** work only for planar surfaces. **Align** places two planar surfaces so that the outward normal vector from the selected surfaces point in the *same direction*, and the surfaces become coplanar. In this way, the planar surfaces face the same direction. **Align** can also be used to make two axes coaxial. **Align Offset** places the surfaces or axes in the same way except that they are offset by a specified distance. **Align** and **Align Offset** work for both planar surfaces and axes. Click **Mate** to close the menu.

Figure 10.5.

Component Reference and **Assembly Reference**—Upon defining a constraint, these areas will contain information about the assembly, pizzacutter.asm, and the component being assembled into it, handle.prt. When you have specified surfaces or datum planes to **Mate** or **Align** with one another, the selections can be verified in this area of the Component Placement window.

Placement Status—Right now the placement status of the handle component is "No Constraints." Once the placement of the handle has been specified in the x, y, and z directions relative to the pizza cutter assembly datum planes, the placement status will state "Fully Constrained." If some of the constraints necessary to position the part have been specified, the placement status will state "Partially Constrained". This means that the component placement is not fully defined in all three dimensions. Pro/ENGINEER will permit the assembly of a partially constrained component, but it will consider that component "packaged." One of the limitations of a packaged component is that other components cannot be assembled to it. There are other limitations with packaged components. We do not recommend using the package feature until you are very comfortable with assemblies.

Now you are ready to specify assembly constraints to position the handle with respect to the datum planes of the assembly to fix the position of the handle in space. The goal is to mate a feature of the handle with a feature of the assembly. Begin by mating DTM2 of the handle to ADTM2 of the assembly. In the Component Placement window, < **click the downward arrow** > in Constraint Type to display the menu. Then click **Mate** for Constraint Type. The particular planes that are to be **Mate**d to one another are selected next. The assembly and part datums may overlay one another like DTM2 and ADTM2 in Figure 10.6. As a result, using **Query Sel** is necessary. **Query Sel**ect DTM2 of the handle. Note that a list of items appears in the **Query Bin** window. Click on the item named **DTM2:F2:HANDLE** to select DTM2 of the handle. The yellow arrow should appear as shown in Figure 10.6.

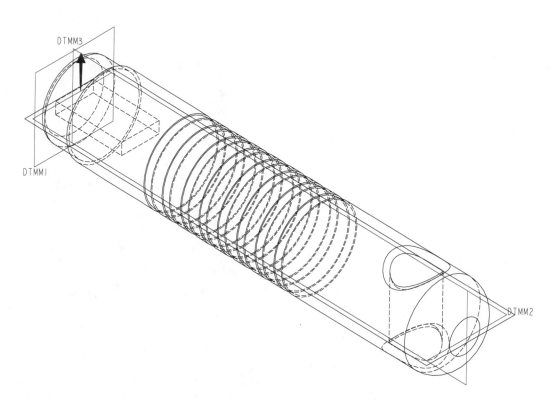

Figure 10.6.

Assemblies are a little different from parts, because the "Flip | Okay" window is not accessible to change the arrow direction. In assembly mode, the side of the datum plane of the part that you want to have face the datum plane of the assembly is selected using the pop-up Datum Orient dialog box shown in Figure 10.7, which should now be on the screen. The arrow in the Graphics window will always be pointing outward from the yellow side of the selected datum plane. In this case, the arrow points outward from the yellow side of the part datum plane, DTM2. You want to choose the red side of DTM2, which is the side of the handle datum plane that is currently facing the yellow side of ADTM2. To do this, < **click on the red button** > in the Datum Orient dialog box.

Figure 10.7.

A quick review of the component placement window shown in Figure 10.8 shows that you have specified the red side of DTM2 of the handle (HANDLE:Dtm2). It may help to move and enlarge the Component Placement window to see this. Now Pro/ENGI-NEER prompts for an assembly feature with which to **Mate** the component.

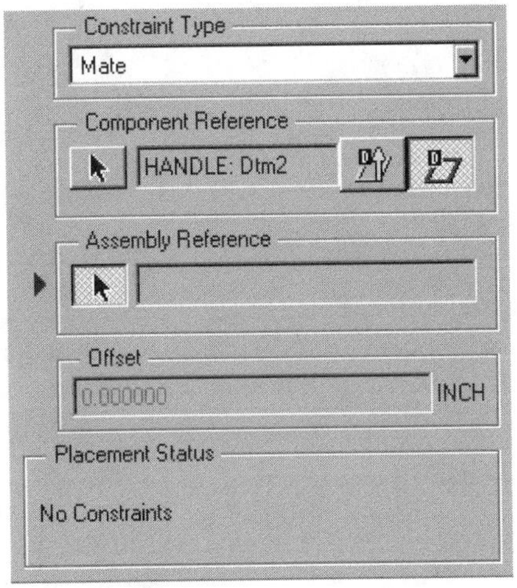

Figure 10.8.

Query Select ADTM2 and the yellow arrow should appear again to indicate the direction that the yellow side of ADTM2 is facing. Select the yellow side of ADTM2 in the Datum Orient dialog box. The datum planes mate against one another so that the red side of DTM2 of the part faces and coincides with the yellow side of ADTM2 of the assembly. As a result the yellow side of both datum planes faces the same direction. (An identical constraint would be to **Align** the yellow sides of both datum planes.)

To review the positioning of DTM2 and ADTM2, click **Mate** in the Constraints window (just above "Defining"). The Component Reference and Assembly Reference show that the red side of DTM2 of the handle is mated (facing) the yellow side of ADTM2 with an offset of .00 inches. (If this is not the case, click **Cancel** at the bottom of the window and start over.)

To continue to constrain the handle to the assembly datum planes, click **Add** just below Constraints in the Component Placement window. Notice that the placement status has changed to "Partially Constrained" as shown in Figure 10.9. In addition, Defining is listed in the Constraints list indicating that you are adding another constraint.

Figure 10.9.

This time you will **Mate** the yellow side of DTM3 and to the red side of ADTM3. **Query Sel**ect DTM3 on the handle component. Select the yellow side of the datum plane. **Query Sel**ect ADTM3 and the red side of the assembly datum plane. The result is that the yellow sides of both planes face the same direction, although the figure will probably not change. The Component Placement window updates to reflect that there are two mates: DTM2 and ADTM2 are mated against one another, and DTM3 and ADTM3 are mated against one another.

The Placement Status of the handle is still Partially Constrained with respect to the assembly datum planes. The position of the handle could move normal to ADTM1 and not violate its two placement constraints. Movement must be constrained by adding a **Mate** in this direction to fully constrain the handle component. This time **Query Sel**ect ADTM1 and the yellow side of the assembly datum plane first. Note that ADTM1 automatically appears as the Assembly Reference, not the Component Reference. Then **Query Sel**ect DTM1 and the red side of the part datum plane. (It does not matter if you choose the Component Reference or the Assembly Reference first.)

The Component Placement window should look like Figure 10.10. There are three mate constraints (in the x, y, and z dimensions) and the handle is Fully Constrained. Click on each constraint to check that the Component and Assembly references match those indicated in Table 10-1. It may be necessary to increase the size of the Component Placement window to see the references. If the correct sides (red or yellow) do not appear, change them in the Component Placement window.

Figure 10.10.

TABLE 10-1 Component and Assembly references

DATUM	COMPONENT	ASSEMBLY
1	red	yellow
2	red	yellow
3	yellow	red

Click **OK** to accept the constraints for the handle. The handle is now assembled into pizzacutter.asm, so that the datum planes of the handle coincide with the datum planes of the assembly. **<u>Save</u>** the assembly.

10.3 ADDING OTHER PARTS TO THE ASSEMBLY

10.3.1 Assembling the Cap

Next, the cap is added to the assembly.

Assemble ⇒ < **cap.prt** > | **Open**

Again, Pro/ENGINEER randomly places the part into the assembly window. Turn off the datum planes, turn on the axes, and set to **<u>No Hidden</u>**, so the assembly looks similar to Figure 10.11.

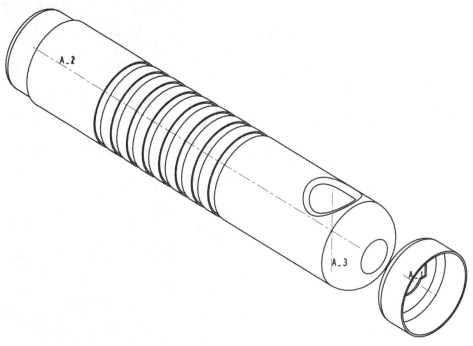

Figure 10.11.

For this component, you will **Align** the axis of the cap to the axis of the handle and then **Mate** the inside surface of the cap to the left-end surface of the handle. In assemblies, a new part can be constrained to datum planes of the assembly, or it can be constrained to other components that are already in the assembly (the handle in this case). The driving factor for how to assemble the parts is the design intent.

Click **Align** using the pull-down menu in the Constraint Type portion of the Component Placement window as shown in Figure 10.12. **Query Sel**ect the axis along the center of the cap and the axis along the center of the handle. Note that the cap axis is automatically used as the Component Reference, and the handle axis is automatically used as the Assembly Reference. Aligning the two axes makes them co-axial.

Click on **Align** under Constraints. The component placement window should look like Figure 10.13, although there might be different numbers for the axes in the References. The cap is now Partially Constrained.

The next assembly constraint will be a **Mate Offset** to offset a surface on the cap with respect to a surface on the handle. To do this, **Add** a new constraint. Then select **Mate Offset** as the Constraint Type in the Component Placement window (Figure 10.14). **Query Sel** the *inner* flat surface of the cap in the plane of the hole of the cap shown in Figure 10.15 as the Component Reference.

Spin the assembly (control and middle mouse button) so that the end of the handle with the rectangular cut is visible, as in Figure 10.16. **Query Sel**ect the flat surface at the end of the handle as the Assembly Reference. The red arrow will appear prompting you for a dimension on the **Mate Offset** in the direction of the arrow. Enter .010 to set the surfaces .010 inches apart. Click the green checkmark. Now the inner flat surface of the cap faces the left end of the handle with a separation of .010 inches.

The cap should now be assembled onto the handle as shown in Figure 10.17. It may be helpful to look at a **Shading** view of the assembly or to spin the assembly. Click

Figure 10.12.

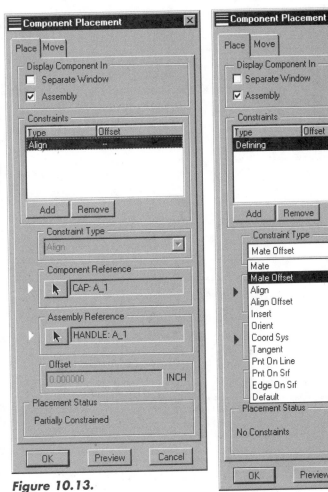

Figure 10.13.

Figure 10.14.

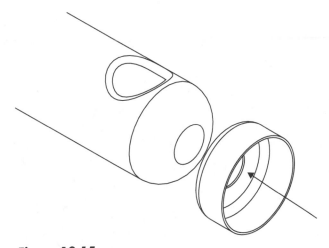

Figure 10.15.

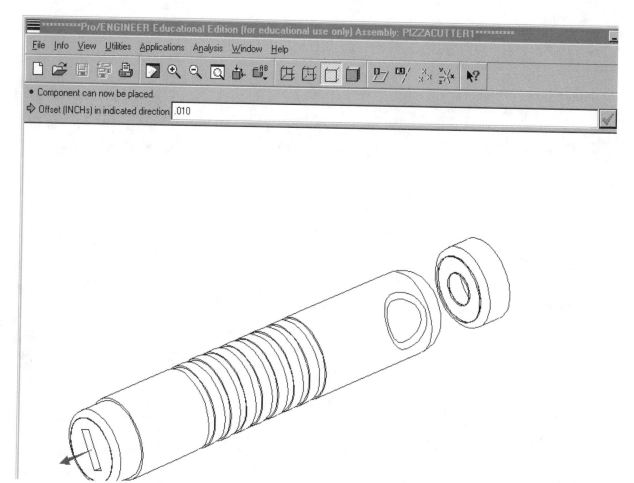

Figure 10.16.

OK to finalize the addition of the cap. Before continuing, return to the default isometric view using the **Saved view list** Tool bar button.

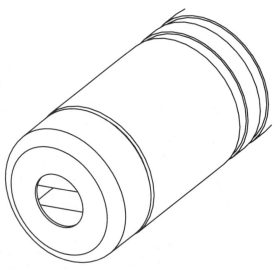

Figure 10.17.

Seeing the cap and handle may be difficult because of their similar color and shading. However it is quite easy to change the color of individual parts. In this case, you will change the color of the handle. This is done by creating a new color.

View ⇒ ***Model Setup*** ⇒ ***Color Appearances***

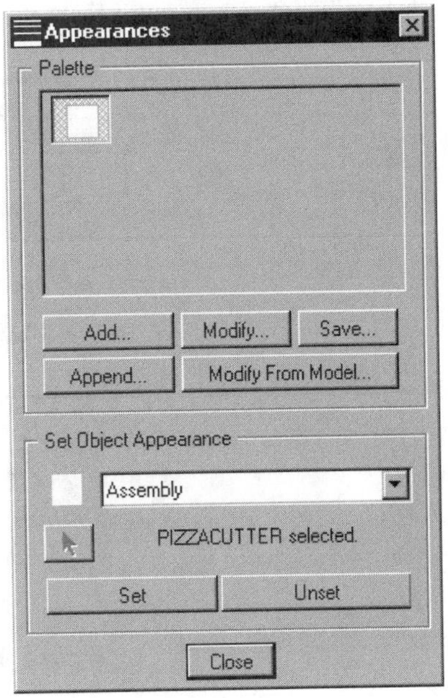

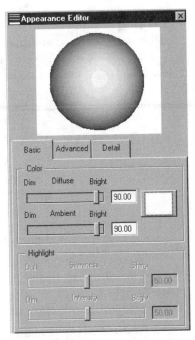

Figure 10.18.

The Appearances window in Figure 10.18 appears. Click **Add** to bring up the Appearance Editor window. Click on the large white button on the right side of the Color portion of the **Basic** tab, shown in Figure 10.19.

Figure 10.19.

This brings up the Color Editor window, shown in Figure 10.20. With the **RGB** box checked, adjust R (red), G (green), and B (blue) sliders to create the color that you want, shown at the top of the Color Editor window. For instance, a red color results from moving the R slider to the right and the G and B sliders to the left. A wood-tone color results from setting the sliders to the approximate values: R = 180, G = 140, and B = 120. Set up any color that you would like for the handle.

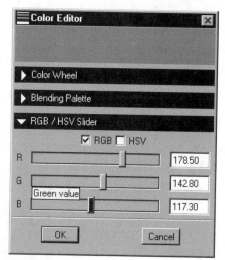

Figure 10.20.

When you have the desired color, click **OK** to return to the Appearance Editor. Click **Add** to add the color to those available in the Palette, then click < **Close** > to return to the Appearances window. The new color should appear in the Palette at the top of the Appearances window. To change the color of the handle, first check that the button of the new color is highlighted in the Palette portion of the Appearances window and that the color appears in the Set Object Appearance portion of the window. If not, click on the desired color button in the Palette portion of the window. Then use the pull-down menu in Set Object Appearances to click **Components**. This results in applying the color to individual components rather than the entire assembly. Select the handle in the Graphics window and **Done Sel**. Finally, click **Set** to color the arm, and click **Close** to finish. The handle should be the color that you just specified, while the cap should still be a gray color.

10.3.2 Adding the Guard

The guard is assembled next.

> **Assemble** ⇒ < **guard.prt** > | **Open**

Pro/ENGINEER randomly places the guard into the assembly window, similar to Figure 10.21. Use **No Hidden** for the display.

The first constraint on the guard is to **Align** the axis of the hole in the guard with the longitudinal axis of the handle. Use **Align** in the Constraint Type window and **Query Sel**ect the axis of the hole in the guard as the Component Reference. Next **Query Sel**ect the axis of the handle as the Assembly Reference.

The second constraint for the guard is a **Mate Offset** to mate the flat surface of the guard against the flat surface of the cap. **Query Sel**ect the front rectangular surface

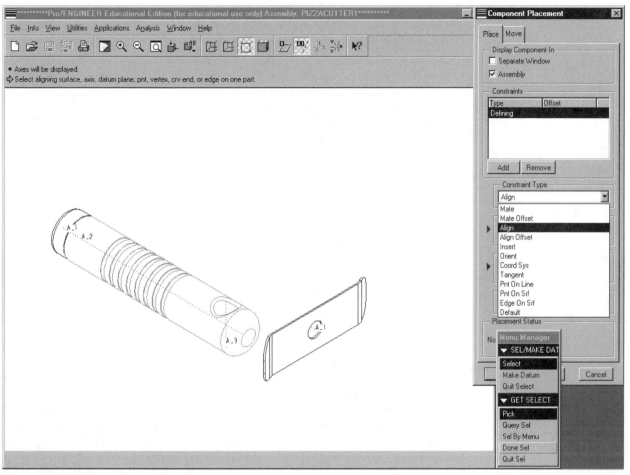

Figure 10.21.

of the guard with the hole in it visible in the isometric view shown in Figure 10.22 for the Component Reference.

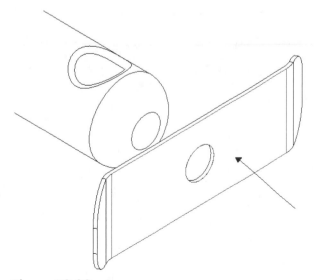

Figure 10.22.

Reorient the assembly as in Figure 10.23. **Query Sel**ect the end face of the cap with the hole in it as the Assembly Reference. The red arrow appears to show the direction of the offset from the cap.

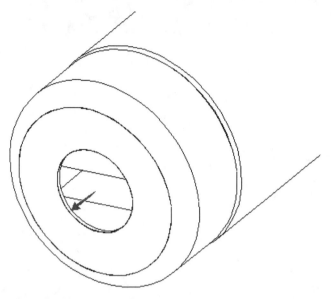

Figure 10.23.

Enter <**1.00**> for the offset distance. The guard is now fully constrained. Click **OK** in the Component Placement window to finish the placement of the guard. It may be necessary to **Repaint the screen** to remove extra lines from the Graphics window. Spin the assembly. The assembly does not yet look like Figure 10.24 because the offset distance was incorrectly set at 1.00. To change the offset:

ASSEMBLY ⇒ **Modify** ⇒ **Mod Assem** ⇒ **Modify Dim | Value** ⇒ <**select the guard**>

The dimension of the offset between the guard and the cap appears in the Graphics window. Click on the 1.00 dimension. Change the offset to .00, and click **Done**.

Regenerate ⇒ **Automatic**

Upon returning to the default isometric view, the result should look like Figure 10.24. Using .00 offset for **Mate Offset** is identical to using **Mate**, but it offers more flexibility for changes if an offset is needed later. To return to the component assembly menu:

ASSEMBLY ⇒ **Component**

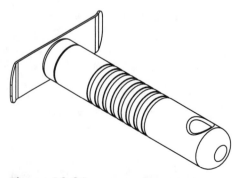

Figure 10.24.

10.3.3 Adding the Arms

The next parts to add to the pizza cutter assembly are the arms. Two copies of the arm are needed, but you will assemble them one arm at a time. Load the arm into the assembly using **Assemble** to result in Figure 10.25. Turn on the datum planes, turn off the axes, and use **No Hidden** with an isometric default view. The assembly looks quite complicated with all of the datum planes visible, but it is necessary to show all datum planes to properly constrain the arm.

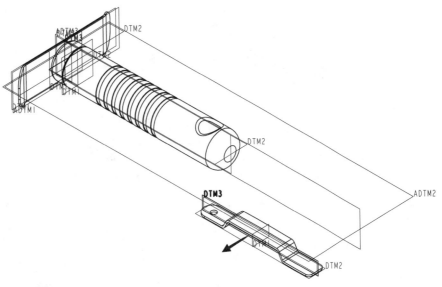

Figure 10.25.

Begin by making DTM3, which bisects the arm along its length, coplanar with ADTM3, which bisects the assembly along its length. Use **Query Sel** to be sure that you select the correct datum. **Mate** the red side of DTM3 for the arm to the yellow side of ADTM3. In this way, the yellow sides of DTM3 and ADTM3 both face the same direction. The view should update as shown in Figure 10.26 after the first constraint is imposed. Note that the arm is now aligned with the handle instead of being off to the side.

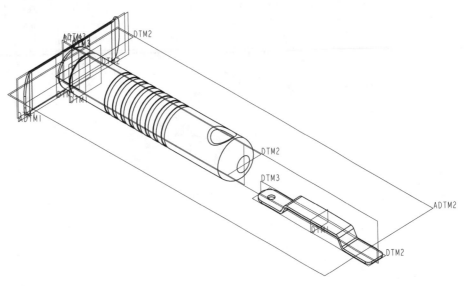

Figure 10.26.

The second assembly constraint is to **Mate Offset** the yellow side of ADTM2 to the red side of DTM2 of the arm. Enter an offset of .025 inches. This will offset the arm in the direction shown by the red arrow in Figure 10.27 to position the arm slightly above ADTM2. The offset is difficult to see in the default orientation. It is readily evident if you spin the part and **Zoom In** to look at the edge of the arm. DTM2 of the arm is slightly above ADTM2. Return to the **Default** view using **Saved view list**.

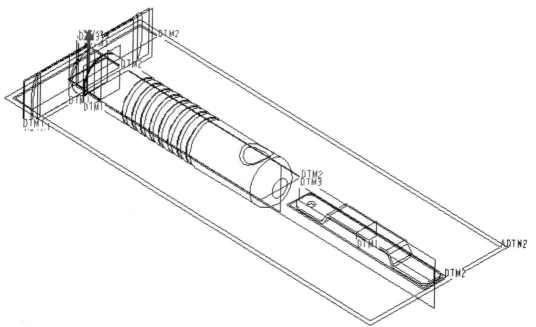

Figure 10.27.

The last assembly constraint is a **Mate Offset** to place the right end of the arm in the rectangular hole of the handle. Select the narrow rectangular face between the rounds that forms the right end of the arm (opposite from the hole) shown in Figure 10.28 for the Component Reference. **Zoom In** and use **Query Sel** to be sure that the correct surface at the end of the arm is highlighted. **Refit the model to the screen** and **Zoom In** on the left end of the assembly. **Query Sel**ect the red side of ADTM1 as the assembly reference. The red arrow shows the direction of the offset of the face of the arm from ADTM1. Use an offset of .76 to insert the arm into the handle. It may help to turn off the datum planes and view in **Wireframe** to see the arm inserted in the handle.

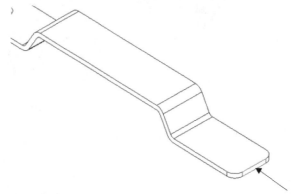

Figure 10.28.

The arm should be assembled as shown in Figure 10.29. Complete the operation with **OK** in the Component Placement window (or **Cancel** to start over). <u>**Refit the model to the screen**</u>.

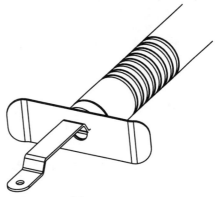

Figure 10.29.

Several identical parts can be included in a single assembly. In this case, another arm will be added to the assembly. Load the arm into the assembly again and turn on the datum planes.

This time instead of mating the datum planes, the second arm will be oriented to the assembly using **Align** command. Recall that **Align** places two planar surfaces so that their outward normal vectors point in the *same direction* and the surfaces are coplanar. Select **Align** as the first constraint type. Before adding this constraint, note that the *yellow* side of DTM3, which bisects the length of the new arm, faces the same direction as the yellow side of ADTM3, which bisects the length of the assembly. If you make the *red* side of DTM3 of the new arm face the same direction as the yellow side of ADTM3 instead, the arm will flip upside down. To do this, **Query Sel**ect the red side of DTM3 of the arm as the Component Reference and the yellow side of ADTM3 as the Assembly Reference. Using these assembly constraints flips the arm upside-down as shown in Figure 10.30.

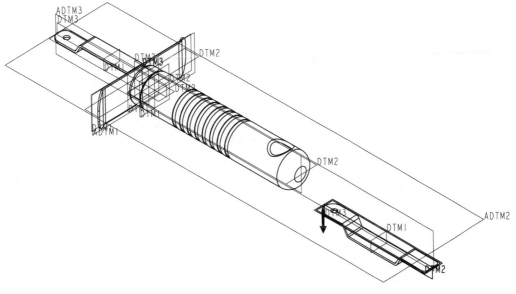

Figure 10.30.

Now the red side of DTM2 of the arm faces the red side of ADTM2. The next constraint is to **Mate Offset** the red side of ADTM2 of the assembly to the red side of DTM2 of the new arm. Use an offset of −.025. The negative value is necessary to place the arm below ADTM2, so the total gap between the two arms is .050 inches. The gap is necessary to accommodate the thickness of the blade when it is added to the assembly.

Now the arm is constrained in two different planes. The Component Placement window states that the component is partially constrained. To fully constrain the arms **Align** the axes of the holes in the two arms. Turn off the datum planes and turn on the axes. **Zoom In** and **Query Sel**ect the axis of the hole in the new arm as the Component Reference. **Zoom Out**, then **Zoom In** on the hole of the first arm. **Query Sel**ect the axis of the hole in the first arm as the Assembly Reference. Now the second arm is fully constrained as shown in Figure 10.31. Click **OK** to complete the placement. Return to the default orientation, and **Save** the Assembly.

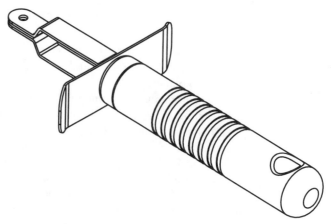

Figure 10.31.

By aligning the axis of the second arm to the first arm, a parent-child relationship was created. Changing the offset of the first arm with respect to ADTM2 will automatically change the position of the second arm. To show this, try the following:

Redefine ⇒ < select first (top) arm >

The first arm is highlighted and the Component Placement window shows the constraints. Select the third constraint (Mate Offset .760). Change the value in the Offset box of the Component Placement window to .20 followed by Enter on the keyboard. The arm is now placed so it is not as deep into the handle. Switch to **Wireframe** and spin the assembly or zoom in to see this. Complete the **Redefine** with **OK**. Because the second arm was placed so the axis of its hole was aligned with the axis of the hole in this first arm, both of the arms have changed their position relative to the handle.

Now use **Redefine** to change the **Mate Offset** of the first arm from .20 back to .76. Return to the default isometric view.

10.3.4 Adding the Blade

Load the blade.prt into the assembly to result in Figure 10.32.

The first assembly constraint is to **Mate** DTM2 of the blade to ADTM2 of the assembly to center the blade between the arms. It does not matter if the red or yellow sides are used for either datum, because the blade is symmetric and can be positioned either way.

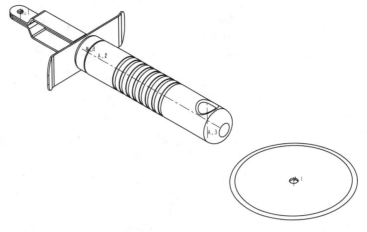

Figure 10.32.

The next assembly constraint is to **Align** the axis of the blade with the axis of the hole in either arm. Use **Query Sel** to be certain that the correct axes are selected. The blade is fully constrained, so click **OK** to assemble as in Figure 10.33. It may be helpful to **Repaint the screen**, turn off the datum planes and axes, and spin the assembly to check the placement of the blade.

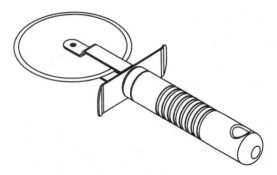

Figure 10.33.

10.3.5 Adding the Rivet

Load the rivet into the assembly as shown in Figure 10.34.

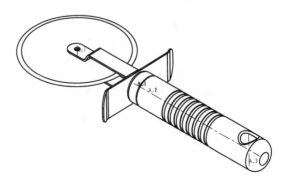

Figure 10.34.

The first assembly constraint is to **Mate Offset** DTM2 of the rivet to ADTM2 of the pizza cutter assembly. Turn on the datum planes. The rivet can be assembled with the rounded head either up or down, depending upon how you mate the datum planes. Assemble the rivet with the rounded head up as shown in Figure 10.35 by choosing the proper sides of the datum planes to face each other. It will be necessary to **Zoom In** on the rivet before **Query Sel**ecting the datum plane. Use an Offset of .00. The **Mate Offset** placement is used rather than **Mate** to permit adjustment of the component later if necessary.

Turn on the axes and turn off the datum planes. **Align** the axis of the rivet to the axis of the hole in either of the arms or the blade. It may help to **Zoom In** on the rivet and hole in the arm before **Query Sel**ecting the axes. The rivet is now Fully Constrained, so click **OK** in the Component Placement window.

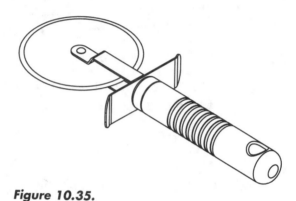

Figure 10.35.

The assembled pizza cutter is complete. All of the parts that have been added to the assembly are listed in the Model Tree window. Clicking on any part in the Model Tree window will highlight the part in the Graphics window. **Repaint the screen** and **Save** the assembly. Spin and shade the assembly to see the virtual pizza cutter from different angles.

10.4 CHECKING INTERFERENCE IN THE ASSEMBLY

Now that you have successfully assembled the pizza cutter, the next task is to determine whether the parts fit together properly. Pro/ENGINEER simply assembles the parts where the placement is specified. It does not immediately check whether any part interferes with another part. However, Pro/ENGINEER has built-in functionality to check for these types of design errors. To do this, analyze the model as shown in Figure 10.36.

> *Analysis ⇒ Model Analysis* [for Pro/ENGINEER Revision 20 use *Info ⇒ Model Analysis*]

The Model Analysis window will appear on the right-hand side of the screen. Click on the Type pull-down menu to see the many types of model analyses that Pro/ENGINEER can perform, as shown in Figure 10.37. For example, the **Mass Properties** options provide the volume, surface area, mass (assuming a user-specified material density), center of gravity, and moments of inertia for the assembly or a part. The

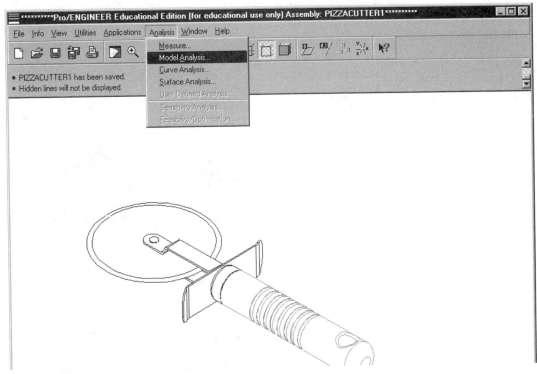

Figure 10.36.

Clearance options are used to determine the clearance distance or amount of interference between specified parts.

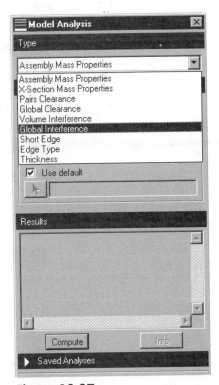

Figure 10.37.

For this design, it is necessary to know whether any of the parts interfere with other parts in the assembly. This type of check is called **Global Interference**. Pro/ENGINEER automatically compares the positions of the solid volumes for every part in the assembly to check for interference between parts. Click on **Global Interferences** in the Type menu. There are several different options for the **Global Interference** check. You need an **Exact Result** for the interference between **Parts Only** (there are no subassemblies or quilts in the model). Set the buttons as shown in Figure 10.38. Then click **Compute**.

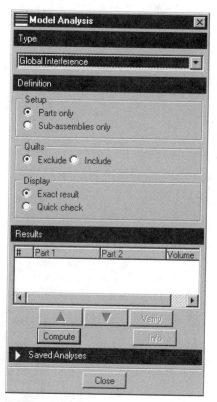

Figure 10.38.

Four items should be listed in the Results window shown in Figure 10.39 (lengthen the Model Analysis window by dragging the lower right corner to see all four items). This means that there are four different places in the assembly where parts interfere, or overlap, with other parts. The Cap interferes with the Arm in two places, and the Guard interferes with the Arm in two places. The total interference volume is listed in the right-most column.

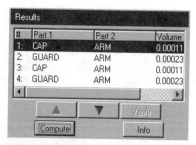

Figure 10.39.

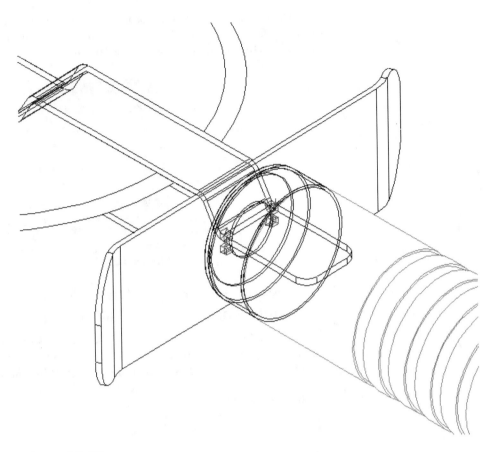

Figure 10.40.

The interfering parts are highlighted in the Graphics window. <u>**Zoom In**</u> on the cap in the assembly and shade the view to see areas that interfere in red, as in Figure 10.40. By clicking on the blue down arrow in the Model Analysis window in Figure 10.39, the next region of the assembly with an interference problem is shown. The interference between the guard and the arm is not surprising. The opening in the guard is round, but the arm has a rectangular shape. Likewise the interference between the arm and the cap results from assembling a rectangular arm into a circular hole in the cap.

10.5 FIXING ERRORS IN PARTS

To fix the interference problems, it will be necessary to **Redefine** the **Feature**s used to create the circular holes in the guard and the cap to change the shape of the hole from a circle to a rectangle. The associative character of Pro/ENGINEER permits modifications to "ripple through" all associated parts. The capability to modify parts quickly and easily without even leaving the assembly mode is very useful.

Open guard.prt in a new window and display with no hidden lines. This window becomes active above the pizza cutter assembly window that is already open. To **Redefine** the circular cut feature in the guard:

> **Feature** ⇒ **Redefine** ⇒ < **click on the circular cut itself or the Cut in the Model Tree** >

The CUT: Extrude feature property box corresponding to the circular cut should appear as shown in Figure 10.41. Because you need to change the shape of the section that outlines the cut, double click on **Section** in the Element column.

Figure 10.41.

Activate the Sketcher mode and **Delete** the circular cut by:

Sketch ⇒ Delete ⇒ < select the edge of the circle >

Now sketch a rectangular cut using **Sketch ⇒ Rectangle** and give it the dimensions as shown in Figure 10.42. If necessary, change the number of digits to three digits using **Sec Tools ⇒ Sec Environ**. You may use a different dimensioning scheme than that shown in the figure. **Regenerate** the sketch and click **Done** when the dimensions match Figure 10.42.

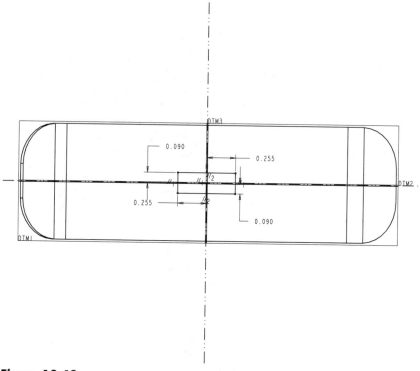

Figure 10.42.

Because only the Section of the cut was modified, Pro/ENGINEER knows to keep the other elements (Depth, Sketching Plane, One Side, etc.) the same. Click **OK** to complete the change in the hole to obtain the corrected guard shown in Figure 10.43. Switch to the **Default** view in <u>**Saved view list**</u> to see the rectangular cut that replaces the circular cut. <u>**Save**</u> the guard and *Close* the guard window.

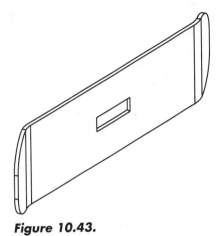

Figure 10.43.

10.6 ASSEMBLY AFTER CORRECTING PART ERRORS

The assembly window should be visible again, but it is not active (the Model Tree and Menu Manager are not visible). To *Activate* the assembly window:

Window ⇒ Activate

Return to the default isometric view. Before checking **Global Interference** again, you will **Regenerate** the assembly so that the changes made to the guard part are incorporated in the assembly. Pro/ENGINEER offers the option to only **Regenerate** selected parts in the assembly (useful if you are dealing with very large assemblies), but it is better practice to use the **Automatic** feature. **Automatic** regeneration updates the assembly constraints and part geometry for all of the parts and features in the assembly. In the ASSEMBLY menu:

Regenerate ⇒ Automatic

Once the assembly is regenerated, the Failure Diagnostics window will appear as shown in Figure 10.44. The Failure Diagnostics window indicates that the guard part has failed regeneration. Why would it fail regeneration? Remember that you assembled the guard by constraining the axis of the hole in the guard with the longitudinal axis of the handle. Now that the hole of the guard is no longer a circle, the axis for the hole no longer exists. The assembly needs to be redefined with different assembly constraints.

To **Redefine** new assembly constraints:

Quick Fix ⇒ Redefine ⇒ Confirm

The only item that can be **Redefine**d (and is highlighted) is the **Placement**, shown in Figure 10.45. Be sure that there is a checkmark in the **Placement** checkbox and click **Done**.

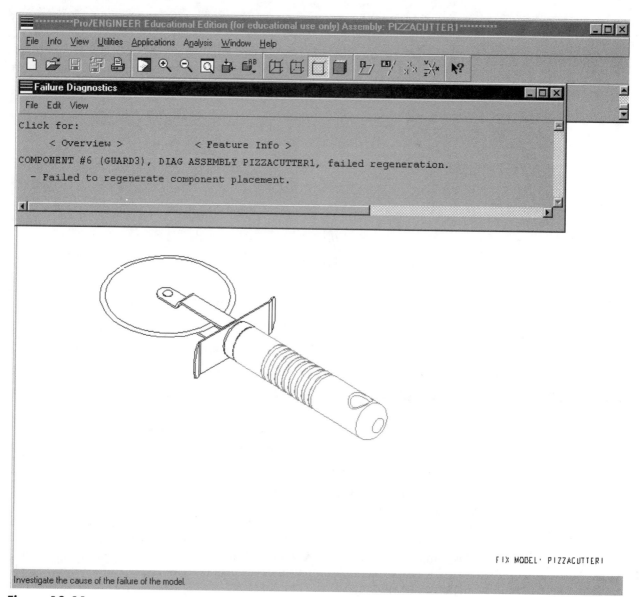

Figure 10.44.

In the Component Placement window that appears (shown in Figure 10.46), the Component Reference related to the **Align** constraint is Missing. This occurred because the axis of the hole in the guard was deleted when you changed the circular cut to a rectangular cut.

Figure 10.45.

Figure 10.46.

If **Align** in the Constraints list is not already highlighted, click on it to highlight it. Then click on the **Remove** button to remove the **Align** constraint. Replace the **Align** constraint by **Add**ing a **Mate Offset** constraint. **Query Sel**ect the yellow side of ADTM3 and the red side of DTM3 of the guard with .00 Offset as shown in Figure 10.47.

A third constraint is still needed. **Add** a **Mate Offset** of .00 between the yellow side of DTM2 of the guard and the red side of ADTM2 of the pizza cutter assembly as shown in Figure 10.48.

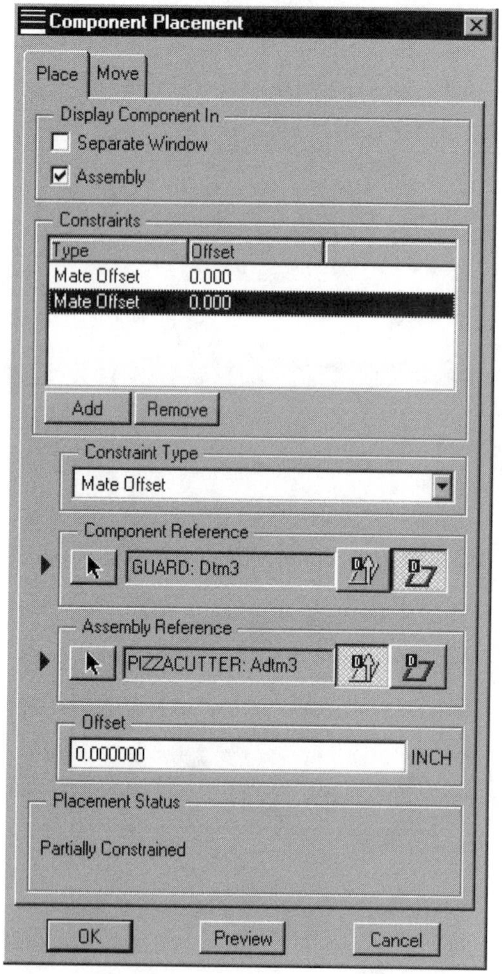

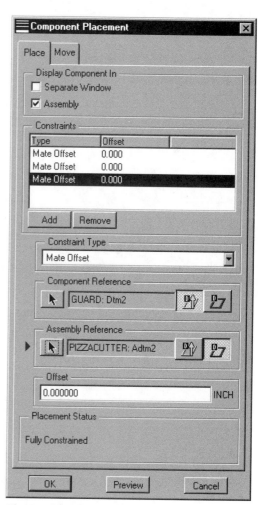

Figure 10.47.

Figure 10.48.

Click **OK** in the Component Placement window to finalize the constraints. Then click **Yes** in the Menu Manager shown in Figure 10.49 to finish resolving the failed feature and **Regenerate**.

Figure 10.49.

Perform the **Global Interference** check again. You should get the results shown in Figure 10.50. The interferences between the guard and the arms have been eliminated, but the cap and the arms still interfere. Of course this is caused by the round hole in the cap interfering with the rectangular arm.

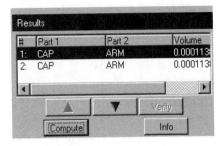

Figure 10.50.

You need to modify the geometry of the cap to eliminate the interference in the assembly. **Open** cap.prt in a new window. **Extrude** a rectangular **Solid Cut** in the cap and retain the circular cut:

Feature ⇒ Create ⇒ Solid ⇒ Cut ⇒ Extrude | Solid | Done ⇒ One Side | Done

In this case you will use an existing surface as the sketch plane rather than using a datum plane. Spin the cap and select the front flat surface of the cap shown Figure 10.51 as the sketching plane. Be sure the arrow is as shown in Figure 10.51 so that the rectangular hole is cut from the front flat surface through the cap. Turn on the datum planes and select DTM2 so it faces the **Top** of screen to orient the sketch plane.

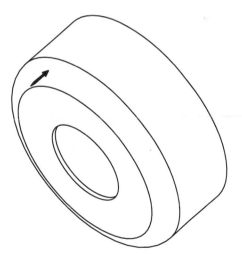

Figure 10.51.

Now **Sketch** a **Rectangle** and **Dimension** it as shown in Figure 10.52. **Regenerate** and **Modify** the dimensions. Upon finishing the sketch, click **Regenerate** and **Done**. Be sure that the red arrow shows that material will be removed in the center of

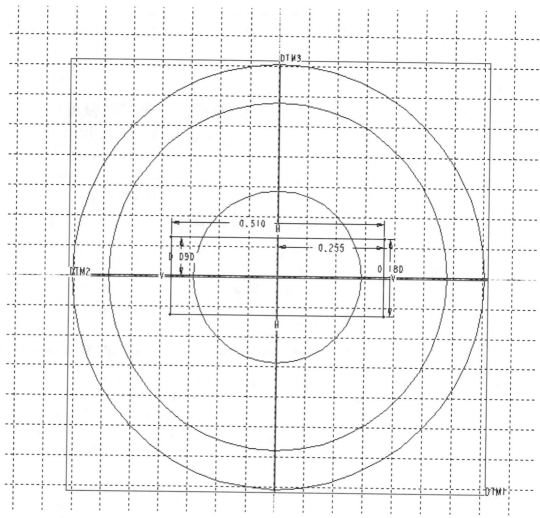

Figure 10.52.

the rectangle. Finish the cut as **Thru All**. The revised cap should look like Figure 10.53. **<u>Save</u>** the cap and **_Close_** the window.

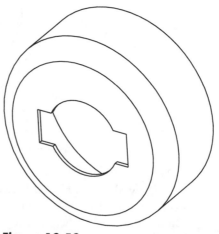

Figure 10.53.

Activate the pizza cutter assembly window. The modified cap automatically appears in the assembly because of the associative character of Pro/ENGINEER. This permits modifications in parts to propagate automatically to associated assemblies (and drawings). It may be difficult to see the modification to the cap while the cap is assembled. To see it more clearly use an exploded view of the assembly:

View ⇒ *Explode*

Spin the exploded assembly in **Wireframe** or **Shading** mode to see the rectangular cut in the cap. Return to the unexploded view:

View ⇒ *Unexplode*

Perform the **Global Interference** check again. Note that it is not necessary to **Regenerate** the model. The axis of the circular hole was used to constrain the cap in the assembly, and this hole was retained in the new version of the cap. There should be nothing in the Results portion of the Model Analysis window, as shown in Figure 10.54, because all of the interferences have been resolved. Double check the Message area above the Graphics window shown in Figure 10.55 to confirm that there are no interfering parts. **Close** the Model Analysis window.

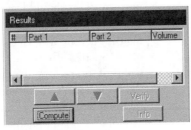

Figure 10.54.

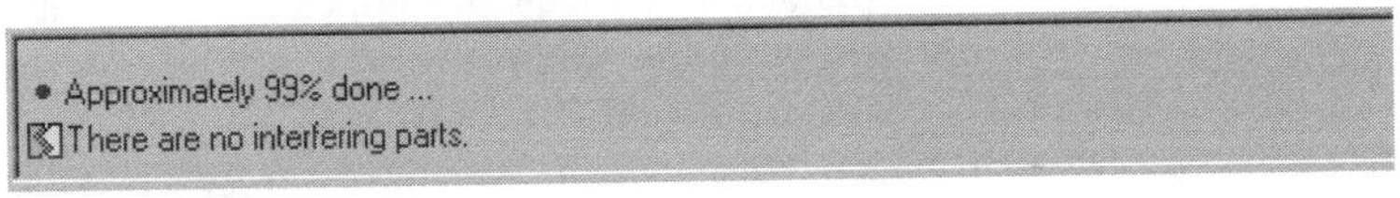

• Approximately 99% done ...
☒ There are no interfering parts.

Figure 10.55.

Congratulations! The final pizza cutter assembly should look like Figure 10.1. You have successfully assembled the pizza cutter and resolved interference errors. **Save** the assembly and *Close* the window.

Exploding the Assembly

When the assembly is exploded, Pro/ENGINEER places parts in default positions. Usually the default positions are not optimal for displaying an exploded view of the assembly. To **Modify** the **Position** of the parts in an exploded view, first turn on the axes and show the assembly as **No Hidden**. Then **Modify** the position of the parts by:

Modify ⇒ **Mod   Expld** ⇒ **Position** ⇒ **Entity/Edge | Translate** ⇒ < **Query Sel the axis of the handle** > ⇒ < **select the handle** > ⇒ < **select a**

new position for the handle after moving it along its axis >

The last two operations can be repeated with other parts. It is often necessary to **Repaint the screen** after parts are moved. Finish with **Done Sel** > **Done**. This operation can be repeated to translate components along other axes. For instance, the rivet can be moved to a location above the blade by selecting its axis and moving as described above. Use **Done/Return** twice to return to the ASSEMBLY menu.

KEY TERMS

Align
Assembly contraints
Assembly references

Associative modeling
Component references
Exploded view

Fully constrained
Interference
Mate

Problems

1. Assemble the pizza cutter beginning with the blade and working toward the handle.

2. Assemble the pizza cutter beginning with the guard and working first toward the handle and then toward the blade.

3. Remove the circular cut from the cap and reassemble the pizza cutter.

4. The current pizza cutter assembly requires a .025" offset of the arms from ADTM2. In a real pizza cutter, there would be nothing to keep the arms at this offset, at the end inserted into the handle. Correct this problem by creating a .050" web of material between the two arms in the rectangular cut in the handle. Then reassemble using the modified parts. (Hint: To do this, delete the rectangular cut and make two rectangular cuts in the handle, each big enough to accept one arm. This should leave .050" of material between the cuts.)

5. Correct the problem described in Problem 4 by modeling a new arm (or modifying the current arm) that is designed so that the flat surface flush with the blade is offset by .025" from the flat surface that is inserted into the handle. Change the width of the rectangular cut in the handle to .100" from .150", so that the ends of the arms that fit in the handle are flush with one another. Then reassemble using the modified parts.

6. Model a wooden pencil. Most pencils have three parts: a hexagonal wooden portion with embedded lead (extruded hexagon with a cut at one end to form the point and a cut at the opposite end to fit the cylindrical eraser holder), a metal eraser holder (thin revolve), and the cylindrical eraser. Assemble the three parts to make a pencil.

7. Model a plastic butter tub and cover. Model the tub as a thin revolve. Model the cover as a thick revolve to be able to form the lip at the bottom edge of the cover.

11

Creating Working Drawings

OVERVIEW

Working drawings are the traditional graphical means of displaying a part or assembly. These drawings provide all of the information necessary to manufacture a part or assemble an assembly. The drawings are based on the part or assemblies that have already been modeled. First, views of the part or assembly are added to the drawing. Then dimensions are added. Notes and a title block are also added to the drawing to include necessary information. Often section views and detail views are used in a drawing to display details of the part or assembly.

11.1 DETAIL DRAWINGS IN PRO/ENGINEER

Now that you have learned how to model parts and put a collection of parts together into an assembly, it is necessary to put this information in the standard engineering graphics format known as an engineering drawing. The Drawing Mode is where the details of the part or assembly are collected and presented in a formal way. There are many variations on the details of and the format for engineering drawings. However, one key guideline is that *a drawing should clearly convey all information necessary to fabricate the part*. In this chapter, you will learn the common Pro/ENGINEER commands for generating engineering drawings.

SECTIONS

OBJECTIVES

After working through this tutorial chapter, you should be able to:

- Open a new drawing
- Place and arrange views on a drawing
- Add dimensions to a drawing
- Add notes to a drawing
- Create tables and a title block
- Create an assembly drawing
- Add a section view to a drawing
- Add a detail view to a drawing
- Label parts in a drawing

Prior to solids modeling software such as Pro/ENGINEER, engineering drawings were created by draftsmen and designers laboriously translating the 3D visual image from their mind or a physical model into detailed orthographic projections. This was slow and inexact. More importantly, changes were very difficult to make. Using Pro/ENGINEER the designer or engineer first creates a 3D virtual model of a part. Based on this model, the Pro/ENGINEER drawing mode extracts the 2D orthographic information exactly and quickly. Any changes to the 3D model are automatically transferred to the drawing because of the associative nature of Pro/ENGINEER.

The drawing in Figure 11.1 shows three 2D orthographic views and one 3D isometric view of the arm. Details such as dimensions, tolerances, material, and so forth, are also displayed on the drawing. The title block, which contains drawing control information, is in the lower right corner of the drawing.

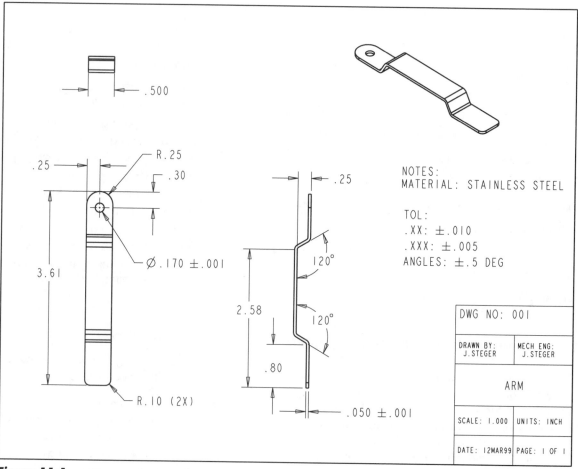

Figure 11.1.

11.2 OPENING A DRAWING

You will make a drawing of the arm of the pizza cutter, shown in Figure 11.1. (Be sure that *File* ⇒ *Working Directory* is set properly to the working directory that you are using. Also set up the **Options** tab in *Utilities* ⇒ *Customize Screen,* as in Section 7.4.) The *Utilities* ⇒ *Environment* should be set to **Spin Center** off, **Query Bin** on, **Hidden Line, Isometric,** and **Coordinate Systems** off. Also be sure that the **Tangent Edges** option in the **Environment** window is set to **Solid.** This controls the way that intersecting tangent surfaces such as the bends in the arm are displayed. Then begin the drawing by creating a **New Drawing File** with the same name as the part that you created earlier.

File ⇒ *New* ⇒ **Drawing** ⇒ < **enter arm** > | < **click OK** > (See Figure 11.2)

Figure 11.2.

The New Drawing pop-up menu window shown in Figure 11.3 appears. The Name box under Optional Default Model allows you to select which part model or assembly will be displayed in the drawing. The associative nature of Pro/ENGINEER makes it necessary for a default model to be associated with any drawing. The drawing is dependent on the part or assembly file that is selected. Once a model is chosen, all of the orthographic views in the drawing will be based on that model. Additional models can be added later. In this case, arm.prt will be the default model:

< **click Browse** > ⇒ < **click on arm.prt if it is not already highlighted** > | < **click Open** >

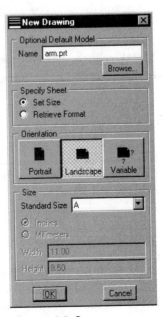

Figure 11.3.

Specify Sheet in the **New Drawing** menu refers to the format of the drawing. Many companies have predefined drawing formats customized for the company. If so, you would select **Retrieve Format** and select the appropriate size format from a standard library. But because you may not have access to standard formats for this exercise, you will use a blank drawing outline and add a title block:

< click Set Size >

Orientation defines the paper orientation. Landscape orientation is almost always used:

< click Landscape >

The Size box allows you to set the height/width parameters of the drawing. Standard sizes for engineering drawings listed in the pull-down Standard Size menu are shown in Table 11-1.

TABLE 11-1 Standard sizes for engineering drawings

ANSI	ISO
A — 8.50" × 11.00"	A4 — 210 mm × 297 mm
B — 11.00" × 17.00"	A3 — 297 mm × 420 mm
C — 17.00" × 22.00"	A2 — 420 mm × 594 mm
D — 22.00" × 34.00"	A1 — 594 mm × 841 mm
E — 34.00" × 44.00"	A0 — 841 mm × 1189 mm

The size of the drawing is based on the size of the part and the degree of detail that needs to be presented. As with everything else in Pro/ENGINEER, you can modify the size selection later. Use an A size drawing:

< click on the Standard Size pull down menu > | < click A > | < click OK >

The screen should look similar to Figure 11.4. You may want to increase the window size by dragging the lower right corner of the window. The large rectangle is the border of the drawing. All of the work should be kept within this border. The scale, type, name, and drawing size are listed just below the rectangle. In this case, the SCALE of 1.000 indicates that 1 inch on the drawing corresponds to 1 inch on a printed page. TYPE indicates that the model is a part as opposed to an assembly or format. The NAME tells the name of the current model. These items will not show up when you print the drawing.

11.3 PLACING VIEWS IN A DRAWING

Begin by adding views of the arm in the drawing. The front view will be placed in the lower left corner. Other orthographic views will be added based on this front view. To **Add** the first **View**:

Views ⇒ Add View ⇒ General | Full View | No Xsec | No Scale | Done

This set of commands creates a **Full View** of the part without a cross-section (**Xsec**). A **General** view is independent of any other views on the drawing, so it is always used for the first view added to a drawing. By selecting **No Scale**, the view defaults to the same scale as the drawing scale, which is indicated below the border outline of the drawing. After executing the above commands, the prompt in the message

Figure 11.4.

window shown in Figure 11.5 asks for the view to be placed on the drawing with the mouse.

⇔ Select CENTER POINT for drawing view.

Figure 11.5.

This view should be placed in the lower left portion of the drawing so:

< select a point in the lower left quadrant of the drawing >

The default isometric projection appears where you clicked. Be sure that the datum planes are visible. If not, turn them on using the Tool bar button and **Repaint the screen**. Now the part needs to be oriented to an orthographic view rather than the isometric view that currently appears. The part is oriented using datum planes in the

Orientation window that has appeared on the right side of the screen, as shown in Figure 11.6. The front view of the part in the drawing should be the flat surfaces of the arm that are parallel to DTM2. Thus, we select the **Front** face of the part to be DTM2 in Reference 1, so that you view the part as if you were viewing the yellow side of DTM2. Reference 1 in the Orientation window should already indicate **Front**. If not, click the pull-down menu and select **Front**. Then:

< Query Sel DTM2 >

After selecting DTM2, Reference 2 is highlighted in the Orientation window. To orient the hole in the arm upward select the yellow side (front) of DTM1 to face toward the **Bottom** of the screen as Reference 2:

< click on the Reference 2 pulldown menu > | < click Bottom > | < Query Sel DTM1 > | < click OK >

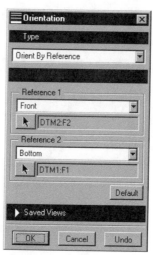

Figure 11.6.

The front face of the arm should appear with the hole toward the top of the drawing. Datum planes, axes, and coordinate systems are not usually shown in a drawing, so turn them off. Refresh the screen, by clicking on the **Repaint the screen** Tool bar button.

Before adding more views, move the front view of the arm to the position shown in Figure 11.1:

Move View

Select the front view with the left mouse button. Move the view to the approximate location shown in Figure 11.1. Click the left mouse button again to place the view.

Now you can **Add** the remaining orthographic **Views**. These views are dependent upon the first view that you placed, so the **Projection** option is used instead of the **General** option. This will let Pro/ENGINEER determine the correct orientation of the view based on the front view that was placed first. The view that is placed will automatically be a top, bottom, right-side, or left-side view, depending on where the mouse is clicked on the drawing.

Add View ⇒ Projection | Full View | No Xsec | No Scale | Done

To place the top view shown in Figure 11.7:

< select a point above the front view >

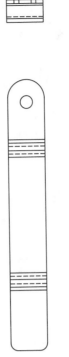

Figure 11.7.

Repeat the same steps to create an orthographic projection to the right of the front view. When complete, the drawing should look similar to Figure 11.8.

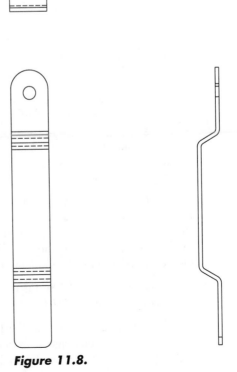

Figure 11.8.

It is usually helpful to show a 3D view of the part on an engineering drawing to help others visualize the part. In this case, you will **Add** an isometric **View** of the arm in the upper right portion of the drawing. Because this new view is independent of the views that have been placed so far, use the **General** option. Recall that the **General** option was also used to place the initial front view of the drawing because it is an independent view. Use the **Full View** | **No Xsec** | **No Scale** options. Place the view in a location similar to the one shown in Figure 11.9. When prompted for an orientation, accept the default isometric view, by clicking **OK**. The datum planes may reappear because they are associated with the default view. Turn them off and **Repaint the screen**.

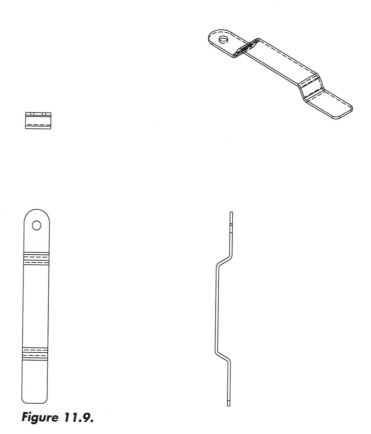

Figure 11.9.

<u>Save</u> the drawing. Remember that this file can have the same name as the part because the filename extension is different. Thus, the drawing of the arm is saved as arm.drw.

The appearance of each view can be controlled individually. Usually, hidden lines should be shown in a drawing. In this case, though, the hidden lines clutter the drawing and are somewhat confusing. (The hidden lines are shown in gray and may not be seen easily on the screen, but they are shown clearly in the printout of the arm shown in Figure 11.9.) Turn off the hidden lines from each view, starting with the front view.

Disp Mode ⇒ **View Disp** ⇒ < **select the front view** > | **Done Sel** ⇒ **No Hidden** | **No Qlt HLR** | **Tan Default** | **Hide Skeleton** | **Done**

The gray hidden lines in the front view are removed. The **Tan Default** option causes edges between tangent surfaces of the model to be shown as the default specified in the Environment window. Examples of such edges in the front view are the horizontal lines located at the bends (where a flat surface meets a curved surface). The Tangent Edges option in the Environment window was set to Solid at the beginning of this chapter, so that solid lines appear at these edges between tangent surfaces. Other options in **View Disp** permit these lines to be shown as dashed lines (**Tan Phantom**) or not at all (**No Disp Tan**). **No Qlt HLR** and **Hide Skeleton** are related to advanced operations of quilts (surfaces with zero thickness) and skeletons, which are not used here.

Repeat the process to remove hidden lines for the remaining views, except select all three remaining views (including the isometric view) before clicking on **Done Sel**. After **Repaint the screen**, the result should resemble Figure 11.10.

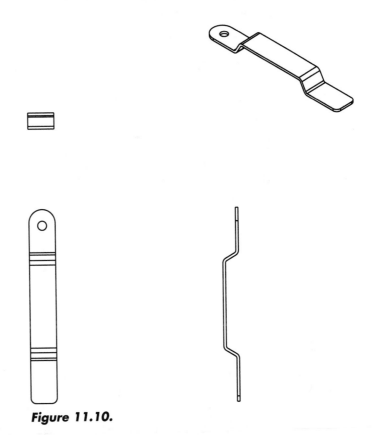

Figure 11.10.

Move each view using **Move View**. The **General** views (front and isometric) are free to move anywhere on the drawing without restriction. The dependent **Projection** views (top and right side) move along with the parent view (front). Furthermore, the dependent views only move so that they remain properly aligned with the parent view. For instance, the right-side view can be moved left or right with respect to the front view, but not up or down. Move the views around to see how they can be placed. Finish by placing the views as in Figure 11.1, then click **Done/Return**.

11.4   DIMENSIONING A DRAWING

The DETAIL submenu in the Menu Manager window has all of the commands necessary to add or modify the various details of the drawing. These details include dimensions, notes, leader lines, tolerances, and so forth.

There are two primary ways to display dimensions on the drawing. One method is to use the **Show/Erase** command. The other method is to **Create** the dimension that you want to display. The **Show/Erase** method displays the dimensions that were used in the part mode to create the model. This works well for a very simple part or if the dimensions that you want to **Show** are the ones you used to create the part. But sometimes the most useful dimensions to show in a drawing are not the ones used to create the part. The alternative method using the **Create** ⇒ **Dimension** command displays the dimensions that you specify on the drawing. Because each method requires different procedures to delete dimensions, it is generally best to use only one dimensioning scheme. Use the **Create** ⇒ **Dimension** command to create **Standard** dimensions, because it is more versatile:

Create ⇒ **Dimension** ⇒ **Standard | New Ref | On Entity | Pick**

Creating a dimension in Drawing mode is exactly the same as creating a dimension in Sketcher mode. Either select the a single edge with the left button, and place the dimension for the length of that edge using the middle mouse button. Or select points on each end of the item to be dimensioned with the left button, and place the dimension with the middle mouse button. Follow this procedure to dimension the width of the arm as shown in Figure 11.11 by selecting the bottom edge in the top view. If you make a mistake in creating the dimension, use **DETAIL** ⇒ **Delete** to remove the dimension. The number of digits after the decimal point may not be the same as shown in Figure 11.11. You will correct this shortly.

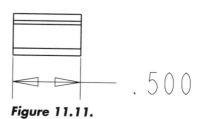

Figure 11.11.

Using the same method, create the 3.61 vertical dimension shown in Figure 11.12. Select the bottom edge and the top rounded edge of the front view. After you place the dimension using the middle mouse button, the dimension will not appear. Pro/ENGINEER needs information on whether it should dimension to the center of the arc forming the top rounded edge or to its tangent. In the Menu Manager, a menu has opened asking whether you wish to use the **Center** or the **Tangent** of the arc. Click on **Tangent** so the dimension extends to the top edge of the arm, and the dimension will appear.

The same situation will occur when dimensioning the .30 dimension from the center of the hole to the top of the arm in the front view. To create this dimension, select the circle forming the hole. Either the circle itself or the center of the circle will be highlighted. Either is okay. Then select the top rounded edge of the arm and place the dimension. Again, more information is needed before the dimension can be finished. In this case, the **Center** or **Tangent** needs to be specified for the top rounded edge and possibly for the hole (if the circle was initially highlighted, not the center of the circle). As each item is highlighted, select **Center** for the hole (if prompted) and **Tangent** for the top rounded edge. Sometimes Pro/ENGINEER will question the orientation of a dimension. As shown in Figure 11.12, .30 is a vertical dimension, so select **Vertical** from the DIM ORIENT menu.

Finish dimensioning the front view and right view following Figure 11.12. Sometimes dimensioning can be quite frustrating, especially when the message < The specified dimension could not be created. Try again > appears in the Message area at the top of the Graphics window. If you have this problem, try the following:

< **Zoom In** to the desired portion of the part > ⇒ **Repaint the screen** ⇒ < select the entity to dimension > ⇒ < **place the dimension** >

Then **Refit the model to the screen** and move to the next dimension. **Query Sel** the lines to make dimensioning easier. To dimension a radius, click once on the arc. Double clicking on the arc will dimension the diameter. If you inadvertently add a dimension that you do not want or position the dimension incorrectly, leave it for now. You can delete or move it shortly. When you are finished dimensioning, click **Return** ⇒ **Done/Return.**

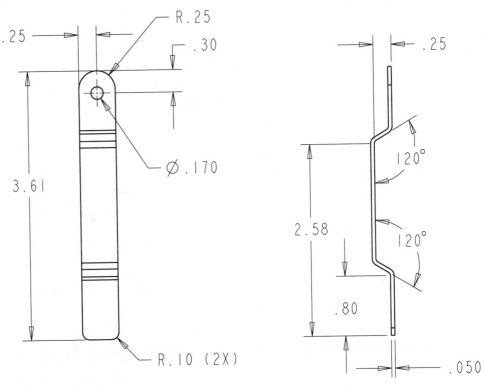

Figure 11.12.

The dimensions are probably not exactly like those shown in Figure 11.12. If a dimension is wrong, it can be deleted and recreated. To **Delete** a dimension:

Delete ⇒ < select the numerical dimension > ⇒ **Done Sel**

Repaint the screen and recreate the dimension.

In some cases, the arrows in the newly created dimension may not be in the direction that makes the dimension most clear. To correct this:

Flip Arrows ⇒ < select .50 dimension (select the numerical value) >

The arrows will reverse as shown in Figure 11.13. **Flip Arrows** for the other dimensions, including the diameter of the hole, to match Figure 11.12.

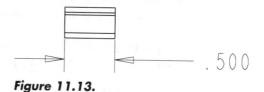

Figure 11.13.

It may also be necessary to reposition some dimensions to match the positions shown in Figures 11.12 and 11.13 using **Move**. Select the numerical dimension to drag it to another position.

Generally, the location of the center of a circular hole is marked with a cross. To do this requires the use of **Show/Erase**. Begin by making sure that datum planes and axes are turned off.

Show/Erase

The dialog box shown in Figure 11.14 appears. Set up the dialog box as shown. **Show** indicates that the items marked will be shown. The **A-1** button should be depressed to **Show** axes. The **View** button indicates that all axes in a particular view will be shown. When the dialog box is set up as shown:

< select the front view in which the circular hole is dimensioned > ⇒ Done Sel ⇒ Close ⇒ <u>Repaint the screen</u>

Perpendicular lines to mark the center of the hole should appear.

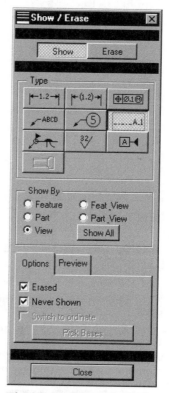

Figure 11.14.

The number of digits following the decimal point in a dimension prescribes the tolerance of the dimension based on the general tolerance that you will specify in a note shortly. Tolerances that are too tight result in a part that is difficult or expensive to manufacture. Tolerances that are not tight enough may result in a poor fit between parts. Therefore, the number of digits following the decimal point in a dimension is quite important, unless the dimension is explicitly toleranced. To **Modify** the **Num**ber of **Dig**its following the decimal point:

> **Modify** ⇒ **Num Digits** ⇒ < enter 0 > | < select both 120° dimensions > ⇒ **Done Sel**

Now change all of the dimensions to match the number of digits in Figure 11.1. For instance, to change 2-digit dimensions to 3-digit dimensions:

> **Num Digits** ⇒ < enter 3 > | < select all 3-digit dimensions to match Figure 11.1 > ⇒ **Done Sel**

Repeat this procedure to change 3-digit dimensions to 2-digit dimensions where necessary. Click **Done/Return** when finished.

The two rounds at the bottom of the front view both have a .100 radius. Rather than dimensioning each round individually, **Modify** the **Text Line** for the dimension of one round to indicate that this radius appears twice (once for each round):

> **Modify** ⇒ **Text** ⇒ **Text Line** ⇒ < **Pick R.10 dimension** > ⇒ < enter (2X) as shown in Figure 11.15 > ⇒ **Done/Return** ⇒ **Done/Return**

> ⇒ Edit line {0:R}{1:@D} (2X)

Figure 11.15.

The **Modify** command can also be used to explicitly tolerance dimensions. Most dimensions will be toleranced using the general tolerance note that you will create shortly. However, it is necessary to specify a tighter tolerance for the .170 dimension on the front view and the .050 dimension on the right-side view:

> **Modify** ⇒ **Text** ⇒ **Text Line** ⇒ < **Pick 0.050 thickness dimension** > ⇒ < enter ± .001 to the right end of the line >

To get the ± to appear, use the Symbol Palette shown in Figure 11.16, which appears automatically. Repeat the procedure for the .170 dimension. Finish with **Done/ Return** ⇒ **Done/Return**.

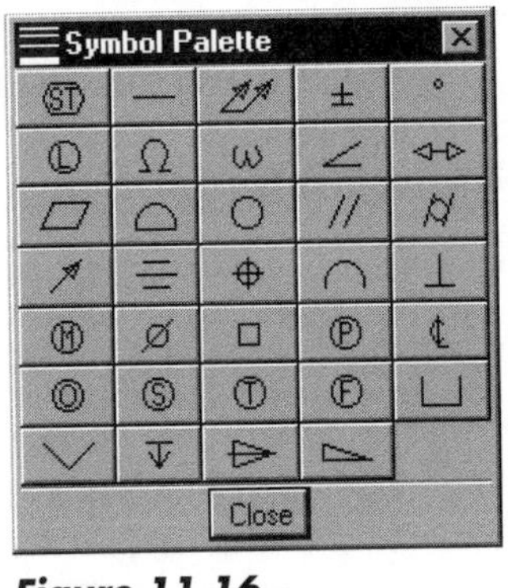

Figure 11.16.

<u>**Repaint the screen**</u> and <u>**Save**</u> the drawing.

Displaying Tolerances

Pro/ENGINEER has an alternate means to display individual tolerances on a drawing. This method requires that the tolerances visibility be turned on in the configuration file. The configuration file is a file that exists in the background of a Pro/ENGINEER session. It consists of a set of keywords for the settings of many options. To turn on the visibility of tolerances in the DRAWING menu:

Advanced ⇒ Modify Val ⇒ < scroll down to "tol_display" > ⇒ < enter YES in place of NO > ⇒ File ⇒ Exit ⇒ Yes ⇒ Done/Return

Now tolerances should be shown on the drawing. Individual tolerances can be changed using

Modify ⇒ Dimension ⇒ < select the dimensions for which the tolerance will be modified > ⇒ Done Sel

The **Modify Dimension** dialog box will appear. The Tolerance, Tolerance Mode, and other aspects of the dimension can be changed using this dialog box. In addition, dimensions can be given geometric tolerance attributes. If tolerances are not to be shown on the drawing, return to the original display with no tolerances by changing "tol_display" to NO.

11.5   CREATING NOTES

Many items other than dimensions are necessary to provide enough information on a drawing to manufacture the part. Items such as general tolerances, material choice, units, and so forth, can be included on a drawing as notes. Notes can stand alone or may have leader lines pointing to a feature on a view. Begin by **Creat**ing a **Note** to specify the material using the DETAIL menu:

Create ⇒ Note ⇒ No Leader | Enter | Horizontal | Standard | Default | Make Note

This note created will have **No Leader** line and the text will be oriented **Horizontally**.

< select a location for the note on the right side of the drawing using the left mouse button >

Enter the following text into the box shown in Figure 11.17:

NOTES: < Enter >

MATERIAL: STAINLESS STEEL < Enter >

< Enter >

⇨ Enter NOTE:

Figure 11.17.

Upon the last <Enter> the text will appear on the drawing in the location selected a moment before. Repeat this procedure to create a note for tolerance information as indicated in Figure 11.18. Use the Symbol Palette that appears automatically for the ± sign. When finished click **Done/Return**.

NOTES:
MATERIAL: STAINLESS STEEL

TOL:
.XX: ±.010
.XXX: ±.005
ANGLES: ±.5 DEG

Figure 11.18.

Use **Move** to position the notes approximately as shown in Figure 11.1. <u>**Save**</u> the drawing.

Geometric Tolerancing and Dimensioning

Geometric Dimensioning and Tolerancing symbols can be added to a drawing by:

Create ⇒ Geom Tol ⇒ Specify Tol

In the Geometric Tolerance dialog box that appears, several items must be set to apply the geometric tolerance on the drawing. For instance, to specify a **flatness form tolerance**:

< **click on the parallelogram symbol for flatness** >

In the Model Refs tab:

< **click on Surface in the Reference menu** > ⇒ < **Query Sel the surface to which the flatness condition is applied** > ⇒ < **click on Leaders in the Placement menu** > ⇒ < **Query Sel an edge to which the leader line will point** > ⇒ **Done Sel** ⇒ **On Entity | Arrow Head | Done** ⇒ < **select a location for the tolerance** >

The Geometric Tolerance should appear on the drawing. In the Tol Value tab:

< **enter the desired Overall Tolerance value** > ⇒ **OK** ⇒ **Done/Return**

The position of the tolerance can be changed using **Move**.

Orientation tolerances such as parallelism or perpendicularity are slightly more difficult to apply, because it is necessary to first set up a reference datum. To do this:

Create ⇒ **Datum** ⇒ **3D Datum** ⇒ < **enter a name for the datum plane such as " B " > ⇒ < click On Surface > ⇒ < Query Sel the desired planar surface or datum plane to be used as a reference for the geometric tolerance > ⇒ < click on the -A- button >** ⇒ **OK** ⇒ **Done/Return**

This creates a datum plane called B that can be used as a reference for the geometric tolerance. To create a parallelism orientation tolerance for a surface with respect to B, use the same steps as for the flatness tolerance except click the parallel lines symbol in the Geometric Tolerance dialog box. In addition, in the Datum Refs tab, the item in the Basic box in the Primary tab is set to B. This makes plane B the reference datum plane for the parallelism tolerance.

11.6 CREATING A TITLE BLOCK

The last item to add to the drawing is a title block. Often standard drawing formats that include a title block, a predefined border, and other items that a company always requires on its drawings are available using the Retrieve Format button of the New Drawing dialog box (Figure 11.3). The engineer would only need to add the views and notes in addition to filling out the title block. Because you may not have a drawing format to use, you will create a title block with the **Table** command:

> **Table** (from DRAWING menu) ⇒ **Create** ⇒ **Descending** | **Rightward** | **By Num Chars** | < **Pick a point to the right of the orthographic views and just below the notes** >

The numbers shown in Figure 11.19 will appear where you clicked the mouse. Each number represents the position of one character. You will be creating a table with each row being added to the bottom of the table (**Descending**), and each column being added to the right of the table (**Rightward**). **Num Chars** means that the row widths and column heights will be determined by character lengths, which you will now specify. Select a point in the Graphics window just after the first 9 to make the first column 9 characters wide.

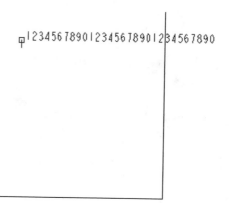

Figure 11.19.

The line of numbers will shift 9 characters to the right and a vertical tick mark will appear marking the right side of the first column, as shown in Figure 11.20. Select a point just after the 9 again, to create a second column.

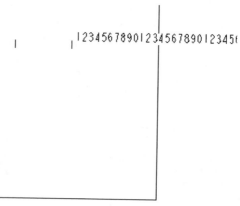

Figure 11.20.

Click **Done** to finish the column creation. The table will look like Figure 11.21.

⌐

1
2
3
4
5

Figure 11.21.

Just as with the columns, select a point just below the number to create a row of that height. Create five rows:

< select below the 2 > | < select below the 2 > | < select below the 4 > | < select below the 2 > | < select below the 2 > | Done

The table is now complete as shown in Figure 11.22. If you make a mistake, use **Delete** after clicking **Done** to delete the table, and start over.

The table still needs to be modified to create the desired look. Specifically, **Merge** the top two boxes (cells) into a single cell:

Modify Table ⇒ Merge ⇒ Rows&Cols ⇒ < select the top left cell (cell 1) by clicking in the center of the cell > < select the top right cell (cell 2) >

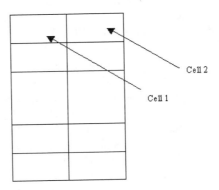

Figure 11.22.

Repeat the **Merge** command, but apply it to cells 3 and 4, shown in Figure 11.23.

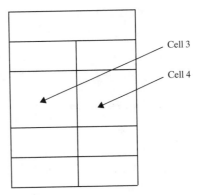

Figure 11.23.

Now **Enter Text** into each table cell according to Figure 11.24:

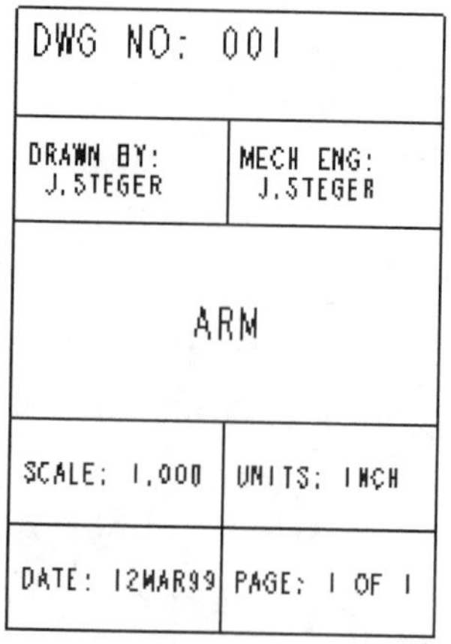

```
DWG NO: 001

DRAWN BY:        MECH ENG:
  J.STEGER          J.STEGER


            ARM


SCALE: 1.000   UNITS: INCH

DATE: 12MAR99  PAGE: 1 OF 1
```

Figure 11.24.

Enter Text ⇒ < select the top cell > ⇒ < enter DWG NO: 001 < Enter > < Enter > >

Continue to fill in text from the top of the table, working downward. Finish the text in each cell by clicking < Enter > a second time after finishing the line. Fill in your name in the DRAWN BY: and MECH ENG: cells. The text may not fit in the cell, but you will correct this later. When you enter the text for the SCALE, type the text exactly (including the case) as shown in Figure 11.25. The "&" triggers predefined variables in Pro/ENGINEER. In this case, "&scale" will place the actual scale from the drawing into the text line automatically. Specifying the scale in this way is quite useful if you modify the scale of the drawing later. Likewise, when typing in the PAGE, use the text shown in Figure 11.26 to automatically bring up the page information.

If you make a mistake and want to change the text, just select the cell you wish to modify and type in the correct text. Click **Done/Return** when finished with all of the text.

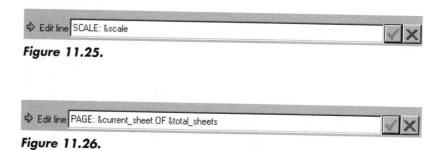

Edit line | SCALE: &scale

Figure 11.25.

Edit line | PAGE: &current_sheet OF &total_sheets

Figure 11.26.

At this point the text will probably look like Figure 11.27. This is because the text height is too large for the cells. To correct the text height and justify the text in the cell:

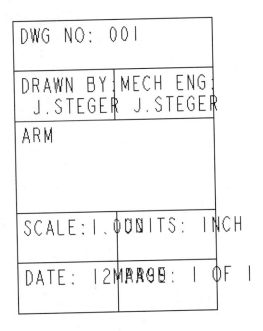

Figure 11.27.

Modify ⇒ **Text** ⇒ **Text Style** ⇒ < select *all* the text in boxes 1–6 in Figure 11.28 > | **Done Sel**

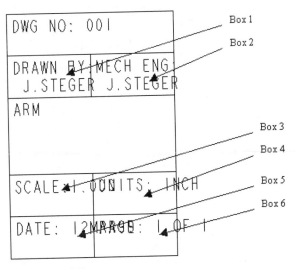

Figure 11.28.

The Text Style menu shown in Figure 11.29 will appear. Modify the **Height** to **.1** < **Enter** > and modify the **Justify Vert** to **Middle**. Then < **click on Apply** > | < **Close or OK** >.

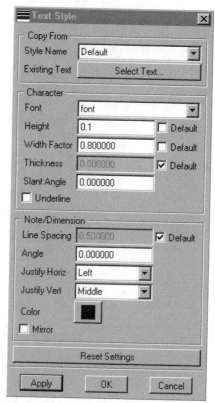

Figure 11.29.

Finally, you need to correct the "ARM" text so that it is centered both horizontally and vertically in its cell:

< select ARM in the table > ⇒ Done Sel

This time use **Justify Horiz: Center | Justify Vert: Middle**. The final table should be similar to Figure 11.30. When finished click **Done/Return ⇒ Done/ Return**.

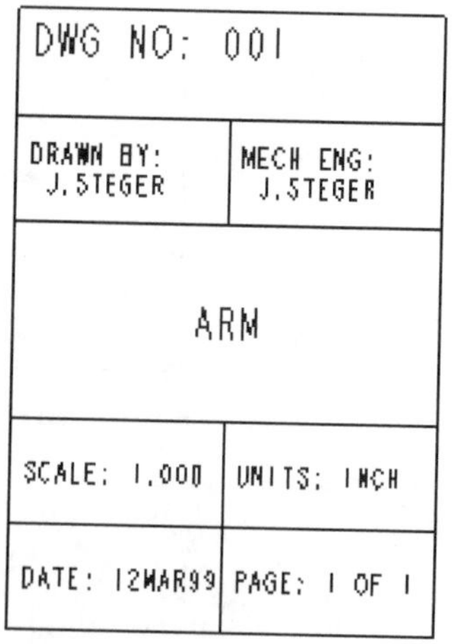

```
DWG NO: 001

DRAWN BY:        MECH ENG:
   J.STEGER          J.STEGER


            ARM


SCALE: 1.000    UNITS: INCH


DATE: 12MAR99  PAGE: 1 OF 1
```

Figure 11.30.

This table will serve as a title block for all the subsequent drawings that you will create. To avoid creating this table again for each drawing, **Store** this table separately from the arm drawing:

> **Table** ⇒ **Save/Retrieve** ⇒ **Store** ⇒ < **select the table** > ⇒ < **enter tblock** >

Now the table is saved as tblock.tbl and can be reused on any drawing by using the **Retrieve** command. Click **Done/Return**.

The final drawing of the arm should look similar to Figure 11.31. If not, use the **Move** command to move the text, dimensions, and tables to the desired location. **Move** will move every entity on a drawing. You can also use the **Views** ⇒ **Move View** command to move views.

Repaint the screen and **Save** the drawing. The drawing can be printed using the **Print** Tool bar button or *File* ⇒ *Print. Close* the window. Drawings for all of the other parts of the pizza cutter can be created in a similar fashion.

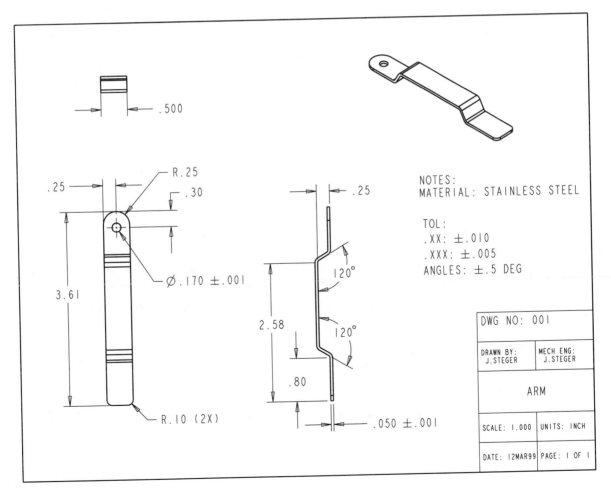

Figure 11.31.

Formats and the Title Block

Pro/ENGINEER has a set of standard drawing formats that include a blank title block. In many cases, using one of these formats is easier than creating a new title block. To create a new drawing using the standard format, open a *New* file for the drawing as usual. When the New Drawing dialog box shown in Figure 11.3 appears, specify the Optional Default Model as usual. Then click on the **Retrieve Format** button. Now it is necessary to **Browse** through the file structure to find the Pro/ENGINEER "formats" folder. This folder is probably not in your working directory. Instead, it should be one of the folders in the folder where Pro/ENGINEER is located on your computer. Open the "formats" folder. The standard drawing sizes should appear as .frm files. Select the appropriate drawing size and open it. Upon clicking **OK** in the New Drawing window, a blank draw-

ing including a border and a title block appears on the screen. Text can be added to the title block using **DETAIL** ⇒ **Create** ⇒ **Note**, as usual. However, the title block itself cannot be modified.

To modify the title block or the standard drawing format, the format itself must be opened before creating a drawing using the format. To do this, use the *Open* command, find the "formats" folder, and click on the desired format. Use **Create** to add a **Note**, use **Delete** to remove lines, use **Move** to move lines, and use **Sketch** to draw new lines. When the format is in its desired form, use *Save As* to save it with a new file name in your working directory. Now this new, customized format can be used whenever a *New* drawing is created by clicking on **Retrieve Format** and using **Browse** to find the revised format.

11.7   CREATING AN ASSEMBLY DRAWING

Assembly drawings are useful in showing how parts fit together to create the entire assembly and in labeling individual parts in an assembly. In the next few sections you will create the assembly drawing of the pizza cutter shown in Figure 11.32.

We will only step through the commands that are new to this drawing. Refer back to previous sections for help with commands that you have already used.

Use the **Create new object** Tool bar button to open a new drawing called pizzacutter based on the Optional Default Model of the pizzacutter.asm. Use a C size drawing. The larger drawing size is necessary to adequately show the details of the pizza cutter assembly.

Typically, an assembly drawing shows the assembly in an isometric view or an exploded view. These views are often accompanied by a table listing the parts that make up the assembly, known as the Bill Of Materials, or BOM. For this drawing, you will only set up the views and label the parts. A bill of materials is not included, because there are only six parts.

Begin by placing a front view of the pizza cutter as shown in Figure 11.33.

Views ⇒ **Add View** ⇒ **General | Full View | No Xsec | Unexploded | No Scale | Done** ⇒ < **select a point on the left side of the sheet** >

It may help to **Zoom In** on the image of the pizza cutter to make it easier to select the datum planes for orientation. Click the middle mouse button to end the zoom.

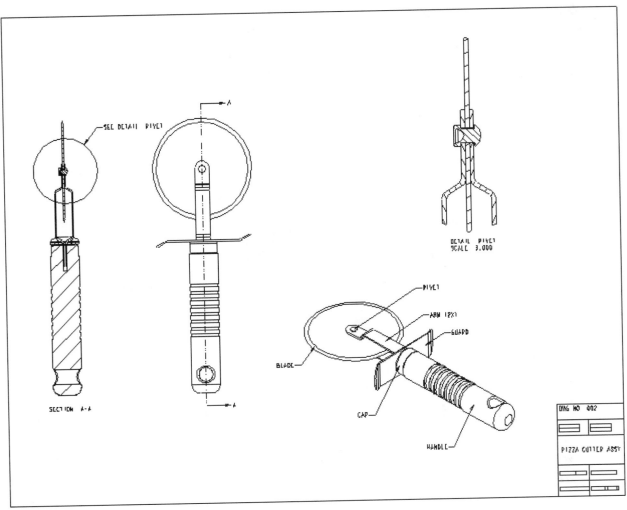

Figure 11.32.

< Query Sel the Front of ADTM2 as Reference 1 > | < Query Sel ADTM1 to face the Bottom as Reference 2 > | < click OK >

The result is the view of the front of the pizza cutter with the blade upward. Turn off the datum planes, **Refit the model to the screen**, and **Repaint the screen**.

Next use **Add View** ⇒ **General** to add an isometric view of the pizza cutter as shown in Figure 11.33. Turn off the datum planes and **Repaint the screen**.

Pro/ENGINEER determines the drawing's scale based on the size of the part or assembly compared to the drawing size selected. In this case, the scale was automatically set to .500, as indicated just below the border of the drawing. This scale is smaller than necessary, as suggested by the small size of the images of the pizza cutter in Figure 11.33. The scale can be modified by:

DETAIL ⇒ **Modify** ⇒ **Value** ⇒ **< select SCALE: .500 at the bottom of the screen > ⇒ < enter 1.0 >**

Now the drawing scale is 1 to 1, and the pizza cutter is shown much larger.

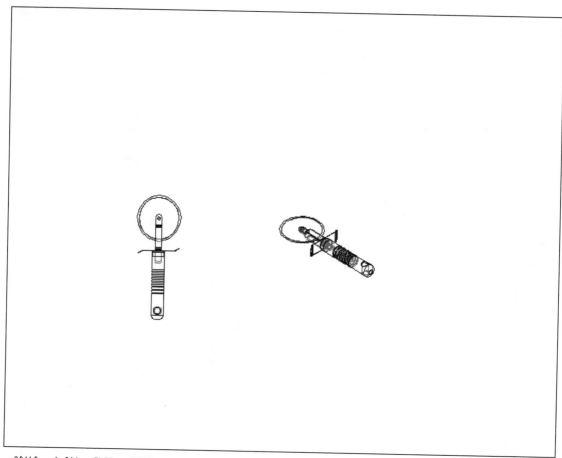

Figure 11.33.

11.8 CREATING A SECTION VIEW

Now you will create a cross-section view of the pizza cutter by slicing the front view of the model along a vertical plane. Section views are often useful to avoid part interferences in assemblies, and to ensure that interior regions of the parts are correct.

Zoom In on the front view of the pizza cutter. Turn on the datum planes if they are off and **Repaint the screen** . Create a **Projection** of a **Section** view of the entire (**Total**) pizza cutter by:

> **Views** ⇒ **Views** ⇒ **Add View** ⇒ **Projection** | **Full View** | **Section** | **Unexploded** | **No Scale** | **Done** ⇒ **Full** | **Total Xsec** | **Done**

In this case, you will **Create** a **Planar** section through a **Single** datum plane.

> **< select a point to the left of the front view >** ⇒ **Create** | **Planar** | **Single** | **Done**

By selecting to the left of the front view (within the boundary of the drawing), Pro/ENGINEER knows that the front view is the parent view for the section that will be generated and that the projection of the section is to the left of the front view. Each section plane needs a name. In addition, a cross-section plane must be identified. Call this section "A," and select assembly datum ADTM3 in the front view to use as the cross-section plane:

< **enter A** > ⇒ **Plane | Query Sel** ⇒ < **select ADTM3 at the top of the blade on the front view** > ⇒ **Done Sel**

Next, Pro/ENGINEER queries for a view perpendicular to the section where the section arrows can be shown. In this case the logical view on which to show the section arrows is the front view:

< **select the front view** >

Turn off the datum planes and **Repaint the screen**. The result should look like Figure 11.34 with **Hidden Lines** on. Then **Refit the model to the screen**.

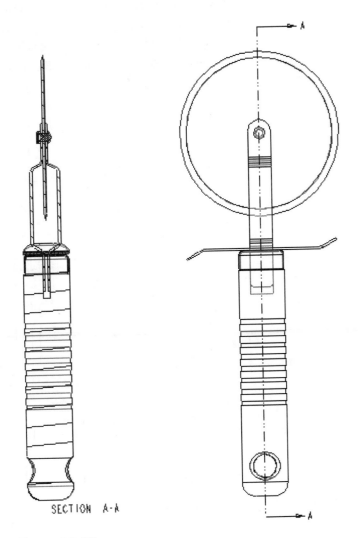

SECTION A-A

Figure 11.34.

11.9   CREATING A DETAIL VIEW

A detail view is a zoomed-in view of a small portion of the drawing. A detail view can be particularly useful to show small details such as the rivet that holds the blade in the pizza cutter. The view is dependent on the parent that is selected, but has a scale that is independent of the rest of the drawing.

To show a **Detailed** view of the cross-section through the rivet:

Add View ⇒ **Detailed** | **Full View** | **No Xsec** | **Unexploded** | **Scale** | **Done**

This is similar to previous **Add View** commands except for selecting **Detailed** to denote that a zoomed-in view is to be created. In addition, **Scale** indicates that a particular scale will be specified for the detailed view. To place the detailed view:

< select a point in the open area in the upper right part of the drawing to place the detail > ⇒ **< enter 5 >**

A 5 to 1 scale is prescribed, making the detailed view 5 times larger than the other views in order to show the detail of the rivet. To define the region that is to be shown in the detailed view:

< Zoom In on the rivet in the section view and click the middle mouse button to end the zoom > ⇒ **< select a point on the rivet >**

A red crosshair will appear near the selected point as shown in Figure 11.35.

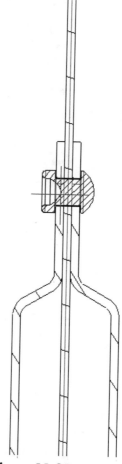

Figure 11.35.

Now a boundary must be sketched around the rivet indicating the area that is to be shown in the detail. To do this, click with the left mouse button below the rivet at about the distance shown by the rough circle in Figure 11.36. Then click at about the same distance to the right of the rivet. Click above the rivet, and then click to the left of the rivet. Close the loop to create a rough circle with the rivet at its center, as shown in Figure 11.36, by clicking near the start point. Then click once with the middle mouse button to finish.

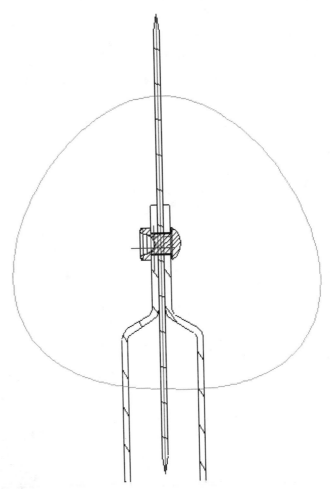

Figure 11.36.

Specify the name for the detail:

< enter rivet >

The type of boundary for the area used in the detail must be specified. In this case, specify a **Circle** to show a detailed section within a circle that is based on the outline that is sketched in Figure 11.36:

Circle ⇒ **Pick Pnt**

Finally it is necessary to specify the location for the note naming the detail. Place the note anywhere outside the newly formed circle, as in Figure 11.37, by clicking the left mouse button above and to the right of the circle. **Refit the model to the screen**. Figure 11.38 shows the detail view. Note that the scale specified earlier is indicated just below the detail view. **Save** the drawing.

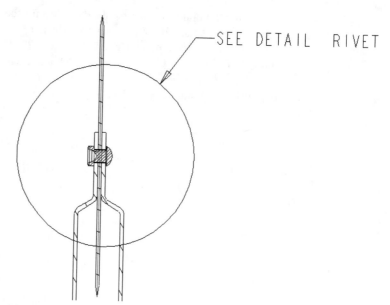

SEE DETAIL RIVET

Figure 11.37.

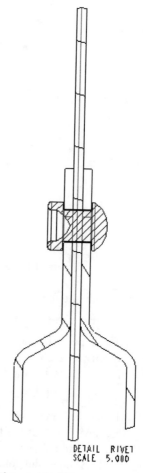

DETAIL RIVET
SCALE 5.000

Figure 11.38.

11.10 CLEANING UP THE VIEWS AND LABELING PARTS

All that is left for the assembly drawing is to remove hidden lines for clarity, reposition the views, add a title block, and label the individual parts of the pizza cutter.

To eliminate the hidden lines, click on **<u>No Hidden</u>** and then **<u>Repaint the screen</u>**.

If the scale of the detail is not quite right, change it by:

Modify View $\Rightarrow$ **Change Scale** $\Rightarrow$ < select the rivet detail view > $\Rightarrow$ < enter a new scale of 3 >

To move the views to the positions shown in Figure 11.39:

Move View

To move the notes (including the cross-section arrows) to the positions shown in Figure 11.32:

DETAIL $\Rightarrow$ **Move**

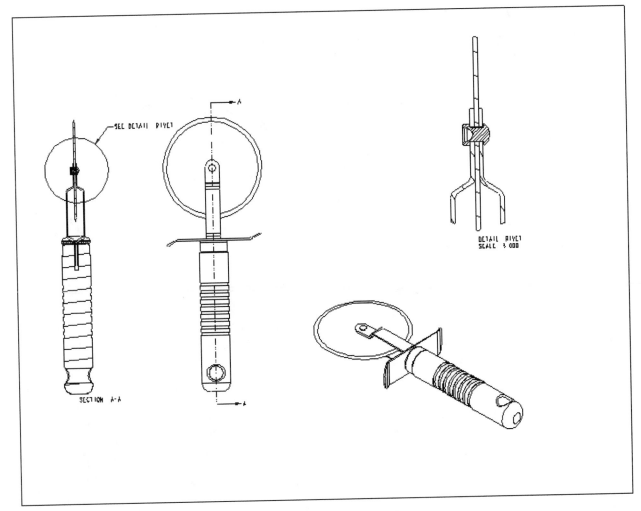

Figure 11.39.

Identifying each part in an assembly helps a reader better understand the assembly. This can be done using notes with a leader line. First, **Zoom In** on the isometric view. To **Create Leader** line notes to each part on in the isometric view:

Create ⇒ **Note** ⇒ **Leader** | **Enter** | **Horizontal** | **Standard** | **Default** | **Make Note** ⇒ **On Surface** | **Arrow Head** | < **select the point shown in Figure 11.40** > | **Done**

On Surface indicates the arrowhead is attached to a surface of a part. If **Free Point** was selected instead, then the selected point on the drawing itself would be the anchor for the endpoint of the leader line. **Arrow Head** puts an arrowhead at the end of the leader line.

< **select a point below the blade for the note as shown in Figure 11.41** > | < **enter BLADE** >

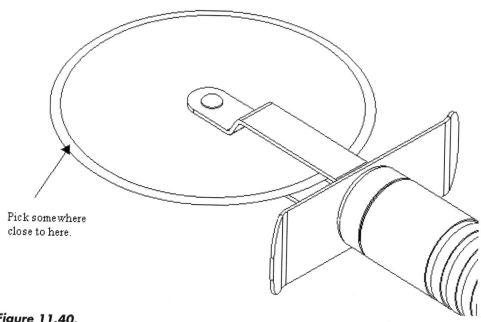

Figure 11.40.

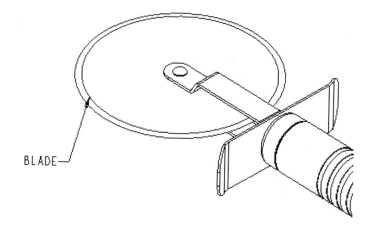

Figure 11.41.

Repeat this process for each part referring to Figure 11.42. The label for the arm should include "(2×)" to indicate that there are two arms in the assembly. After all the labels are created, click **Done/Return**. The labels can be moved using **Move**. Finally **Refit the model to the screen**.

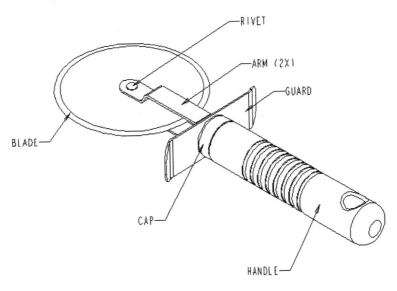

Figure 11.42.

Because you saved the title block from the arm drawing, creating the title block in this drawing will be much simpler. You only need to add the title block table to this drawing and modify the text. To retrieve the title block:

Table ⇒ **Save/Retrieve** ⇒ **Retrieve** ⇒ **< Double click on tblock.tbl > ⇒ < Place the block in the lower right corner of the drawing as shown in Figure 11.43 >**

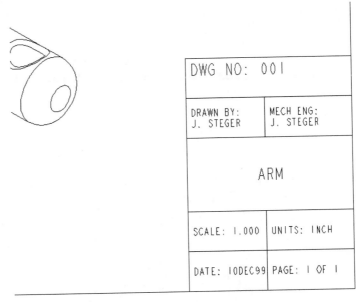

Figure 11.43.

Zoom In on the title block and change the text:

DETAIL ⇒ **Modify** ⇒ **Text** ⇒ **Text Line** ⇒ < **select the text you are changing** >

The only lines that you need to change are the drawing number, the title of the drawing, and the date. Match the title block to Figure 11.44.

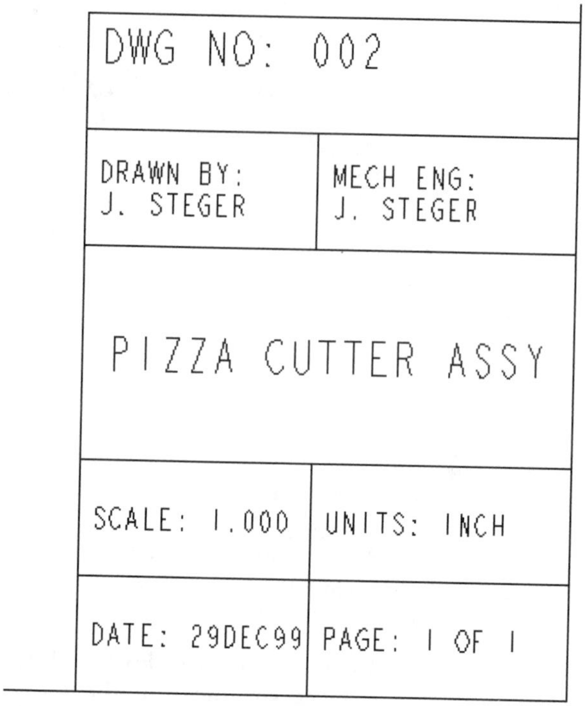

```
┌─────────────────────────────────────┐
│  DWG NO:  002                        │
├──────────────────┬──────────────────┤
│  DRAWN BY:       │  MECH ENG:        │
│  J. STEGER       │  J. STEGER        │
├──────────────────┴──────────────────┤
│                                      │
│    PIZZA CUTTER ASSY                 │
│                                      │
├──────────────────┬──────────────────┤
│  SCALE: 1.000    │  UNITS: INCH      │
├──────────────────┼──────────────────┤
│  DATE: 29DEC99   │  PAGE: 1 OF 1     │
└──────────────────┴──────────────────┘
```

Figure 11.44.

After making all of the changes, click **Done/Return**. Then **Refit the model to the screen**.

Finally, the **cross-hatching** of the section view needs minor modification to make it more clear. Cross-hatching defines the solid material in a section view. Angled lines are used to show what part of solid material has been cut to form the section view. To **Modify** the cross-hatch lines on the A-A section view:

DETAIL ⇒ **Modify** ⇒ **Xhatching** ⇒ < **Pick anywhere on the view of SECTION A-A** > | **Done Sel**

Even though you selected the entire SECTION A-A, the cross-hatching is only changed on one part of the assembly at a time. The part for which the cross-hatching will be changed first remains highlighted in blue with the cross-hatching highlighted in red. Usually the first part that is highlighted is the rivet in this drawing. **Zoom In** on the rivet to see it more clearly. To change the spacing of the cross-hatching:

Spacing | **Hatch** ⇒ **Overall** | **Half**

Repeat clicking on **Half** to reduce the spacing by half. Or click on **Double** to increase the spacing by a factor of two. Use **Half** or **Double** until the cross-hatching looks like Figure 11.45. If a specific spacing value was desired, then the **Value** command could be used.

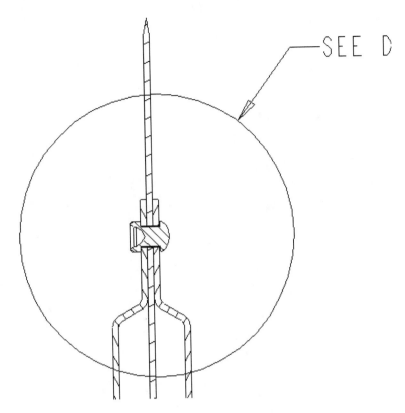

Figure 11.45.

The angle of the cross-hatch lines can also be changed to help the reader of the drawing distinguish between the different parts in the cross-section. Usually the largest sections in a drawing are set to 45 degrees with respect to horizontal. Smaller sections are set to 30 or 60 degrees with respect to horizontal. To change the angle of the cross-hatch in the rivet from its current angle to 135 degrees with respect to horizontal:

Angle | Hatch ⇒ Overall | 135

To modify the next part, click on **Next Xsec**. This will highlight the blade. Repeat the **Angle** and **Spacing** commands to improve the visibility of the blade. Use 30 degrees for the angle. Repeat **Next Xsec**, **Angle**, and **Spacing** for the subsequent parts, using the following angles to avoid adjacent parts from having the same cross-hatch angle. **<u>Zoom Out</u>** when necessary.

120 degrees: left arm

60 degrees: right arm

30 degrees: guard

120 degrees: cap

45 degrees: handle

Click **Done** when all angles have been changed. To apply the same angles and spacing in the detail of the rivet as in the **Parent** Section A-A:

Xhatching ⇒ < Pick anywhere on the view of the detail of the RIVET > |
Done Sel ⇒ From Parent | Done

The final assembly drawing should look similar to Figure 11.46. **<u>Save</u>** the drawing.

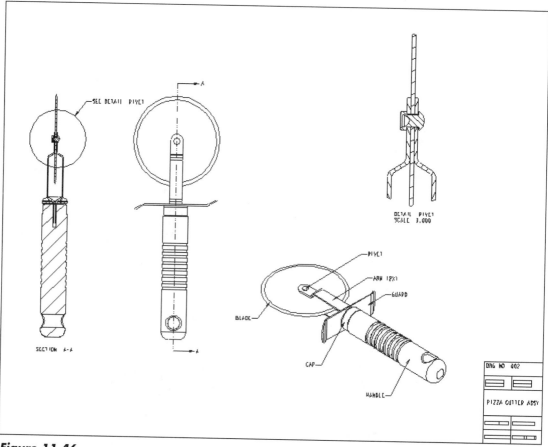

Figure 11.46.

Congratulations! You have completed this tutorial. ***Close*** the window and ***Exit***. Pro/ENGINEER has many more capabilities than were covered in this tutorial, but now you have the basics necessary to model fairly complex parts. As you become more proficient with Pro/ENGINEER, you will be able to explore the advanced capabilities of the software. To learn more, several advanced guides to the use of Pro/ENGINEER are listed in the References.

File Transfer Between CAD Systems

As the engineering world becomes more interconnected with email and the internet, engineering graphics are routinely transferred both within a company and outside of a company. Sometimes this involves the necessity of importing drawings created using one CAD system to a different CAD system. Each CAD system seems to have its own format for files that are saved. Fortunately, several standard formats exist. Translators are usually available within most CAD software to import and export data files that are in a standard file format.

The most commonly used format is the Initial Graphics Exchange Specification, or IGES. Models may be imported to or exported from most CAD systems if the file is stored as an IGES transfer file (.igs). Unfortunately, IGES translators vary quite a bit and may sometimes give unexpected results, especially for the inexperienced user. Nevertheless, IGES is frequently used. Other standard file formats are available. STEP is capable of translating a solids model and maintaining it as a solids model. DXF and DWG formats are intended for 2D data such as drawings. Use the ***Import*** and ***Export*** commands in the ***File*** menu to use other standard file formats.

KEY TERMS

Assembly drawing
Detail view
Dimensioning
Drawing format
Drawing size
General view

Hidden lines
Leader line
Orthographic view
Projection
Scale
Section view

Table
Tangent surfaces
Title block
Tolerances

Problems

Use drawing size A for the following problems. Be sure to include a title block and appropriate notes.

1. Create a drawing of the guard. Include three orthographic views and an isometric view.

2. Create a drawing of the cap using a scale of 2:1. Include two orthographic views, an isometric view, and a section through the cap.

3. Create a drawing of the blade. Include two orthographic views, an isometric view, and a detail view of the cutting edge.

4. Create a drawing of the rivet using a scale of 5:1. Include two orthographic views, an isometric view, and a section view through the rivet. (Note that it is unlikely that a drawing of the rivet *after it is deformed* would be necessary in a practical situation.)

5. Create a half-scale drawing of the handle. Include two orthographic views, an isometric view, a section view through the diameter of the handle, and a detail section view of one of the grooves.

References

G. Graham, J. Proctor, and, P. Berg, *Inside the New Pro/ENGINEER Solutions*, Santa Fe, NM: Onword Press, 1999.

L. G. Lamit, *Pro/ENGINEER 2000i*. Pacific Grove, CA: Brooks/Cole, 2000.

Parametric Technology Corporation web site: http://www.ptc.com/.

R. Rizza, *Getting Started with Pro/ENGINEER*. Upper Saddle River, NJ: Prentice Hall, 2000.

S. G. Smith, *Basic Pro/ENGINEER Design*. Harrisburg, PA: CADQuest, 1998.

J. Utz and W. R. Cox, *Inside Pro/ENGINEER*. Sante Fe, NM: Onword Press, 1995.

Index